SENECA

17 LETTERS

with translation and commentary by

C. D. N. Costa

British Library Cataloguing in Publication Data

Seneca, Lucius Annaeus, 4 B.C. — 65
    Letters. — (Classical texts).
    I. Title   II. Costa, C.D.N.   III. Series
    876'.01   PA 6661.E7

ISBN 0 85668 354 X *cloth*
ISBN 0 85668 355 8 *limp*

Classical texts ISSN 0953 — 7961

Printed and published in England by ARIS & PHILLIPS Ltd, Teddington House, Warminster, Wiltshire, BA12 8PQ. U.K.

CONTENTS

TO

SIMON AND CLARE

PREFACE

Seneca's Letters are arguably his greatest achievement, as they have certainly been his most popular work, and English readers have been well served by the Macmillan selection, edited by W.C. Summers in 1910. But, valuable as that edition is, especially for its extensive introduction, it has inevitably dated, and students now need different kinds of help from a commentary. The present selection tries to be representative in giving some idea of the flavour and tone of the Letters and the range of topics which they cover. One principle of the edition is that the chosen letters are not abbreviated, and they therefore vary greatly in length. The commentary concentrates on elucidating the subject matter, though help is offered on grammatical and linguistic points: the translation itself should go some way to supplying a commentary of the more conventional pedagogic type. The text is that of the Oxford Classical Texts, edited by L.D. Reynolds, but without the Apparatus. In the few places where a textual point is discussed the lack of a printed Apparatus will not affect the understanding of the note, and a reference to the Apparatus simply directs anyone interested to the OCT for further information.

It is a pleasure to thank for their guidance and help Emeritus Professor A.E. Douglas and Professor D.A. Russell, who read drafts of the commentary; and I am also most grateful to the staff of Aris & Phillips for their encouragement and their patience.

May 1988   C. D. N. C.

INTRODUCTION

The Letter in Greek and Latin Literature

The letter is one of the most interesting and attractive of the literary forms which have come down to us from the Graeco—Roman world. A large number of the Greek ones which survive are not in fact what we would call letters, in the sense of vehicles for news and chat between friends. (Clear examples of this class in Latin are of course to be found in Cicero's voluminous correspondence). There are certainly many Greek private letters surviving in papyri, but we are concerned with the collections of formal letters dating mainly from the fourth century B.C. onwards, e.g. letters dealing with the official business of government and the bureaucracy of the Hellenistic world; letters used for instruction in philosophical, educational and literary theory (like those of Plato, Epicurus and St. Paul); stylistic exercises on real or imaginary themes, dating from the period of the Second Sophistic and intended like a novelette for entertainment (Alciphron, Aelian, Aristaenetus).

The Greeks took the theory of letter—writing seriously, and Demetrius discussed it in an important section of his treatise *On Style* (date uncertain but perhaps late Hellenistic). This is our major surviving treatment of the subject, and especially interesting is Demetrius' idea that a letter is an 'image of the writer's soul' (*On Style* 227). This way of putting it would have appealed to the writers of didactic or protreptic letters, and in particular to Seneca, who regarded his letters as a means of passing on his thoughts and philosophical experience to Lucilius.

In Latin there were two major collections of letters prior to Seneca, Cicero's correspondence and the verse epistles of Horace. Neither of these were models for him in any strict sense, though there are some similarities with Horace's frequent moralizing tone .and his informal anecdotal style. There is a possible link with Cicero if one accepts the arguments that the correspondence *Ad Atticum* was published some time under Nero.[1] The appearance of this corpus might have suggested to Seneca the idea of writing a sequence of letters himself, however different they might be in kind. (Seneca himself quotes from the correspondence to Atticus at 97.4 and 118.1—2.)

The Letters to Lucilius

The Letters belong to the last period of Seneca's life and probably occupied him during the years 63—4. He seems to have written obsessively fast during the time between his retirement from public life in 62 and his death in 65: *De Otio*, *De Providentia* and *Naturales Quaestiones* also appeared in this period, and it is not fanciful to imagine that the thought of his advancing years and the precariousness of life under Nero stimulated him to get out of his system works which he might have been pondering for some time. This would explain some of the recurrent themes in the Letters, especially the injunctions to Lucilius (and thereby to himself) to make the right use of *otium* and to cultivate the right attitude to death.

We have 124 letters addressed to Lucilius, divided into twenty books — perhaps by Seneca himself, but this is uncertain. [2] It is probably not a real correspondence, though epistolary signposts are used quite often, as Seneca claims to be taking up a point or answering a question put to him by Lucilius. We must also allow that genuine consolation was offered to Lucilius at times of trouble, like his law—suit (24) and his illness (78). [3] No doubt Seneca was sincerely interested in Lucilius and his moral welfare, and it would be reasonable to assume that Lucilius saw the letters, individually or in groups; but Seneca seems to have had his eye on a wider readership and to have envisaged publication, whether piecemeal or as a complete *opus*. In fact Lucilius tends to fade from view in some of the later long letters, as though having given the letters their initial impetus his presence as a notional recipient becomes less necessary afterwards. [4]

The Letters derive their form clearly from the Greek philosophical letter (see above), and their underlying aim is to discuss in Stoic terms a variety of mainly ethical questions. This emphasis reflects the preoccupation which Stoicism had by now acquired in the minds of its leading adherents. Early Stoic theories had already been significantly adapted by the Middle Stoa of the second and first centuries B.C., chiefly through the teaching of Panaetius and Posidonius, and by the time of the Late Stoa in the Roman period interest centred much less on theoretical questions about logic and physics than on practical discussion of human conduct. In this process of adaptation Seneca himself, and Epictetus after him, played a leading part, and the Letters are a major document for Stoic thinking of this period. In both Seneca and Epictetus the relaxing of earlier doctrine shows itself in a greater awareness of human weakness and an acceptance that most of us must be content with a reasonable advance towards a perfection which is virtually unattainable. This is Seneca's stance in the Letters with regard to Lucilius: he like Lucilius is a novice, *proficiens*, on the journey towards becoming the Stoic ideal *sapiens*, but he is a little further on the way and can give Lucilius the benefit of his experiences and his mistakes. It is one of the attractions of the Letters that Seneca disclaims anything like perfection in himself, occasionally makes fun of himself, and generally regards his own position as simply that of a more advanced student.

Another symptom of this mellowing of Stoicism, and also an indication that the Letters cannot be called a strict Stoic treatise, is Seneca's willingness to tap the wisdom of other thinkers, especially Epicurus, the founder of the school which in many ways was in sharp contrast with Stoicism. Many letters, particularly the earlier ones, end with a quotation, a 'tag' which arises from and rounds off the preceding argument, and these quotations are often from Epicurus.[5] Seneca was himself a master of the crisp thought pungently expressed, and recognizing this quality in Epicurus he was happy to acknowledge it by quoting him — and to defend himself for doing so (12.11). It is interesting to note that another great Stoic, Marcus Aurelius, also quotes Epicurus (7.64, 9.41).

Besides the example of the Greek philosophical letter the most important influences on Seneca's Letters are techniques derived from Hellenistic sermonizing and from rhetorical practice. There was a kind of moralizing discourse (sometimes ·called diatribe by modern authorities) much in vogue in Hellenistic times, especially in the hands of Cynic and Stoic philosophers. It used popular language, introduced anecdotes to enliven its ethical teaching, and frequently set up imaginary objections in order to demolish them. Throughout the Letters, as in his ethical treatises, one of Seneca's own favourite techniques is the use of anecdotes and *exempla* to make a point emphatically or humorously; and the imaginary objector too is time after time introduced by *inquit, dicet aliquis*, or the like. It is a well—tried trick and it adds variety to the lesson.

From his rhetorical training Seneca derived his style, and in this he was both a child of his time and the most dominant figure in Silver Latin prose literature. The schools of rhetoric trained their students in all the tricks of style by which a weak argument could appear a good one, and a strong argument unassailable, and Seneca was a master of every declamatory device in the book — the polished epigram (*sententia*), the elaborately balanced antithesis, the sophisticated use of word—order, an almost obsessive concern for rhythm. Practically every page of his works reveals the artist in words revelling in his own virtuosity. All this is obvious, and yet Seneca claims that his letters aim to be, like his conversation, *inlaboratus et facilis* (75.1). This looks paradoxical to us, but it must mean that he is not trying for special effects beyond the ordinary range of intelligent discourse, and that conversational elements like colloquialisms and anecdotes are often to be found. The declamatory features are not intended to lift the Letters above the grasp of the unsophisticated.

Rhythm has just been mentioned, and no account of Seneca's prose style could ignore this feature of it. It was characteristic of Greek and Latin formal prose to be self−consciously rhythmical, and the effective use of prose−rhythm was seriously discussed by rhetorical theorists.[6] Writers and speakers were especially conscious of the effects which could be produced by certain metrical cadences, or clausulae, at sentence−endings. Cicero asserted that sentence−endings were rhythmically the most important (*de Orat.* 3.192), and Seneca would certainly have agreed with him, for it is here that we can see his constant use of certain cadences. He has two favourite clausulae, $-u-/-\underset{\smile}{u}$ and $-u-/-u-$ (with resolutions), and either or both of these will be found to occur several times on virtually every page of the Letters.[7] Taking at random the sections 7.3−5, for example, we find the following clausulae:

frustra mānum mittunt; postulaticiis praeferunt; repellitur ferrum; detinent caedem; pugnantium mors est; incurrit in ferrum; audacter occidit

(giving seven examples in twelve lines of the O.C.T., and not counting those involving resolution of long syllables).

There is no other collection of Latin letters like Seneca's, and they are widely thought to be his finest work. The reasons for this judgment are not hard to see, and they arise partly from the freshness and informality of the epistolary style and partly through comparison with the treatises. Choosing the letter−form not only allowed Seneca to set up a recipient of his news and views and teaching within an informal two−way relationship, but also encouraged him to talk about himself, as we do in letters. These autobiographical details are an obvious feature of the Letters and of great interest, whether we are hearing about Seneca's hypochondria, his pride in his vineyards, his love for his wife, his feelings on getting old. He can keep a light touch and puncture his own *gravitas*, as in the conversation with an old retainer (12), and where he admits that his solution to the problem of noisy neighbours was not philosophical detachment but moving house (56).

Other topics of interest occur when Seneca diversifies the predominantly Stoic teaching on the moral life, contentment and death, and talks about, for example, education (88), literary style (114) and anthropology (90). In fact these three letters are of great importance to us as witnesses to ancient ideas on their respective topics, as well as revealing the views of one of the most intelligent men of his time.

This kind of variety − personal details about the writer, and wide−ranging and important topics − are part of the attraction of the Letters, and one reason for their popularity compared with the treatises. Another reason is their on the whole lighter touch. The treatises generally have a formal theme − Anger, Providence, Clemency − and Seneca characteristically wades into it with a massive battery of arguments, often supported by a procession of *exempla* to prove his case; and the whole thesis is presented with all the technical virtuosity of the trained declaimer. These works are interesting, clever and no doubt sincere performances, and the themes are usually of fundamental importance; but many modern readers feel that the author protests too much and goes on too long. From this point of view the Letters, although they deal with many of the same topics, have a greater appeal to us because of their more relaxed and free-wheeling style.

Lucilius

At the time the Letters were written Lucilius was procurator of Sicily. He was younger than Seneca and clearly an old friend, to whom *De Providentia* and *Naturales Quaestiones* were also addressed, but we have no idea why Seneca should have singled him out as the notional recipient of advice on moral improvement. We need not assume that he was particularly in need of it, though Seneca maintains the pose of an instructor (4.1, 20.1, 31.1): a shared interest in Stoic ethics would be sufficient grounds for what can be regarded as a mutual exploration steered by Seneca as the more experienced philosopher. As we have seen, the letter was a well-tried vehicle for philosophical discussion, and, given the form, the addressee clearly has a rôle to play. In any case, Seneca and Lucilius had other interests in common: Lucilius was a cultivated man of literary pretensions, and Seneca mentions his poetic activities in several of the letters (see notes on 7.9, 24.19, 79.5).[8] Lucilius was clearly more than just the ideal pupil-addressee, and whether or not he actually received all the letters, in many of them his presence and his reported thoughts and activities add life and interest to the topic concerned. (See above p. 2.)

Postscript to the Letters

The Letters to Lucilius were by far the most popular of Seneca's works in the Middle Ages, especially from the twelfth century onwards;[9] and they were not the only letters that circulated under his name. A group of letters has survived which were allegedly written by Seneca to St. Paul, and they have become attached to the Letters to Lucilius in some of the manuscripts. They are certainly spurious, and were probably forged sometime in the fourth century, perhaps in an effort to associate Seneca with Christianity because his moral teaching elsewhere qualified him for such a link.[10]

Because of the features of style and content which have been outlined above the Letters are perhaps the nearest form in Latin literature to the modern essay, and they are the recognizable forerunners of the essays of Bacon and Montaigne.[11]   But in many ways the most interesting parallel in English comes in the eighteenth century with the letters of Lord Chesterfield to his son.   These letters with their advice on good manners and clear thinking, their firm and patient moralizing, their quotations from a diversity of authors, their mixture of worldliness, urbanity and affection, would give anyone who could not read Seneca's Letters a very fair idea of their spirit and intention.[12]

The Letters, however, survive because of their own qualities and not through their descendants.   Seneca did not have a notably original mind, and many have been repelled by some aspects of his public life and his work for Nero (which was to some extent forced upon him).   But in his writings he is unequalled as a brilliant formulator of received wisdom, and the Letters remain as a witness to his affection for a friend and his final thoughts before death − his own *meditatio mortis*.   He has kept his promise to Lucilius, and through these Letters has given him immortality (21.5).

Manuscripts

The manuscript tradition of the Letters is a double one.   Sometime in antiquity they were divided into two groups, comprising 1−88 and 89−124, and apart from one tenth century manuscript, Q, the two sections of the text were not combined again until the twelfth century.   For the group 1−88 the most important manuscripts are p P L V O Q b g M (all dating from the ninth to the eleventh centuries); for 89−124 the main witnesses are B (ninth century) Q (containing 89−120.12) p (containing 121.12 ad fin. and 122).[13]

There are several unresolved cruces in this selection of letters, but in no case is the general sense seriously in doubt.

NOTES TO THE INTRODUCTION

1. See D.R. Shackleton Bailey, *Cicero's Letters to Atticus* I 59—73.
2. The division into books in any case goes back to Aulus Gellius in the second century A.D., who knew of at least twenty—two books (12.2): we must therefore presume that some more letters have not survived.
3. See Albertini, *La Composition dans les ouvrages philosophiques de Sénèque*, 136ff., for the view that the whole correspondence was a genuine one.
4. For a discussion along these lines see D.A. Russell in C.D.N. Costa (ed.) *Seneca*, 78—9.
5. In our selection see, for example, Letters 7, 12, 24. Seneca also asserts the eclectic principles governing his philosophical beliefs at 21.9, 64.10.
6. For many technical details and a bibliography on the subject see *OCD* s.v. 'Prose—Rhythm'.
7. See Summers, Introd. xc—xci; Norden, *Antike Kunstprosa* I 310—12.
8. For other biographical details about Lucilius see 19.3, 26.7, 31.9, 44.2, 45.1, 49.1, 79.1.
9. See L.D. Reynolds, *The Medieval Tradition of Seneca's Letters*, 104ff. The Letters were the subject of two early commentaries: one by the monk Domenico Peccioli (died 1408), and one written in 1408—11 by Gasparino Barzizza, professor of rhetoric at the University of Milan. (See L.A. Panizza in *Traditio* 33 (1977) 297—358.)
10. See L.D. Reynolds, op.cit. Chap. 6.
11. See Summers, Introd. xcvi—cxiv, for a comprehensive account of the influence of Seneca's prose works generally on later authors.
12. Though Chesterfield is full of classical quotations I can find no evidence that he was particularly fond of Seneca. Nevertheless, the following two quotations, taken at random from the letters to his son, will illustrate the similarity of tone and themes.

September 12, O.S. 1749

Dear Boy,
    It seems extraordinary, but it is very true, that my anxiety for you increases in proportion to the good accounts which I receive of you from all hands. I promise myself so much from you, that I dread the least disappointment. You are now so near the port, which I have so long wished and laboured to bring you safe into, that my concern would be doubled, should you be shipwrecked within sight of it...
    (Everyman ed. p.112: cf. Sen. *Ep.* 2.1., 20.1.)

February 5, O.S. 1750

My Dear Friend,

Very few people are good economists of their fortune, and still fewer of their time; and yet of the two the latter is the most precious. I heartily wish you to be a good economist of both; and you are now of an age to begin to think seriously of these two important articles...

(Everyman ed. p.155: cf. Sen. *Ep.* 1.)

13. For a full discussion of the manuscript tradition of the Letters see L.D. Reynolds, op.cit., esp. Chapters 2 and 3.

SELECT BIBLIOGRAPHY

Editions
(Post — Renaissance)

Schweighäuser, J.   Strasbourg, 1809.
Fickert, C.K.   Leipzig, 1842.
Haase, F.   Leipzig, 1853.
Hense, O.   Leipzig, 1914.² (Teubner)
Beltrami, A.   Rome, 1931.
Préchac, F.   Paris, 1945—64. (Budé: French translation
by H. Noblot)

Reynolds, L.D.   Oxford, 1965.

Translations

Gummere, R.M.   London, 1917—25. (Loeb)
Barker, E.P.   Oxford, 1932.
Noblot, H.   (Budé: see above)
Campbell, R.   *Seneca, Letters from a Stoic* (selection),
Harmondsworth, 1969.

Commentaries

Summers, W.C.   *Select Letters of Seneca*, London, 1910.
Blankert, S.   *Seneca, Epist. 90*, Amsterdam, 1940.
Stückelberger, A.   *Senecas 88. Brief*, Heidelberg, 1965.
Scarpat, G.   *Lettere a Lucilio* (Libro primo, Epp. i—xii),
Brescia, 1975.

Note also a useful, detailed discussion of Letter 92 (not a formal commentary) by K. Reinhardt in *RE* s.v. 'Poseidonios', 757 ff.

General

(Square brackets indicate the form in which the work is referred to in the commentary.)

Albertini, E. *La Composition dans les ouvrages philosophiques de Sénèque*, Paris, 1923.
Cançik, H. *Untersuchungen zu Senecas Epistulae Morales*, Hildesheim, 1967.
Coleman, R. 'The Artful Moralist: a Study of Seneca's Epistolary Style', *CQ* 24 (1974) 276—89.

Delatte—Evrard—Govaerts—Denooz (edd.)   *L.A. Seneca Opera Philosophica Index Verborum*, Hildesheim, 1981.

Diels, H. and Kranz, W.   *Die Fragmente der Vorsokratiker*, Berlin, 1954 [7] [D—K].

Griffin, Miriam T.   *Seneca: a Philosopher in Politics*, Oxford, 1976.

Guillemin, A.   'Sénèque directeur d'âmes', *REL* 30 (1952) 202 ff.; 31 (1953) 215 ff.; 32 (1954) 250 ff.

Hadot, I.   *Seneca und die griechisch—römische Tradition der Seelenleitung*, Berlin, 1969.

Hofmann, J.B. and Szantyr, A.   *Lateinische Syntax und Stilistik*, Munich, 1965 [Hofmann—Szantyr].

Koskenniemi, H.   *Studien zur Idee und Phraseologie des griechischen Briefes*, Helsinki, 1956.

Kühner, R. and Stegmann, C.   *Ausführliche Grammatik der lateinischen Sprache*, Munich, 1962 [4] [K—S].

Liddell—Scott—Jones,   *A Greek—English Lexicon*, Oxford, 1940—68 [L—S—J].

Long, A.A.   *Hellenistic Philosophy*, London, 1974.

Martha, C.   *Les Moralistes sous l'empire romain*, Paris, 1865.

Maurach, G.   *Der Bau von Senecas Epistulae Morales*, Heidelberg, 1970.

Oxford Classical Dictionary, Oxford, 1970 [2] [OCD].

Oxford Latin Dictionary, Oxford, 1968—82 [OLD]

Peter, H.   *Der Brief in der Römischen Literatur*, Leipzig, 1901.

Reynolds, L.D.   *The Medieval Tradition of Seneca's Letters*, Oxford, 1965.

Rist, J.M.   *Stoic Philosophy*, Cambridge, 1969.

Russell, D.A.   'Letters to Lucilius' in C. D. N. Costa (ed.) *Seneca*, London, 1974, 70—95.

Sandbach, F.H.   *The Stoics*, London, 1975.

Steyns, D.   *Métaphores et comparaisons de Sénèque le philosophe*, Ghent, 1906.

Thesaurus linguae Latinae, Leipzig, 1900— .   [TLL]

Usener, H.   *Epicurea*, Leipzig, 1887 [Usener]

Abbreviated references to ancient works and authors generally follow the conventions of *L—S—J* and *OLD*. Untitled references to other works of Seneca are to the Letters.

SENECA: 17 LETTERS

LETTER 7

1.   Quid tibi vitandum praecipue existimes quaeris? turbam. Nondum illi tuto committeris. Ego certe confitebor inbecillitatem meam: numquam mores quos extuli refero; aliquid ex eo quod composui turbatur, aliquid ex iis quae fugavi redit. Quod aegris evenit quos longa inbecillitas usque eo adfecit ut nusquam sine offensa proferantur, hoc accidit nobis quorum animi ex long morbo reficiuntur.

2.   Inimica est multorum conversatio: nemo non aliquod nobis vitium aut commendat aut inprimit aut nescientibus adlinit. Utique quo maior est populus cui miscemur, hoc periculi plus est. Nihil vero tam damnosum bonis moribus quam in aliquo spectaculo desidere; tunc

3.   enim per voluptatem facilius vitia subrepunt. Quid me existimas dicere? avarior redeo, ambitiosior, luxuriosior? immo vero crudelior et inhumanior, quia inter homines fui. Casu in meridianum spectaculum incidi, lusus expectans et sales et aliquid laxamenti quo hominum oculi ab humano cruore adquiescant. Contra est: quidquid ante pugnatum est misericordia fuit; nunc omissis nugis mera homicidia sunt. Nihil habent quo tegantur; ad ictum totis corporibus expositi numquam

4.   frustra manum mittunt. Hoc plerique ordinariis paribus et postulaticiis praeferunt. Quidni praeferant? non galea, non scuto repellitur ferrum. Quo munimenta? quo artes? omnia ista mortis morae sunt. Mane leonibus et ursis homines, meridie spectatoribus suis obiciuntur. Interfectores interfecturis iubent obici et victorem in aliam detinent caedem; exitus pugnantium mors est. Ferro et igne res geritur.

5.   Haec fiunt dum vacat harena. 'Sed latrocinium fecit aliquis, occidit hominem.' Quid ergo? quia occidit, ille meruit ut hoc pateretur: tu quid meruisti miser ut hoc spectes? 'Occide, verbera, ure! Quare tam timide incurrit in ferrum? quare parum audacter occidit? quare parum libenter moritur? Plagis agatur in vulnera, mutuos ictus nudis et obviis pectoribus excipiant.' Intermissum est spectaculum: 'interim iugulentur homines, ne nihil agatur'. Age, ne hoc quidem intellegitis, mala exempla in eos redundare qui faciunt? Agite dis immortalibus gratias quod eum docetis esse crudelem qui non potest discere.

LETTER 7

1.   You ask me what you should regard as particularly to be avoided. A crowd. You can't yet safely entrust yourself to it. At any rate I will confess my own weakness: I never come home with the same moral character I set out with. Some of the peace of mind I have achieved is disturbed, one or other of those things which I have banished returns. You know how invalids are so reduced by prolonged weakness that they cannot venture outside without ill effects: it is the same with those of us who are recovering from a long

2.   spiritual illness. Associating with crowds is dangerous: someone is bound to seduce us with some vice, or stamp or smear it on us even without our being conscious of it. Obviously the larger the crowd the greater the danger of this. Indeed there is nothing so damaging to good character as to take a seat at a show, for then faults sneak up

3.   on us more easily through our enjoyment. Do you think I mean that I go home more greedy, more ambitious, more self—indulgent? Yes — and more cruel and inhuman because I have been among humans.

        I happened to drop in on a midday show, looking for entertainment, wit, and some relaxation in which human eyes could take a rest from human blood. It was quite the opposite. All the fights beforehand were acts of mercy in comparison: now the frivolities are banished and we are offered sheer butchery. The combatants wear no protection: their whole bodies are exposed to

4.   strokes and they never aim a blow in vain. Most of the spectators prefer this to the regular matches and the special demand ones. Naturally: there's neither helmet nor shield to ward off the weapon. What's the point of protection or skill? All that just delays death. In the morning men are thrown to lions and bears and at midday to their own spectators. The crowd insists that those who have killed their man are thrown against those who will kill them in turn, and reserves each victor for another slaughter. The only outcome for the

5.   combatants is death, while fire and steel keep things moving. All this happens between the main shows. 'But', you say, 'the man was a brigand, a murderer.' So what? Because he killed he deserved this fate; but what have *you* done, poor wretch, to deserve this spectacle? 'Kill him, beat him, burn him! Why is he so fearful of running against the sword? Why does he kill so timidly? Why is he so loth to die? Let him be driven by blows to receive his wounds; let them face and batter each other with unprotected breasts.' And when there's an interval: 'Let some throats be cut meanwhile, to keep things going'. Come now, don't you even know this, that evil examples recoil on those who offer them? Give the immortal gods thanks that you are giving a lesson in cruelty to a man who cannot

6.   Subducendus populo est tener animus et parum tenax recti: facile transitur ad plures.   Socrati et Catoni et Laelio excutere morem suum dissimilis multitudo potuisset: adeo nemo nostrum, qui cum maxime concinnamus ingenium, ferre impetum vitiorum tam magno

7. comitatu venientium potest.   Unum exemplum luxuriae aut avaritiae multum mali facit: convictor delicatus paulatim enervat et mollit, vicinus dives cupiditatem inritat, malignus comes quamvis candido et simplici rubiginem suam adfricuit: quid tu accidere his moribus credis

8. in quos publice factus est impetus?   Necesse est aut imiteris aut oderis.   Utrumque autem devitandum est: neve similis malis fias, quia multi sunt, neve inimicus multis, quia dissimiles sunt.   Recede in te ipse quantum potes; cum his versare qui te meliorem facturi sunt, illos admitte quos tu potes facere meliores.   Mutuo ista fiunt, et homines

9. dum docent discunt.   Non est quod te gloria publicandi ingenii producat in medium, ut recitare istis velis aut disputare; quod facere te vellem, si haberes isti populo idoneam mercem: nemo est qui intellegere te possit.   Aliquis fortasse, unus aut alter incidet, et hic ipse formandus tibi erit instituendusque ad intellectum tui.   'Cui ergo ista didici?'   Non est quod timeas ne operam perdideris, si tibi didicisti.

10.   Sed ne soli mihi hodie didicerim, communicabo tecum quae occurrunt mihi egregie dicta circa eundem fere sensum tria, ex quibus unum haec epistula in debitum solvet, duo in antecessum accipe. Democritus ait, 'unus mihi pro populo est, et populus pro uno'.

11. Bene et ille, quisquis fuit (ambigitur enim de auctore), cum quaereretur ab illo quo tanta diligentia artis spectaret ad paucissimos perventurae, 'satis sunt' inquit 'mihi pauci, satis est unus, satis est nullus'.   Egregie hoc tertium Epicurus, cum uni ex consortibus studiorum suorum scriberet: 'haec' inquit 'ego non multis, sed tibi;

12. satis enim magnum alter alteri theatrum sumus'.   Ista, mi Lucili, condenda in animum sunt, ut contemnas voluptatem ex plurium adsensione venientem.   Multi te laudant: ecquid habes cur places tibi, si is es quem intellegant multi? introrsus bona tua spectent.   Vale.

learn it.

6.   When a mind is impressionable and has only a shaky hold on what is right, it must be protected from the crowd: it is too easy to follow the majority. Even Socrates or Cato or Laelius could have had their moral principles knocked out of them by a crowd that differed from them, so true is it that no one of us, however well—ordered our personality, can withstand the attack of vices which

7.   come in such numbers. One example of self—indulgence or greed does much harm: a luxurious companion gradually debilitates and softens us; a rich neighbour stirs us to greed; a spiteful comrade rubs off his malice even on a frank and open—hearted person. Can you imagine what happens to characters on which there is an onset from

8.   all sides? You are bound either to imitate or to hate what you see, but you should really avoid both reactions. Do not either become like the wicked because they are many, or hate the many because they are unlike you. Retreat into yourself as much as you can; associate with those who will make you a better man; welcome those whom you can make better men. This is a two—way process, and

9.   men learn while they teach. And there is no reason to let pride in publicising your ability entice you before the public to give readings and lectures. I'd be happy for you to do that if your merchandise was suitable for that type of crowd; but in fact no one could really understand you. Perhaps you will find one or two, but you will have to mould and train them before they can understand your instruction. 'For whose benefit then did I acquire my learning?' You need not fear that you have wasted your efforts if you acquired it for your own.

10.   But not to keep for my benefit alone what I have learnt to—day, I shall share with you three excellent sayings I have come across, all making roughly the same point: one of them will pay this letter's debt to you, and you can have the other two as an advance payment. Democritus says 'To me an individual is a crowd and a

11.   crowd is an individual'. Then there was a good reply too from the man (his name is uncertain) who, when asked what was the point of taking such pains over a work of art which very few would notice, said 'Few are enough for me; one is enough; none is enough'. Thirdly there is this fine remark of Epicurus in a letter to one of his philosophical colleagues: 'I write this not to the many but just to you, for we are a big enough audience for each other, you and I'.

12.   Store these quotations in your heart, Lucilius, so that you may despise the pleasure that comes from the approval of the majority. Many praise you, but have you any grounds for self—approval if you are the sort of man the many understand? Let your good qualities face inwards.

LETTER 12

1.   Quocumque me verti, argumenta senectutis meae video. Veneram in suburbanum meum et querebar de inpensis aedificii dilabentis.   Ait vilicus mihi non esse neglegentiae suae vitium, omnia se facere, sed villam veterem esse.   Haec villa inter manus meas crevit: quid mihi futurum est, si tam putria sunt aetatis meae saxa?

2.   Iratus illi proximam occasionem stomachandi arripio.   'Apparet' inquam 'has platanos neglegi: nullas habent frondes.   Quam nodosi sunt et retorridi rami, quam tristes et squalidi trunci!   Hoc non accideret si quis has circumfoderet, si inrigaret.'   Iurat per genium meum se omnia facere, in nulla re cessare curam suam, sed illas vetulas esse.   Quod intra nos sit, ego illas posueram, ego illarum

3.   primum videram folium.   Conversus ad ianuam 'quis est iste?' inquam 'iste decrepitus et merito ad ostium admotus? foras enim spectat. Unde istunc nanctus es? quid te delectavit alienum mortuum tollere?' At ille 'non cognoscis me?' inquit: 'ego sum Felicio, cui solebas sigillaria adferre; ego sum Philositi vilici filius, deliciolum tuum'. 'Perfecte' inquam 'iste delirat: pupulus, etiam delicium meum factus est?   Prorsus potest fieri: dentes illi cum maxime cadunt.'

4.   Debeo hoc suburbano meo, quod mihi senectus mea quocumque adverteram apparuit.   Conplectamur illam et amemus; plena < est> voluptatis, si illa scias uti.   Gratissima sunt poma cum fugiunt; pueritiae maximus in exitu decor est; dedits vino potio extrema delectat, illa quae mergit, quae ebrietati summam manum inponit;

5.   quod in se iucundissimum omnis voluptas habet in finem sui differt. Iucundissima est aetas devexa iam, non tamen praeceps, et illam quoque in extrema tegula stantem iudico habere suas voluptates; aut hoc ipsum succedit in locum voluptatium, nullis egere.   Quam dulce est cupiditates fatigasse ac reliquisse!   'Molestum est' inquis 'mortem

6.   ante oculos habere.'   Primum ista tam seni ante oculos debet esse quam iuveni (non enim citamur ex censu); deinde nemo tam senex est ut inprobe unum diem speret.   Unus autem dies gradus vitae est. Tota aetas partibus constat et orbes habet circumductos maiores minoribus: est aliquis qui omnis conplectatur et cingat (hic pertinet a natali ad diem extremum); est alter qui annos adulescentiae excludit; est qui totam pueritiam ambitu suo adstringit; est deinde per se annus

LETTER 12

1.   Wherever I turn I see proofs that I am growing old. I visited my country place and began to complain about the expense of maintaining the building, which was falling into disrepair. My farm manager said its dilapidated condition wasn't his fault: he was doing all he could but the house was old. That house grew under my own hands: what's in store for me if a building of my age is crumbling?

2.   I was cross with him and took the first opportunity of venting my spleen. 'These plane trees', I said, 'are clearly being neglected: they have lost their leaves, and look how knotted and shrivelled the branches are, and how wretched and rough the trunks! This wouldn't happen if somebody dug round and watered them.' He swore by my guardian spirit that he was doing everything and not relaxing his efforts, but they were old. Now don't tell anyone, but I had planted those trees myself and watched the first leaves appearing.

3.   Turning to the front door I asked him 'Who is that old fossil there? The door is the right place to put him — he's obviously about to leave us. Where did you find him?, Why do you like to take in other people's dead for burial?' But the other man replied 'Don't you recognize me? I'm Felicio: you used to bring me toy figures. I'm the son of Philositus, the manager — your little pal.' 'The man is completely mad,' I said; 'has he become a little boy again — and my playmate too? It's quite possible: he's certainly losing his teeth.'

4.   I owe it to my estate that my old age became obvious to me wherever I looked. Well, let us embrace and cherish old age: it is full of pleasure if you know how to use it. Fruit are sweetest when their season is ending; the charm of youth is greatest as it passes; drunkards love the last drink, the one that sinks them and gives the finishing touch to intoxication.

5.   Every pleasure reserves its highest delight till its end. So the pleasantest time of life is that which is beginning to decline, but not yet sinking headlong, and to my mind even the age which is teetering on the brink has its own delights — or their place is taken by our no longer wanting them. How good it is to have exhausted our desires and left them behind us!

6.   'It is unpleasant', you say, 'to have death before your eyes.' Well, firstly, a young man should have death before his eyes as much as an old man, for we aren't summoned according to our places on the register. Secondly, no one is so old that it is unreasonable for him to hope for one more day; yet one day is a stage in the journey of life.

The whole of our lifetime consists of sections formed by concentric circles. The outermost one covers the time from birth to death and encloses all the others. The next one marks off the years of our early manhood. The next contains all our boyhood. Then

in se omnia continens tempora, quorum multiplicatione vita componitur; mensis artiore praecingitur circulo; angustissimum habet dies gyrum, sed et hic ab initio ad exitum venit, ab ortu ad occasum.

7. Ideo Heraclitus, cui cognomen fecit orationis obscuritas, 'unus' inquit 'dies par omni est'. Hoc alius aliter excepit. Dixit enim *** parem esse horis, nec mentitur; nam si dies est tempus viginti et quattuor horarum, necesse est omnes inter se dies pares esse, quia nox habet quod dies perdidit. Alius ait parem esse unum diem omnibus similitudine; nihil enim habet longissimi temporis spatium quod non et in uno die invenias, lucem et noctem, et in alternas mundi vices plura

8. facit ista, non <alia> *** alias contractior, alias productior. Itaque sic ordinandus est dies omnis tamquam cogat agmen et consummet atque expleat vitam. Pacuvius, qui Syriam usu suam fecit, cum vino et illis funebribus epulis sibi parentaverat, sic in cubiculum ferebatur a cena ut inter plausus exoletorum hoc ad symphoniam caneretur:

9. βεβίωται, βεβίωται. Nullo non se die extulit. Hoc quod ille ex mala conscientia faciebat nos ex bona faciamus, et in somnum ituri laeti hilaresque dicamus,

vixi et quem dederat cursum fortuna peregi.

Crastinum si adiecerit deus, laeti recipiamus. Ille beatissimus est et securus sui possessor qui crastinum sine sollicitudine expectat; quisquis dixit 'vixi' cotidie ad lucrum surgit.

10. Sed iam debeo epistulam includere. 'Sic' inquis 'sine ullo ad me peculio veniet?' Noli timere: aliquid secum fert. Quare aliquid dixi? multum. Quid enim hac voce praeclarius quam illi trado ad te perferendam? 'Malum est in necessitate vivere, sed in necessitate vivere necessitas nulla est.' Quidni nulla sit? patent undique ad libertatem viae multae, breves faciles. Agamus deo gratias quod nemo

11. in vita teneri potest: calcare ipsas necessitates licet. 'Epicurus' inquis 'dixit: quid tibi cum alieno?' Quod verum est meum est; perseverabo Epicurum tibi ingerere, ut isti qui in verba iurant nec quid dicatur aestimant, sed a quo, sciant quae optima sunt esse communia. Vale.

there is the year—circle, containing the whole sequence of seasons whose periodic repetition makes up our lives. Then there is the smaller circle of the month; and then the tiniest circuit of the day,

7. but this too has a beginning and an end, a rising and a setting. For this reason Heraclitus, whose obscure style of utterance gave him his nickname, said 'One day equals all', a remark which has been understood in different ways. One interpretation is that the day is equal in hours, which is true enough; for if we regard a day as a period of twenty—four hours, all days are necessarily equal as night has what daytime has lost. Another view is that one day equals all by analogy. For not even the longest period of time has more than the two elements you find in one day, light and darkness, so that these cosmic alternations are just more numerous, not different, and the length of the period determines the number of days and nights.

8. So every day should be regulated as if it rounded off and closed the series and completed our life. Pacuvius, who acquired prescriptive rights over Syria, celebrated his own death with wine and the usual funeral feast, and had himself carried from the meal into his bedroom while his boy—friends applauded and there was a musical chant, 'His life is o'er, his life is o'er'. This funeral parade took

9. place every day. What he did through a bad conscience let us do from a good one, and as we go to sleep let us repeat with happiness and joy:

'I have lived and run the course that fate prescribed'.

If god offers us to—morrow let us joyfully accept it. He is beyond others happy and calmly independant who waits for to—morrow without anxiety. Whoever has said 'I have lived' rises each morning to a surplus of time.

10. But I must now close my letter. 'Just like that?' you'll say; 'will it come to me without any offering?' Never fear: it brings something with it. 'Something' did I say? A lot. For what could be nobler than these words which my letter brings you? 'It is grim to live under constraint, but there is no constraint to live under constraint.' How so? Because there are on all sides many short and easy roads to freedom. Let us thank god that no one can be forced

11. to stay alive: we can trample down our very constraints. 'Epicurus said that', you protest; 'what are you doing with somebody else's property?' What is true belongs to me too, and I shall continue to inflict Epicurus on you, so that those who swear allegiance to individual teachers and don't weigh up the substance of what is said, only its author, may realize that the best things are common property.

LETTER 24

1.　　　　Sollicitum esse te scribis de iudici eventu quod tibi furor inimici denuntiat; existimas me suasurum ut meliora tibi ipse proponas et adquiescas spei blandae.　Quid enim necesse est mala accersere, satis cito patienda cum venerint praesumere, ac praesens tempus futuri metu perdere?　Est sine dubio stultum, quia quandoque sis futurus

2. miser, esse iam miserum.　Sed ego alia te ad securitatem via ducam: si vis omnem sollicitudinem exuere, quidquid vereris ne eveniat eventurum utique propone, et quodcumque est illud malum, tecum ipse metire ac timorem tuum taxa: intelleges profecto aut non magnum aut

3. non longum esse quod metuis.　Nec diu exempla quibus confirmeris colligenda sunt: omnis illa aetas tulit.　In quamcumque partem rerum vel civilium vel externarum memoriam miseris, occurrent tibi ingenia aut profectus aut impetus magni.　Numquid accidere tibi, si damnaris, potest durius quam ut mittaris in exilium, ut ducaris in carcerem? Numquid ultra quicquam ulli timendum est quam ut uratur, quam ut pereat?　Singula ista constitue et contemptores eorum cita, qui non

4. quaerendi sed eligendi sunt.　Damnationem suam Rutilius sic tulit tamquam nihil illi molestum aliud esset quam quod male iudicaretur. Exilium Metellus fortiter tulit, Rutilius etiam libenter; alter ut rediret rei publicae praestitit, alter reditum suum Sullae negavit, cui nihil tunc negabatur.　In carcere Socrates disputavit et exire, cum essent qui promitterent fugam, noluit remansitque, ut duarum rerum gravissi—

5. marum hominibus metum demeret, mortis et carceris.　Mucius ignibus manum inposuit.　Acerbum est uri: quanto acerbius si id te faciente patiaris! Vides hominem non eruditum nec ullis praeceptis contra mortem aut dolorem subornatum, militari tantum robore instructum, poenas a se inriti conatus exigentem; spectator destillantis in hostili foculo dexterae stetit nec ante removit nudis ossibus fluentem manum quam ignis illi ab hoste subductus est.　Facere aliquid in illis castris felicius potuit, nihil fortius.　Vide quanto acrior sit ad occupanda pericula virtus quam crudelitas ad inroganda: facilius Porsina Mucio ignovit quod voluerat occidere quam sibi Mucius quod non occiderat.

6.　　　　'Decantatae' inquis 'in omnibus scholis fabulae istae sunt; iam mihi, cum ad contemnendam mortem ventum fuerit, Catonem

LETTER 24

1.   You write that you are worried about the outcome of a lawsuit which an enraged enemy is bringing against you. You think that I'll persuade you to view the future with confidence and calm yourself with comforting hope. For what need is there to summon troubles, to anticipate them, all too soon to be endured when they come, and squander the present in fears of the future? It is certainly foolish to make yourself wretched now just because you are going to be wretched sometime in the future.

2.   But I shall lead you to tranquillity by another route. If you want to be rid of all anxiety, suppose that anything you are afraid of happening is going to happen in any case, then mentally calculate all the evil involved in it and appraise your own fear: you will undoubtedly come to realize that what you fear is either not great or

3. not long lasting. It won't take long to assemble examples to convince you: every age has produced them. Cast your mind back to any sphere of life, whether at home or abroad, and you will think of minds which showed either philosophical maturity or great natural energy. If you are condemned can you think of a harsher fate than exile or imprisonment? Is anything more fearful than burning or death? Set up these horrors one by one and summon forth those who have despised them: we don't have to hunt for them, but to

4. select them. Rutilius bore his condemnation as though the only thing that hurt him was the false judgment. Metellus endured his exile bravely, Rutilius even willingly; the former afforded the state the chance to recall him, the latter refused to return for Sulla — a man to whom one did not then refuse anything. Socrates debated when in prison, and refused to accept the promise of escape, remaining there so that he could free men from their two worst fears, death and

5. prison. Mucius put his own hand in the fire. Being burnt is ghastly: how much more so if you submit to it voluntarily! Here you see a man neither clever nor fortified by precepts against death or pain, simply a product of tough military discipline, punishing himself for a failed attempt. He stood and watched his right hand dripping into the enemy's brazier, and did not remove the bare bones of his dissolving hand until his enemy took the fire away. He could have done something more successful in that campaign, but nothing more brave. You can see how much more keen is virtue to anticipate dangers than cruelty to inflict them: Porsina was more ready to spare Mucius for wishing to kill him than Mucius was to spare himself because he had failed to do so.

6.   'These stories are chanted in all the rhetorical schools,' you say; 'soon you'll be coming to the theme Contempt for Death and

narrabis.' Quidni ego narrem ultima illa nocte Platonis librum legentem posito ad caput gladio? Duo haec in rebus extremis instrumenta prospexerat, alterum ut vellet mori, alterum ut posset. Compositis ergo rebus, utcumque componi fractae atque ultimae poterant, id agendum existimavit ne cui Catonem aut occidere liceret

7. aut servare contingeret; et stricto gladio quem usque in illum diem ab omni caede purum servaverat, 'nihil' inquit 'egisti, fortuna, omnibus conatibus meis obstando. Non pro mea adhuc sed pro patriae libertate pugnavi, nec agebam tanta pertinacia ut liber, sed ut inter liberos, viverem: nunc quoniam deploratae sunt res generis humani,

8. Cato deducatur in tutum.' Inpressit deinde mortiferum corpori vulnus; quo obligato a medicis cum minus sanguinis haberet, minus virium, animi idem, iam non tantum Caesari sed sibi iratus nudas in vulnus manus egit et generosum illum contemptoremque omnis potentiae spiritum non emisit sed eiecit.

9. Non in hoc exempla nunc congero ut ingenium exerceam, sed ut te adversus id quod maxime terribile videtur exhorter; facilius autem exhortabor, si ostendero non fortes tantum viros hoc momentum efflandae animae contempsisse sed quosdam ad alia ignavos in hac re aequasse animum fortissimorum, sicut illum Cn. Pompei socerum Scipionem, qui contrario in Africam vento relatus cum teneri navem suam vidisset ab hostibus, ferro se transverberavit et quaerentibus ubi

10. imperator esset, 'imperator' inquit 'se bene habet'. Vox haec illum parem maioribus fecit et fatalem Scipionibus in Africa gloriam non est interrumpi passa. Multum fuit Carthaginem vincere, sed amplius mortem. 'Imperator' inquit 'se bene habet': an aliter debebat

11. imperator, et quidem Catonis, mori? Non revoco te ad historias nec ex omnibus saeculis contemptores mortis, qui sunt plurimi, colligo; respice ad haec nostra tempora, de quorum languore ac delicis querimur: omnis ordinis homines suggerent, omnis fortunae, omnis aetatis, qui mala sua morte praeciderint. Mihi crede, Lucili, adeo

12. mors timenda non est ut beneficio eius nihil timendum sit. Securus itaque inimici minas audi; et quamvis conscientia tibi tua fiduciam faciat, tamen, quia multa extra causam valent, et quod aequissimum est spera et ad id te quod est iniquissimum compara. Illud autem ante omnia memento, demere rebus tumultum ac videre quid in quaque re sit: scies nihil esse in istis terribile nisi ipsum timorem.

13. Quod vides accidere pueris, hoc nobis quoque maiusculis pueris evenit:

telling me about Cato.' And why not tell you about him reading Plato's dialogue on that last night, with a sword near his pillow? He had taken care to have these two aids in his extremity, the will to die and the means to die. And so, arranging his affairs so far as his final disaster allowed, he determined to act so that no one would

7. have the choice whether to kill Cato or to spare him. He then drew his sword which until that day he had kept unstained by any slaughter, and said 'Fortune, you have achieved nothing by blocking all my efforts. So far I have fought for my country's liberty, not my own, and all my determination was aimed at living, not a free man myself, but among free men. But now that mankind's affairs are

8. hopeless let Cato be led to safety. Then he dealt himself a fatal wound on the head. This was bound up by the doctors, but, though his blood and his strength were failing him, his courage failed him not, and by now angry not just with Caesar but with himself he tore at his wound with his bare hands, and not so much let forth as cast out that noble spirit which despised any kind of tyranny.

9. I am not piling up examples just to exercise my wits but to support you against a horrifying prospect; and I shall do this the better by showing you ' that not only brave men have treated with contempt this moment when life ceases, but some who were in other respects indolent have here matched the courage of the bravest. Such was Scipio, father—in—law of Gnaeus Pompey, who, carried back by adverse winds to Africa and seeing his ship in the power of his enemies, fell on his sword, and when men asked where was the

10. general he replied 'All is well with the general'. These words raised him to the stature of his ancestors and ensured the continuance of that renown which destiny granted the Scipios in Africa. It was a great achievement to conquer Carthage, but a greater one to conquer death. 'All is well with the general' he said: should a general —

11. and what is more Cato's general — die otherwise? I'm not referring you to the history books or assembling from all past ages the very many who have despised death. Look at these times of ours whose apathy and affected manners we complain about: they will still offer you individuals of every rank, fortune and age who have cut short their sufferings by death. Trust me, Lucilius, death is so far

12. not to be feared that thanks to it nothing is to be feared. So listen with tranquillity to your enemy's threats, and though your good conscience gives you confidence, since there are many powerful factors outside the case, you must both hope for the most favourable outcome and gird yourself to face the most unfavourable one. But this above all remember: to banish life's turbulence and see clearly the essence of everything. You will then realize that there is nothing fearful

13. there except fear itself. What you see happen with children is true

illi quos amant, quibus adsueverunt, cum quibus ludunt, si personatos vident, expavescunt: non hominibus tantum sed rebus persona demenda

14. est et reddenda facies sua. Quid mihi gladios et ignes ostendis et turbam carnificum circa te frementem? Tolle istam pompam sub qua lates et stultos territas: mors es, quam nuper servus meus, quam ancilla contempsit. Quid tu rursus mihi flagella et eculeos magno apparatu explicas? quid singulis articulis singula machinamenta quibus extorqueantur aptata et mille alia instrumenta excarnificandi particulatim hominis? Pone ista quae nos obstupefaciunt; iube conticiscere gemitus et exclamationes et vocum inter lacerationem elisarum acerbitatem: nempe dolor es, quem podagricus ille contemnit, quem stomachicus ille in ipsis delicis perfert, quem in puerperio puella perpetitur. Levis es si ferre possum; brevis es si ferre non possum.

15. Haec in animo voluta, quae saepe audisti, saepe dixisti; sed an vere audieris, an vere dixeris, effectu proba; hoc enim turpissimum est quod nobis obici solet, verba nos philosophiae, non opera tractare. Quid? tu nunc primum tibi mortem inminere scisti, nunc exilium, nunc dolorem? in haec natus es; quidquid fieri potes; quasi futurum

16. cogitemus. Quod facere te moneo scio certe fecisse: nunc admoneo ut animum tuum non mergas in istam sollicitudinem; hebetabitur enim et minus habebit vigoris cum exsurgendum erit. Abduc illum a privata causa ad publicam; dic mortale tibi et fragile corpusculum esse, cui non ex iniuria tantum aut ex potentioribus viribus denuntiabitur dolor: ipsae voluptates in tormenta vertuntur, epulae cruditatem adferunt, ebrietates nervorum torporem tremoremque,

17. libidines pedum, manuum, articulorum omnium depravationes. Pauper fiam: inter plures ero. Exul fiam: ibi me natum putabo quo mittar. Alligabor: quid enim? nunc solutus sum? ad hoc me natura grave corporis mei pondus adstrinxit. Moriar: hoc dicis, desinam aegrotare posse, desinam alligari posse, desinam mori posse.

18. Non sum tam ineptus ut Epicuream cantilenam hoc loco persequar et dicam vanos esse inferorum metus, nec Ixionem rota volvi nec saxum umeris Sisyphi trudi in adversum nec ullius viscera et renasci posse cotidie et carpi: nemo tam puer est ut Cerberum timeat

of us slightly older children too. If they see their own friends and regular playfellows wearing masks they become frightened of them. Well, not only people but things must have their masks stripped off and their true features restored.

14.   Why do you show me swords and flames and a crowd of executioners clamouring around you? Away with that parade behind which you lurk to terrify fools: you are death, whom lately my slave and my handmaid despised. Why display again all that equipment of whips and racks? — the instruments specially designed to tear apart individual joints, and a thousand other tools for slaughtering a man bit by bit? Lay aside those means of paralysing us with horror; silence the groans, the shrieks, the hoarse cries extorted under torture. Of course you are pain — pain which the gouty man scorns, the dyspeptic suffers while he indulges himself, the girl endures in child—birth. You are mild if I can bear you and short—lived if I cannot.

15.   Think these things over: you have often heard them and often said them yourself, but you must give practical proof that you have really absorbed them from others and uttered them sincerely. For this is the most shocking charge commonly brought against us, that we deal in the words of philosophy and not its works. Well, then, have you just now realized that death looms over you, or exile, or anguish? You were born to these things. Let us reflect that

16. whatever can happen is going to happen. I am sure you have done what I'm telling you to do: my point now is not to let your mind be overwhelmed by this anxiety of yours, for it will be deadened and lose its vigour when the time comes for it to bestir itself to action. Divert it from your individual case to a general one. Tell yourself that you have only a little body, frail and mortal, and threatened by pain not only from ill—treatment by superior strength. Pleasures themselves lead to pain, banquets bring indigestion, excessive drinking brings muscular paralysis and fits of trembling, lust brings deformity in

17. hands, feet and all the joints. I shall become poor: I'll be among the majority. I shall become an exile: I'll suppose myself a native of my place of banishment. I shall be bound in fetters: so what? Am I free now? Nature has tied me to this grievous weight of my body. I shall die: what you mean is this — I shall cease to be liable to illness, I shall cease to be liable to bonds, I shall cease to be liable to death.

18.   I am not so gauche as to keep repeating the Epicurean refrain here, that fears about the underworld are groundless, and there is no Ixion turning on his wheel, no Sisyphus heaving a stone uphill with his shoulders, no possibility of anyone's entrails being daily devoured and reborn. No one is so childish as to fear Cerberus and darkness

et tenebras et larvalem habitum nudis ossibus cohaerentium.   Mors nos
aut consumit aut exuit; emissis melior restant onere detracto,
19. consumptis nihil restat, bona pariter malaque summota sunt.   Permitte
mihi hoc loc referre versum tuum, si prius admonuero ut te iudices
non aliis scripsisse ista sed etiam tibi.   Turpe est aliud loqui, aliud
sentire: quanto turpius aliud scribere, aliud sentire!   Memini te illum
locum aliquando tractasse, non repente nos in mortem incidere sed
20. minutatim procedere.   Cotidie morimur; cotidie enim demitur aliqua
pars vitae, et tunc quoque cum crescimus vita decrescit.   Infantiam
amisimus, deinde pueritiam, deinde adulescentiam.   Usque ad
hesternum quidquid transît temporis perît; hunc ipsum quem agimus
diem cum morte dividimus.   Quemadmodum clepsydram non extremum
stilicidium exhaurit sed quidquid ante defluxit, sic ultima hora qua esse
desinimus non sola mortem facit sed sola consummat; tunc ad illam
21. pervenimus, sed diu venimus.   Haec cum descripsisses quo soles ore,
semper quidem magnus, numquam tamen acrior quam ubi veritati
commodas verba, dixisti,

mors non una venit, sed quae rapit ultima mors est.

Malo te legas quam epistulam meam; apparebit enim tibi hanc quam
timemus mortem extremam esse, non solam.
22.   Video quo spectes: quaeris quid huic epistulae infulserim, quod
dictum alicuius animosum, quod praeceptum utile.   Ex hac ipsa
materia quae in manibus fuit mittetur aliquid.   Obiurgat Epicurus non
minus eos qui mortem concupiscunt quam eos qui timent, et ait:
'ridiculum est currere ad mortem taedio vitae, cum genere vitae ut
23. currendum ad mortem esset effeceris'.   Item alio loco dicit: 'quid tam
ridiculum quam adpetere mortem, cum vitam inquietam tibi feceris
metu mortis?'   His adicias et illud eiusdem notae licet, tantam
hominum inprudentiam esse, immo dementiam, ut quidam timore
24. mortis cogantur ad mortem.   Quidquid horum tractaveris, confirmabis
animum vel ad mortis vel ad vitae patientiam; [at] in utrumque enim
monendi ac firmandi sumus, et ne nimis amemus vitam et ne nimis
oderimus.   Etiam cum ratio suadet finire se, non temere nec cum
25. procursu capiendus est impetus.   Vir fortis ac sapiens non fugere
debet e vita sed exire; et ante omnia ille quoque vitetur adfectus qui
multos occupavit, libido moriendi.   Est enim, mi Lucili, ut ad alia,
sic etiam ad moriendum inconsulta animi inclinatio, quae saepe

and the spectral forms of skeletons. Death either destroys us or sets us free. If we are released, the better part of us remains having lost its burden; if we are destroyed, nothing remains and good and evil

19. alike are removed. Allow me at this point to quote your own verse, first warning you to deem it written not for others but even for yourself. It is shocking to say one thing and think another: how much worse to write one thing and think another! I recall that you once treated this topic, that we don't suddenly meet death but

20. gradually approach it. Every day we die, for every day part of our life is lost, and even when we are growing bigger our life is growing shorter. We have lost successively childhood, boyhood, youth. Right up to yesterday all the time which has passed has been lost, and this present day itself we share with death. It is not the last drop of water which empties the water—clock, but all that dripped out previously. In the same way the final hour when we actually die does not alone bring our death but simply completes the process. At that point we have arrived at death, but we have been journeying

21. thither for a long time. When you had established this with your usual eloquence, always noble but never more pungent than when your words match the truth, you then said

'We face more deaths than one: 'tis the last one takes us off.' I'd rather you read your own words than my letter: you will see clearly that this death which we fear is not the only one, only the last.

22. I see what you are looking for: you are wondering what I've packed into this letter, what spirited remark of somebody, what useful precept. I'll send you something straight from my current reading. Epicurus rebukes equally those who wish for death and those who fear it, saying 'It is silly to run to meet death through boredom with life, when it is just because of your life—style that you have created the

23. need to do so'. Similarly he remarks elsewhere: 'What is so silly as to seek death when it is the fear of death which has made your life anxious?'. You can add this reflection too which makes the same point: so great is human thoughtlessness, even madness, that certain people are driven to death by the fear of it.

24. Pondering over any of these thoughts will fortify your mind to endure either death or life; for we have to be advised and strengthened to face both without either loving or hating our life too much. Even when reason persuades us to end our lives we should

25. not follow this urge rashly or impetuously. A brave and wise man should not flee from life but step out of it, and that mood above all must be avoided which grips many men — a passion for dying. For, Lucilius, there is an unthinking tendency towards death, as towards other things, which often gets hold of men of noble and most

26. generosos atque acerrimae indolis viros corripit, saepe ignavos iacentesque: illi contemnunt vitam, hi gravantur. Quosdam subit eadem faciendi videndique satietas et vitae non odium sed fastidium, in quod prolabimur ipsa inpellente philosophia, dum dicimus 'quousque eadem? nempe expergiscar dormiam, < edam> esuriam, algebo aestuabo. Nullius rei finis est, sed in orbem nexa sunt omnia, fugiunt ac sequuntur; diem nox premit, dies noctem, aestas in autumnum desinit, autumno hiemps instat, quae vere conpescitur; omnia sic transeunt ut revertantur. Nihil novi facio, nihil novi video: fit aliquando et huius rei nausia.' Multi sunt qui non acerbum iudicent vivere sed supervacuum. Vale.

LETTER 47

1. Libenter ex iis qui a te veniunt cognovi familiariter te cum servis tuis vivere: hoc prudentiam tuam, hoc eruditionem decet. 'Servi sunt.' Immo homines. 'Servi sunt.' Immo contubernales. 'Servi sunt.' Immo humiles amici. 'Servi sunt.' Immo conservi, si

2. cogitaveris tantundem in utrosque licere fortunae. Itaque rideo istos qui turpe existimant cum servo suo cenare: quare, nisi quia superbissima consuetudo cenanti domino stantium servorum turbam circumdedit? Est ille plus quam capit, et ingenti aviditate onerat distentum ventrem ac desuetum iam ventris officio, ut maiore opera

3. omnia egerat quam ingessit. At infelicibus servis movere labra ne in hoc quidem, ut loquantur, licet; virga murmur omne conpescitur, et ne fortuita quidem verberibus excepta sunt, tussis, sternumenta, singultus; magno malo ulla voce interpellatum silentium luitur; nocte tota ieiuni

4. mutique perstant. Sic fit ut isti de domino loquantur quibus coram domino loqui non licet. At illi quibus non tantum coram dominis sed cum ipsis erat sermo, quorum os non consuebatur, parati erant pro domino porrigere cervicem, periculum inminens in caput suum

5. avertere; in conviviis loquebantur, sed in tormentis tacebant. Deinde eiusdem adrogantiae proverbium iactatur, totidem hostes esse quot servos: non habemus illos hostes sed facimus. Alia interim crudelia,

energetic character, and often men who are indolent and spiritless:
26. the former despise life, the latter are flattened by it. Some people suffer from a surfeit of doing and seeing the same things. Theirs is not contempt for life but boredom with it, a feeling we sink into when influenced by the sort of philosophy which makes us say 'How long the same old things? I shall wake up and go to sleep, I shall eat and be hungry, I shall be cold and hot. There's no end to anything, but all things are in a fixed cycle, fleeing and pursuing each other. Night follows day and day night; summer passes into autumn, hard on autumn follows winter, and that in turn is checked by spring. All things pass on only to return. Nothing I do or see is new: sometimes one gets sick even of this.' There are many who think that life is not harsh but superfluous.

LETTER 47

1.   I'm glad to hear from those who have come from you that you live on familiar terms with your slaves: this conforms to your good sense and your culture. 'They are slaves' you might say. No, they are human beings. 'They are slaves.' But they share your house. 'They are slaves.' Rather they are humble friends. 'They are slaves.' No, our fellow—slaves, if you reflect that fortune has just
2. the same power over us as over them. This makes me laugh at those who think it degrading to eat with their slaves. Why should this be except for the arrogant fashion which surrounds the master at his dinner with a troupe of standing slaves? He eats more than he can hold and with enormous greed he loads his swollen belly, which has long since forgotten the function of a belly and is more occupied
3. in vomiting back everything than in filling itself. But the wretched slaves are not allowed to move their lips even to speak: every murmur is checked with the lash, and not even accidental sounds are spared a beating, like coughing, sneezing, hiccoughs. Harsh punishment is the price paid for breaking the silence: they must
4. stand all night, hungry and silent. The result is that those who are not allowed to talk in front of their master talk about him; whereas when slaves were allowed to talk not just in front of their masters but actually with them, when their mouths were not sealed, they were ready to face execution in defence of their master and to divert to themselves any danger that threatened him. They talked at meal—
5. times but they were silent under torture. Again, it is the same haughty attitude which has given rise to the common proverb 'You have as many enemies as you have slaves'. We don't acquire them as enemies: we make them enemies.

inhumana praetereo, quod ne tamquam hominibus quidem sed tamquam iumentis abutimur. [quod] Cum ad cenandum discubuimus,

6. alius sputa deterget, alius reliquias temulentorum < toro> subditus colligit. Alius pretiosas aves scindit; per pectus et clunes certis ductibus circumferens eruditam manum frusta excutit, infelix, qui huic uni rei vivit, ut altilia decenter secet, nisi quod miserior est qui hoc

7. voluptatis causa docet quam qui necessitatis discit. Alius vini minister in muliebrem modum ornatus cum aetate luctatur: non potest effugere pueritiam, retrahitur, iamque militari habitu glaber retritis pilis aut penitus evulsis tota nocte pervigilat, quam inter ebrietatem domini ac

8. libidinem dividit et in cubiculo vir, in convivio puer est. Alius, cui convivarum censura permissa est, perstat infelix et expectat quos adulatio et intemperantia aut gulae aut linguae revocet in crastinum. Adice obsonatores quibus dominici palati notitia subtilis est, qui sciunt cuius illum rei sapor excitet, cuius delectet aspectus, cuius novitate nauseabundus erigi possit, quid iam ipsa satietate fastidiat, quid illo die esuriat. Cum his cenare non sustinet et maiestatis suae deminutionem putat ad eandem mensam cum servo suo accedere. Di melius! quot

9. ex istis dominos habet! Stare ante limen Callisti dominum suum vidi et eum qui illi inpegerat titulum, qui inter reicula manicipia produxerat, aliis intrantibus excludi. Rettulit illi gratiam servus ille in primam decuriam coniectus, in qua vocem praeco experitur: et ipse illum invicem apologavit, et ipse non iudicavit domo sua dignum. Dominus Callistum vendidit: sed domino quam multa Callistus!

10. Vis tu cogitare istum quem servum tuum vocas ex isdem seminibus ortum eodem frui caelo, aeque spirare, aeque vivere, aeque mori! tam tu illum videre ingenuum potes quam ille te servum. Variana clade multos splendidissime natos, senatorium per militiam auspicantes gradum, fortuna depressit: alium ex illis pastorem, alium custodem casae fecit. Contemne nunc eius fortunae hominem in quam transire dum contemnis potes.

11. Nolo in ingentem me locum inmittere et de usu servorum

For the time being I pass over other cruel and inhuman behaviour by which we abuse them, not even as though they were human beings but as if they were beasts of burden. When we have arranged ourselves for dinner, one slave wipes up our spittle; another stationed by the couch collects the scraps left by the drunken diners;

6. another carves the costly poultry: with deft strokes his practised hand goes round, cutting slices from the breast and rump. Poor wretch, whose one purpose in life is to carve fowl skilfully — except that he is more pitiable who teaches this art for pleasure's sake than he who

7. learns it because he has to. Another one who serves the wine is dressed like a girl and struggles with his age. He is not allowed to escape his boyhood but is dragged back to it, and though he now has a soldier's bearing he is kept smooth—skinned by having his hair rubbed away or pulled out, and he spends a sleepless night divided between serving his master's drunkenness and his lust — a man in the

8. bedroom and a boy at the dining—table. Another one has the job of classifying the guests, and he, poor wretch, has to remain standing and watching to see which of them by their flattery and their unrestrained appetite or language will earn them another invitation next day. There are the caterers too who have a refined knowledge of their master's palate: they know the flavour that stirs his appetite, the sight that appeals to him, the novel dish to tempt him when nausea is setting in, what he cannot face when really sated, what he fancies on that particular day. These are the men he cannot bear to eat with, and he thinks it lowers his dignity to sit at the same table with his slave. Good heavens! How many masters does he have

9. from these ranks! I've seen his former master standing at Callistus' threshold and refused entry when others were let in — the master who had once stuck a sale—ticket on Callistus and offered him for sale as part of a job lot of slaves. That particular slave paid his master back for being pushed into the first lot for disposal, the one on which the auctioneer practises his voice: it was his turn to reject his master and judge him unworthy of his house. His master sold Callistus — and that sale cost him dear!

10. Perhaps you should reflect that the man you call your slave comes from the same seed as you do, enjoys the same sky above, breathes, lives and dies as you do. You can just as easily regard him as free—born as he can see you a slave. When Varus suffered his disaster fortune humbled many men of most distinguished birth, who were beginning their senatorial career by military service: she made one a shepherd, another a shopkeeper. Despise if you can such a man's lot in life — which might become yours at the moment you are despising it.

11. I don't want to involve myself in an extensive topic and discuss

disputare, in quos superbissimi, crudelissimi, contumeliosissimi sumus. Haec tamen praecepti mei summa est: sic cum inferiore vivas quemadmodum tecum superiorem velis vivere. Quotiens in mentem venerit quantum tibi in servum < tuum> liceat, veniat in mentem

12. tantundem in te domino tuo licere. 'At ego' inquis 'nullum habeo dominum.' Bona aetas est: forsitan habebis. Nescis qua aetate Hecuba servire coeperit, qua Croesus, qua Darei mater, qua Platon,

13. qua Diogenes? Vive cum servo clementer, comiter quoque, et in sermonem illum admitte et in consilium et in convictum.

Hoc loco adclamabit mihi tota manus delicatorum 'nihil hac re humilius, nihil turpius'. Hos ego eosdem deprehendam alienorum

14. servorum osculantes manum. Ne illud quidem videtis, quam omnem invidiam maiores nostri dominis, omnem contumeliam servis detraxerint? Dominum patrem familiae appellaverunt, servos, quod etiam in mimis adhuc durat, familiares; instituerunt diem festum, non quo solo cum servis domini vescerentur, sed quo utique; honores illis in domo gerere, ius dicere permiserunt et domum pusillam rem

15. publicam esse iudicaverunt. 'Quid ergo? omnes servos admovebo mensae meae?' Non magis quam omnes liberos. Erras si existimas me quosdam quasi sordidioris operae reiecturum, ut puta illum mulionem et illum bubulcum. Non ministeriis illos aestimabo sed moribus: sibi quisque dat mores, ministeria casus adsignat. Quidam cenent tecum quia digni sunt, quidam ut sint; si quid enim in illis ex

16. sordida conversatione servile est, honestiorum convictus excutiet. Non est, mi Lucili, quod amicum tantum in foro et in curia quaeras: si diligenter adtenderis, et domi invenies. Saepe bona materia cessat sine artifice: tempta et experire. Quemadmodum stultus est qui equum empturus non ipsum inspicit sed stratum eius ac frenos, sic stultissimus est qui hominem aut ex veste aut ex condicione, quae

17. vestis modo nobis circumdata est, aestimat. 'Servus est.' Sed fortasse liber animo. 'Servus est.' Hoc illi nocebit? Ostende quis non sit: alius libidini servit, alius avaritiae, alius ambitioni, < omnes spei>, omnes timori. Dabo consularem aniculae servientem, dabo ancillulae divitem, ostendam nobilissimos iuvenes mancipia pantomimorum: nulla servitus turpior est quam voluntaria. Quare non est quod fastidiosi isti te deterreant quominus servis tuis hilarem te praestes et non superbe superiorem: colant potius te quam timeant.

the treatment of slaves, to whom we are extremely arrogant, cruel and insulting. But the substance of my advice is this: treat your inferior just as you would like your superior to treat you. Whenever you think how much power you have over your slave, think that your

12. own master has just as much over you. 'But I have no master' you object. You are young: perhaps you will. Don't you know how old Hecuba was when she became a slave, or Croesus, or Darius' mother,

13. or Plato, or Diogenes? Treat your slave gently, even genially, and let him join in your talk, your plans, and your social life.

At this point I hear all the elegant fops exclaiming 'Nothing would be more humiliating and degrading than that'. But these are the very men I shall catch kissing the hands of other men's slaves.

14. Don't you even notice how our ancestors took away all odium from masters and all indignity from slaves? They called the master 'father of the household' and the slaves 'householders', a name that still survives in mimes. They established a holiday, not as the only day but as one on which especially masters and slaves would eat together. They allowed slaves to enjoy some privileges and authority in the

15. house, and they regarded the household as a miniature state. 'So? Am I then to invite all my slaves to my table?' No more than you invite all free men. But you are wrong if you think that I will exclude certain ones on the grounds of their menial jobs, like this muleteer or that cowhand. I shall value them according to their characters, not their tasks. Each man is responsible for his own character, whereas chance assigns him his tasks. Let some of them share your table because they deserve it, and others so that they may learn to deserve it. For if they have any slavish qualities arising from their coarse associations they will cast them off in the company of respectable men.

16. You don't have to find your friends only in the Forum and the Senate, Lucilius: if you look carefully you'll find them at home too. Often good material lies idle for want of a craftsman: try and see. It is a foolish purchaser who inspects the saddle and reins and not the horse itself: far more foolish is it to judge a man from his

17. clothes or social status — which is only a sort of clothes. 'He is a slave.' But he may be free in spirit. 'He is a slave.' Must this be damaging to him? Show me who isn't. One man is a slave to lust, another to greed, another to ambition, everyone to hopes and fears. I can show you an ex−consul who is a slave to his ageing mistress, a sugar−daddy who is a slave to a slave−girl, well−born young men completely ruled by pantomime−dancers. There is no servitude more disgraceful than a self−imposed one. So do not let snobbish people put you off from being pleasant to your slaves instead of proud and high−handed. Let them feel respect rather than fear towards you.

18.   Dicet aliquis nunc me vocare ad pilleum servos et dominos de fastigio suo deicere, quod dixi, 'colant potius dominum quam timeant'. 'Ita' inquit 'prorsus? colant tamquam clientes, tamquam salutatores?' Hoc qui dixerit obliviscetur id dominis parum non esse quod deo sat est.   Qui colitur, et amatur: non potest amor cum timore misceri.

19. Rectissime ergo facere te iudico quod timeri a servis tuis non vis, quod verborum castigatione uteris: verberibus muta admonentur.   Non quidquid nos offendit et laedit; sed ad rabiem cogunt pervenire

20. deliciae, ut quidquid non ex voluntate respondit iram evocet.   Regum nobis induimus animos; nam illi quoque obliti et suarum virium et inbecillitatis alienae sic excandescunt, sic saeviunt, quasi iniuriam acceperint, a cuius rei periculo illos fortunae suae magnitudo tutissimos praestat.   Nec hoc ignorant, sed occasionem nocendi captant querendo; acceperunt iniuriam ut facerent.

21.   Diutius te morari nolo; non est enim tibi exhortatione opus. Hoc habent inter cetera boni mores: placent sibi, permanent.   Levis est malitia, saepe mutatur, non in melius sed in aliud.   Vale.

LETTER 54

1.   Longum mihi commeatum dederat mala valetudo; repente me invasit. 'Quo genere?' inquis.   Prorsus merito interrogas: adeo nullum mihi ignotum est.   Uni tamen morbo quasi adsignatus sum, quem quare Graeco nomine appellem nescio; satis enim apte dici suspirium potest.   Brevis autem valde et procellae similis est impetus; intra

2. horam fere desinit: quis enim diu exspirat?   Omnia corporis aut incommoda aut pericula per me transierunt: nullum mihi videtur molestius.   Quidni? aliud enim quidquid est aegrotare est, hoc animam egerere.   Itaque medici hanc 'meditationem mortis' vocant; facit enim aliquando spiritus ille quod saepe conatus est.   Hilarem me putas haec

3. tibi scribere quia effugi? Tam ridicule facio, si hoc fine quasi bona valetudine delector, quam ille, quisquis vicisse se putat cum vadimonium distulit.

      Ego vero et in ipsa suffocatione non desii cogitationibus laetis

4. ac fortibus adquiescere.   'Quid hoc est?' inquam 'tam saepe mors

18.   Because of that last remark I shall now be accused of advocating freedom for slaves and of undermining the authority of masters. 'Are you really saying that slaves should just feel the same respect as dependants and early morning callers?' This objector forgets that what is sufficient for a god is not too little for masters. One who is respected is also loved, and love and fear cannot go

19. together. So I feel that your policy is absolutely right in that you don't want your slaves to fear you and you punish them by words only: beatings are for animals. We aren't damaged by anything that annoys us; but our fastidious tastes drive us out of our wits so that we get enraged at anything which does not exactly please our fancy.

20. We assume the pride of tyrants; for they too forget their own strength and the weakness of others, and they blaze up in such a fury as if they have received an injury from something they have no reason whatever to fear through their own exalted position. They know this too, but they make their grievance an excuse for hurting someone. They claim an injury as a pretext for inflicting one.

21.   I won't keep you longer, for you don't need exhortation. It is the mark of a 'virtuous character that it satisfies itself and it lasts. Vicious behaviour is fickle and always changing, not for the better but just into something different.

LETTER 54

1.   My ill—health has suddenly attacked me after giving me a long respite. 'In what way?' you ask — and well you may, as there's absolutely no illness I've not suffered. But there is one complaint which as it were' has me in charge. I don't know why I should call it by its Greek name since it is quite adequately described as laboured breathing. Its attack lasts a very short time and hits you with the force of a gale; it is over within about an hour — for who could go

2. on dying for long? I have suffered every kind of unpleasant or dangerous physical complaint, but none is worse than this. Not surprising, for anything else is just an illness, while this is gasping out your life—breath. That is why doctors call it a 'rehearsal for death', since eventually the breath does what it has often been trying to do.

3. Do you think that I am writing to you in a cheerful mood because I've escaped this time? If I were delighted with this remission as though it meant I was in good health, I would be as foolish as the man who thinks he has won his case when he has been given an adjournment of the trial.

    However, even as I gasped for breath I did not cease to

4. comfort myself with brave and cheerful reflections. 'So', I said, 'is

experitur me?   Faciat: [at] ego illam diu expertus sum.'   'Quando?' inquis.   Antequam nascerer.   Mors est non esse.   Id quale sit iam scio: hoc erit post me quod ante me fuit.   Si quid in hac re tormenti est, necesse est et fuisse, antequam prodiremus in lucem; atqui nullam

5.   sensimus tunc vexationem.   Rogo, non stultissimum dicas si quis existimet lucernae peius esse cum extincta est quam antequam accenditur?   Nos quoque et extinguimur et accendimur: medio illo tempore aliquid patimur, utrimque vero alta securitas est.   In hoc enim, mi Lucili, nisi fallor, erramus, quod mortem iudicamus sequi, cum illa et praecesserit et secutura sit.   Quidquid ante nos fuit mors est; quid enim refert non incipias an desinas, cum utriusque rei hic sit effectus, non esse?

6.   His et eiusmodi exhortationibus (tacitis scilicet, nam verbis locus non erat) adloqui me non desii; deinde paulatim suspirium illud, quod esse iam anhelitus coeperat, intervalla maiora fecit et retardatum est. At remansit, nec adhuc, quamvis desierit, ex natura fluit spiritus; sentio haesitationem quandam eius et moram.   Quomodo volet,

7.   dummodo non ex animo suspirem.   Hoc tibi de me recipe: non trepidabo ad extrema, iam praeparatus sum, nihil cogito de die toto. Illum tu lauda et imitare quem non piget mori, cum iuvet vivere: quae est enim virtus, cum eiciaris, exire?   Tamen est et hic virtus: eicior quidem, sed tamquam exeam.   Et ideo numquam eicitur sapiens quia eici est inde expelli unde invitus recedas: nihil invitus facit sapiens; necessitatem effugit, quia vult quod coactura est.   Vale.

LETTER 56

1.   Peream si est tam necessarium quam videtur silentium in studia seposito.   Ecce undique me varius clamor circumsonat: supra ipsum balneum habito.   Propone nunc tibi omnia genera vocum quae in odium possunt aures adducere: cum fortiores exercentur et manus plumbo graves iactant, cum aut laborant aut laborantem imitantur, gemitus audio, quotiens retentum spiritum remiserunt, sibilos et acerbissimas respirationes; cum in aliquem inertem et hac plebeia unctione contentum incidi, audio crepitum inlisae manus umeris, quae

death making all these trials of me? Let him: I made trial of him long ago.' 'When?' you ask. Before I was born. Death is non—existence. I already know what that is like, and it will be the same after me as it was before me. If there is any torment in the after state it must have been present in the state before we came to
5. birth; yet we felt no distress then. I ask you, wouldn't you call anyone an utter idiot who thought that a lamp was worse off when it was extinguished than before it was lit? We too are lit and extinguished: between these times we suffer somewhat, but on either side of the interval there is utter tranquillity. Unless I'm wrong, Lucilius, our mistake is in supposing that death follows, whereas it both has preceded and will follow. Death is everything that was before us. What difference does it make whether you cease or you never begin, when the result of either state is non—existence?

6. I kept up these and similar adjurations to myself — silently, of course, as I was in no fit state to speak — and then gradually the laboured gasping, which had slowly improved to a panting, had longer periods of remission and abated. But it has lingered, and though the worst is over my breath is still not coming naturally: I am conscious that it falters and has a catch in it. Well, let it come as it likes, so
7. long as my sighs are not emotional ones. You can be reassured on this point: I shall not be afraid when the end comes; I am already prepared; my plans never assume a full day ahead of me. You should admire and imitate the man who is not reluctant to die even when life is still sweet: for where is the virtue in departing from life when you are actually being expelled from it? Yet there is a virtue in my case: I am indeed being expelled, but the manner of it is a departure. And this is why the wise man is never expelled: for expulsion means being driven out reluctantly. But the wise man does nothing reluctantly: he escapes necessity because he himself wills what it is going to force upon him.

LETTER 56

1. I can't for the life of me see that silence is as essential as people think for someone studying in seclusion. Look how various kinds of uproar echo all around me: I live over a public bath—house. Now imagine to yourself every type of sound which can make you sick of your ears: when hearty types are exercising by swinging dumb—bells around — either working hard at it or pretending to — I hear their grunts, and then a sharp hissing whenever they let out the breath they've been holding. Or again, my attention is caught by someone who is content to relax under an ordinary massage and I hear the

2. prout plana pervenit aut concava, ita sonum mutat. Si vero pilicrepus supervenit et numerare coepit pilas, actum est. Adice nunc scordalum et furem deprensum et illum cui vox sua in balineo placet, adice nunc eos qui in piscinam cum ingenti inpulsae aquae sono saliunt. Praeter istos quorum, si nihil aliud, rectae voces sunt, alipilum cogita tenuem et stridulam vocem quo sit notabilior subinde exprimentem nec umquam tacentem nisi dum vellit alas et alium pro se clamare cogit; iam biberari varias exclamationes et botularium et crustularium et omnes popinarum institores mercem sua quadam et insignita modulatione vendentis.

3. 'O te' inquis 'ferreum aut surdum, cui mens inter tot clamores tam varios, tam dissonos constat, cum Chrysippum nostrum adsidua salutatio perducat ad mortem.' At mehercules ego istum fremitum non magis curo quam fluctum aut deiectum aquae, quamvis audiam cuidam genti hanc unam fuisse causam urbem suam transferendi, quod

4. fragorem Nili cadentis ferre non potuit. Magis mihi videtur vox avocare quam crepitus; illa enim animum adducit, hic tantum aures implet ac verberat. In his quae me sine avocatione circumstrepunt essedas transcurrentes pono et fabrum inquilinum et serrarium vicinum, aut hunc qui ad Metam Sudantem tubulas experitur et tibias, nec

5. cantat sed exclamat: etiamnunc molestior est mihi sonus qui intermittitur subinde quam qui continuatur. Sed iam me sic ad omnia ista duravi ut audire vel pausarium possim voce acerbissima remigibus modos dantem. Animum enim cogo sibi intentum esse nec avocari ad externa; omnia licet foris resonent, dum intus nihil tumultus sit, dum inter se non rixentur cupiditas et timor, dum avaritia luxuriaque non dissideant nec altera alteram vexet. Nam quid prodest totius regionis silentium, si adfectus fremunt?

6. Omnia noctis erant placida composta quiete.

Falsum est: nulla placida est quies nisi quam ratio composuit; nox exhibet molestiam, non tollit, et sollicitudines mutat. Nam dormientium quoque insomnia tam turbulenta sunt quam dies: illa

7. tranquillitas vera est in quam bona mens explicatur. Aspice illum cui somnus laxae domus silentio quaeritur, cuius aures ne quis agitet sonus, omnis servorum turba conticuit et suspensum accedentium propius vestigium ponitur: huc nempe versatur atque illuc, somnum inter aegritudines levem captans; quae non audit audisse se queritur.

smack of a hand whacking his shoulders, the sound changing as the hand comes down flat or curved.   If on top of all that there is a

2.   game—scorer beginning to call out the score, I've had it!   Then there's the brawler, the thief caught in the act, the man who likes the sound of his voice in the bath, the folk who leap into the pool with an enormous splash.   Besides those whose voices are, if nothing else, natural, think of the depilator constantly uttering his shrill and piercing cry to advertise his services: he is never silent except when plucking someone's armpits and forcing him to yell instead.   Then there are the various cries of the drink—seller; there's the sausage—seller and the pastry—cook and all the eating—house pedlars, each marketing his wares with his own distinctive cry.

3.   'You must be made of iron', you say, 'or deaf, for your mind to remain undisturbed amid such a varied and discordant uproar, when never—ending early—morning greetings were the death of the Stoic Chrysippus.'   But honestly I don't care about that babel any more than I do about the waves of the sea or a waterfall, though I'm told of a people who moved the site of their city for the sole reason that

4.   they could not stand the roar of a Nile cataract.   I find voices more distracting than loud, noises, as they claim the mind's attention, whereas noises just fill and batter the ears.   In the class of noises which can surround without distracting me I include passing carriages, the carpenter living in the same block, the neighbouring sawyer, the man who tunes horns and pipes near the Cone Fountain — he isn't

5.   making music, just a loud noise.   Moreover, it is an intermittent noise which I find more of a nuisance than a continuous one.   But now I have inured myself to all these things, so that I can even put up with the sound of the boatswain's hoarse cry giving time to the oarsmen.   I force my mind to concentrate and not to be distracted by external things.   There can be complete turmoil without so long as there is tranquillity within, so long as greed and fear are not contending with each other, and meanness and extravagance are not at odds and assailing one another.   For what is the good of having silence all around you if your passsions are in uproar?

6.   'Night's peaceful quiet had lulled all things to rest.'
Rubbish: there is no peaceful quiet unless reason has lulled it to rest.   Night causes rather than removes anxiety, and only changes our worries.   Even when we are asleep our dreams are as disturbed as our days: the only true tranquillity is that in which a virtuous mind

7.   can unwind.   Consider the man whose sleep requires complete silence throughout his spacious house.   To prevent any sound disturbing him every slave is mute and everyone approaching him walks on tip—toe.   Yet he tosses about, snatching fitful naps between his worrying

8.   thoughts, and he complains of noises he never heard.   The reason?

8. Quid in causa putas esse? Animus illi obstrepit. Hic placandus est, huius conpescenda seditio est, quem non est quod existimes placidum, si iacet corpus: interdum quies inquieta est; et ideo ad rerum actus excitandi ac tractatione bonarum artium occupandi sumus, quotiens nos
9. male habet inertia sui inpatiens. Magni imperatores, cum male parere militem vident, aliquo labore conpescunt et expeditionibus detinent: numquam vacat lascivire districtis, nihilque tam certum est quam otii vitia negotio discuti. Saepe videmur taedio rerum civilium et infelicis atque ingratae stationis paenitentia secessisse; tamen in illa latebra in quam nos timor ac lassitudo coniecit interdum recrudescit ambitio. Non enim excisa desît, sed fatigata aut etiam obirata rebus parum sibi
10. cedentibus. Idem de luxuria dico, quae videtur aliquando cessisse, deinde frugalitatem professos sollicitat atque in media parsimonia voluptates non damnatas sed relictas petit, et quidem eo vehementius quo occultius. Omnia enim vitia in aperto leniora sunt; morbi quoque tunc ad sanitatem inclinant cum ex abdito erumpunt ac vim sui proferunt. Et avaritiam itaque et ambitionem et cetera mala mentis humanae tunc perniciosissima scias esse cum simulata sanitate
11. subsidunt. Otiosi videmur, et non sumus. Nam si bona fide sumus, si receptui cecinimus, si speciosa contempsimus, ut paulo ante dicebam, nulla res nos avocabit, nullus hominum aviumque concentus
12. interrumpet cogitationes bonas, solidasque iam et certas. Leve illud ingenium est nec sese adhuc reduxit introsus quod ad vocem et accidentia erigitur; habet intus aliquid sollicitudinis et habet aliquid concepti pavoris quod illum curiosum facit, ut ait Vergilius noster:

> et me, quem dudum non ulla iniecta movebant
> tela neque adverso glomerati ex agmine Grai,
> nunc omnes terrent aurae, sonus excitat omnis
> suspensum et pariter comitique onerique timentem.

13. Prior ille sapiens est, quem non tela vibrantia, non arietata inter <se> arma agminis densi, non urbis inpulsae fragor territat: hic alter inperitus est, rebus suis timet ad omnem crepitum expavescens, quem una quaelibet vox pro fremitu accepta deiecit, quem motus levissimi

His mind is in a turmoil. This is what must be appeased; here is the revolt to be quelled: you cannot assume the mind is at rest just because the body is lying down. Sometimes rest is restless, which is why we have to be stirred to action and busied with worthwhile pursuits whenever we are afflicted by the indolence which wearies of
9. itself. Great generals deal with undisciplined troops by giving them work to do and keeping them occupied with excursions. People who are busy have no time to run riot, and nothing is so certain as that the faults arising from idleness are dispelled by activity.

We often appear to have retired into private life because we are sick of the political world and disgusted with a sterile and unpopular post. Yet sometimes ambition starts up again in that very retirement to which our fears and our weariness consigned us. For it did not cease by being exterminated but because it was tired and
10. angry at not having a clear path before it. The same is true of extravagance. Sometimes this seems to have left us, and then when we have settled for temperate habits it tempts us, and in the midst of our policy of moderation it looks for the pleasures we have put away but not finally condemned − and this campaign against us is all the more vigorous for our being unaware of it. For all vices are less serious when they' are visible: so too diseases are on the way to a cure once they have become manifest and have revealed their intensity. Thus you must realize that greed, ambition and all the other ailments of the human mind are at their most dangerous stage just when they have subsided and give a false impression of being
11. cured. We look as though we are in retirement and yet we are not. For if we really mean to be, if we have sounded the retreat, if we have come to despise the outward show of things, then, as I said just now, nothing will distract us, no joint chorus of men and birds will interrupt meditations that are good and have now become steady and assured.
12. It is a sign of an unstable temperament and one that has not yet achieved detachment if it is startled by a voice and by chance sounds. It has some inward disquiet, a sort of deep−rooted dread, that makes it morbidly anxious; as Virgil puts it:
'And I who shuddered not before at flying spears,
Nor troops of Greeks advancing to attack,
Now shrink at every breeze and fear each sound,
In terror both for what I lead and what I bear.'
13. At his earlier stage this character is the wise man, who has no fear of darting weapons, arms clashing together in the dense ranks, the crash of the city in destruction. Later he is ignorant, he fears for his own while in terror at every sound; any single voice prostrates him as he takes it for the eremy's shouts; the slightest movement

14. exanimant; timidum illum sarcinae faciunt. Quemcumque ex istis felicibus elegeris, multa trahentibus, multa portantibus, videbis illum 'comitique onerique timentem'. Tunc ergo te scito esse compositum cum ad te nullus clamor pertinebit, cum te nulla vox tibi excutiet, non si blandietur, non si minabitur, non si inani sono vana 15. circumstrepet. 'Quid ergo? non aliquando commodius est et carere convicio?' Fateor; itaque ego ex hoc loco migrabo. Experiri et exercere me volui: quid necesse est diutius torqueri, cum tam facile remedium Ulixes sociis etiam adversus Sirenas invenerit? Vale.

LETTER 57

1.   Cum a Bais deberem Neapolim repetere, facile credidi tempestatem esse, ne iterum navem experirer; et tantum luti tota via fuit ut possim videri nihilominus navigasse. Totum athletarum fatum mihi illo die perpetiendum fuit: a ceromate nos haphe excepit in 2. crypta Neapolitana. Nihil illo carcere longius, nihil illis facibus obscurius, quae nobis praestant non ut per tenebras videamus, sed ut ipsas. Ceterum etiam si locus haberet lucem, pulvis auferret, in aperto quoque res gravis et molesta: quid illic, ubi in se volutatur et, cum sine ullo spiramento sit inclusus, in ipsos a quibus excitatus est recidit? Duo incommoda inter se contraria simul pertulimus: eadem via, eodem die et luto et pulvere laboravimus.

3.   Aliquid tamen mihi illa obscuritas quod cogitarem dedit: sensi quendam ictum animi et sine metu mutationem quam insolitae rei novitas simul ac foeditas fecerat. Non de me nunc tecum loquor, qui multum ab homine tolerabili, nedum a perfecto absum, sed de illo in quem fortuna ius perdidit: huius quoque ferietur animus, mutabitur 4. color. Quaedam enim, mi Lucili, nulla effugere virtus potest; admonet illam natura mortalitatis suae. Itaque et vultum adducet ad tristia et inhorrescet ad subita et caligabit, si vastam altitudinem in crepidine eius constitutus despexerit: non est hoc timor, sed naturalis 5. adfectio inexpugnabilis rationi. Itaque fortes quidam et paratissimi

scares him silly: it is the burden he carries which makes him fearful.

14. Single out any of your successful men, those with much to carry and much in their wake, and you will see the man 'in terror both for what I lead and what I bear'. You can be sure, then, that you will be 'lulled to rest' only when no uproar concerns you, no voices shake your inner poise, whether they are flattering or menacing or just making an empty, meaningless sound around you.

15. 'That's all very well,' you say, 'but isn't it sometimes more convenient just to avoid a racket?' True — so I'm going to move. I wanted to test and train myself, but why must I go on being tormented when Ulysses found such an easy remedy for his comrades even against the Sirens?

LETTER 57

1. When I was due to return to Naples from Baiae I easily persuaded myself that the weather was too stormy to try a second sea — voyage. And yet the whole of my route was so muddy that anyone would think I had sailed nevertheless. That day I had to go through everything that athletes endure: after our anointment with

2. mud we then faced a sand — dusting in the Naples tunnel. Nothing is longer than that prison, nothing more gloomy than the torches there, which intensify the darkness rather than enabling us to see through it. In any case, even if the place had any light, the dust would conceal it. Dust is a serious nuisance even in the open: you can imagine what it's like in that place, where it just eddies around, and since there's no ventilation it settles on those who have stirred it up. We suffered simultaneously from two normally opposing inconveniences: on the same journey and the same day we had to cope with both mud and dust.

3. And yet that darkness gave me something to think about: I felt a sort of mental shock and confusion, though without fear, caused by the novelty and also the unpleasantness of an unusual experience. I'm not now talking to you about myself — I'm far from being even a passable man, let alone a perfect one — but about the sort of man over whom Fortune has lost her rights: even *his* mind will suffer a

4. blow and his colour change. For there are some things, dear Lucilius, which no courage can escape — nature warns that courage of its own mortality. And so this man will contort his features at sad news, and shudder at sudden occurrences, and turn giddy if he stands on the edge of a great height and looks down. This isn't fear but a

5. natural reaction which cannot be conquered by reason. And so some brave men who are more than willing to shed their own blood cannot

6. fundere suum sanguinem alienum videre non possunt; quidam ad vulneris novi, quidam ad veteris et purulenti tractationem inspectionemque succidunt ac linquuntur animo; alii gladium facilius recipiunt quam vident. Sensi ergo, ut dicebam, quandam non quidem perturbationem, sed mutationem: rursus ad primum conspectum redditae lucis alacritas rediit incogitata et iniussa. Illud deinde mecum loqui coepi, quam inepte quaedam magis aut minus timeremus, cum omnium idem finis esset. Quid enim interest utrum supra aliquem vigilarium ruat an mons? nihil invenies. Erunt tamen qui hanc ruinam magis timeant, quamvis utraque mortifera aeque sit; adeo non effectus, sed efficientia timor spectat.

7. Nunc me putas de Stoicis dicere, qui existimant animam hominis magno pondere extriti permanere non posse et statim spargi, quia non fuerit illi exitus liber? Ego vero non facio: qui hoc dicunt videntur

8. mihi errare. Quemadmodum flamma non potest opprimi (nam circa id diffugit quo urgetur), quemadmodum aer verbere atque ictu non laeditur, ne scinditur quidem, sed circa id cui cessit refunditur, sic animus, qui ex tenuissimo constat, deprehendi non potest nec intra corpus effligi, sed beneficio subtilitatis suae per ipsa quibus premitur erumpit. Quomodo fulmini, etiam cum latissime percussit ac fulsit, per exiguum foramen est reditus, sic animo, qui adhuc tenuior est

9. igne, per omne corpus fuga est. Itaque de illo quaerendum est, an possit inmortalis esse. Hoc quidem certum habe: si superstes est corpori, opteri illum nullo genere posse, [propter quod non perit] quoniam nulla inmortalitas cum exceptione est, nec quicquam noxium aeterno est. Vale.

LETTER 78

1. Vexari te destillationibus crebris ac febriculis, quae longas destillationes et in consuetudinem adductas sequuntur, eo molestius mihi est quia expertus sum hoc genus valetudinis, quod inter initia contempsi — poterat adhuc adulescentia iniurias ferre et se adversus morbos contumaciter gerere — deinde succubui et eo perductus sum ut

2. ipse destillarem, ad summam maciem deductus. Saepe impetum cepi abrumpendae vitae: patris me indulgentissimi senectus retinuit. Cogitavi enim non quam fortiter ego mori possem, sed quam ille fortiter desiderare non posset. Itaque imperavi mihi ut viverem; aliquando enim et vivere fortiter facere est.

bear to see someone else's. Some people collapse and faint at the sight and handling of a fresh wound, others at an old and festering one. Some receive a sword—thrust more easily than they see one
6. given. Well, as I was saying, my feeling was not really a serious disturbance but a sort of confusion, and at the first glimpse of the return of daylight my natural cheerfulness returned without thought or volition.

Then I began to say to myself how foolishly we fear some things more or less although the same end awaits us all. For what difference does it make whether a watch—tower or a mountain collapses on somebody? None, of course. Yet you will find people who are more afraid of the mountain falling though both are equally fatal. So true is it that fear contemplates not results but what brings them about.

7. Do you imagine I am now talking about the Stoics, who believe that the soul of a man crushed by a great weight cannot survive and is straightway broken up because there was not a clear outlet for it?
8. Not in the least: those who say this seem to me wrong. Just as a flame cannot be crushed (for it escapes around whatever is pressing it), nor can air be damaged or even divided by hitting and striking it, but flows around that which it gives way to; so the soul, which is composed of the most rarefied material, cannot be trapped or crushed within the body, but thanks to its fine texture it forces its way right through any overpowering weight. Just as however widely a thunderbolt's force and flash is diffused it returns through a tiny opening, so the soul, which is even more rarefied than fire, can
9. escape through any part of the body. And so we must ask this question: can it be immortal? Well, be sure of this: if it survives the body it can in no way be destroyed, since no sort of immortality is qualified and nothing can damage what is eternal.

LETTER 78

1. I am all the more distressed that you are being plagued with frequent catarrh and the feverishness which attends protracted and chronic catarrh, because I too suffer from this disorder. In its early stages I made light of it — being young I could still put up with afflictions and bid defiance to illness. But then I succumbed to it and was reduced to a skeleton as the whole of me oozed away.
2. Often I had the urge to end my life, but the advanced age of my most loving father restrained me. For I reflected not on how bravely I could die, but on how he could not bravely bear my loss. So I ordered myself to live — sometimes even to live is an act of courage.

3. Quae mihi tunc fuerint solacio dicam, si prius hoc dixero, haec ipsa quibus adquiescebam medicinae vim habuisse; in remedium cedunt honesta solacia, et quidquid animum erexit etiam corpori prodest. Studia mihi nostra saluti fuerunt; philosophiae acceptum fero quod surrexi, quod convalui; illi vitam debeo et nihil illi minus debeo.

4. Multum autem mihi contulerunt ad bonam valetudinem < et> amici, quorum adhortationibus, vigiliis, sermonibus adlevabar. Nihil aeque, Lucili, virorum optime, aegrum reficit atque adiuvat quam amicorum adfectus, nihil aeque expectationem mortis ac metum subripit: non iudicabam me, cum illos superstites relinquerem, mori. Putabam, inquam, me victurum non cum illis, sed per illos; non effundere mihi spiritum videbar, sed tradere. Haec mihi dederunt voluntatem adiuvandi me et patiendi omne tormentum; alioqui miserrimum est, cum animum moriendi proieceris, non habere vivendi.

5. Ad haec ergo remedia te confer. Medicus tibi quantum ambules, quantum exercearis monstrabit; ne indulgeas otio, ad quod vergit iners valetudo; ut legas clarius et spiritum, cuius iter ac receptaculum laborat, exerceas; ut naviges et viscera molli iactatione concutias; quibus cibis utaris, vinum quando virium causa advoces, quando intermittas ne inritet et exasperet tussim. Ego tibi illud praecipio quod non tantum huius morbi sed totius vitae remedium est: contemne mortem. Nihil triste est cum huius metum effugimus.

6. Tria haec in omni morbo gravia sunt: metus mortis, dolor corporis, intermissio voluptatum. De morte satis dictum est: hoc unum dicam, non morbi hunc esse sed naturae metum. Multorum mortem distulit morbus et saluti illis fuit videri perire. Morieris, non quia aegrotas, sed quia vivis. Ista te res et sanatum manet; cum convalueris, non mortem sed valetudinem effugeris.

7. Ad illud nunc proprium incommodum revertamur: magnos cruciatus habet morbus, sed hos tolerabiles intervalla faciunt. Nam summi doloris intentio invenit finem; nemo potest valde dolere et diu; sic nos amantissima nostri natura disposuit ut dolorem aut tolerabilem

3.   I'll tell you the consolations I found at that time, first pointing out that the very means by which I achieved tranquillity had a potency like that of medicine. Honourable sources of comfort bring about a cure, and whatever cheers us mentally helps us physically. It was my studies which proved my salvation: I owe it to philosophy that I rose from my bed and grew well. My debt to her is my life,

4.   and yet it is the least of my debts to her. But my friends too helped a great deal towards my recovery, cheered as I was by their encouraging words when they sat by my bed and talked to me. Nothing, my good Lucilius, so helps to restore a sick man as the sympathy of his friends, nothing so well banishes the expectation and fear of death. I began to consider that I was not really going to die when these were the people I was leaving behind me. What I mean is that I realized that I would go on living not among them but through them, and that death meant not breathing away my life but handing it on to them. These thoughts gave me the willingness to aid myself and endure all my pains; otherwise, you really are in a bad way, if having abandoned the will to die you haven't the will to live.

5.   So these are your remedies. Your doctor will prescribe how much walking you should do and the right amount of exercise — not to spend too much time doing nothing, as listless invalids tend to; that you read in a loud voice to exercise your breathing (since your trouble lies in your breathing tubes and receptacle): that you take a cruise to stimulate your internal organs by the gentle rocking of the boat. He'll prescribe your diet, and tell you when to take wine as a tonic and when to avoid it in case it sets you off coughing or makes the cough worse. My prescription is for a remedy not just for this ailment but for your life as a whole: pay no heed to death. Nothing depresses us when we have escaped that fear.

6.   There are three serious elements in every illness: the fear of death, the physical pain, and the interruption to our pleasures. I have said enough about death, and will add the one point that this fear arises from nature, not from the disease. For many people the disease has postponed death, and feeling that death was near gave them a new lease of life. You will die not because you are ill but because you are alive. That fate awaits you even when you have been cured, and when you have recovered it is illness not death that you have escaped.

7.   Let us now return to the misfortune which really is peculiar to illness, the severe physical sufferings it brings. Yet these are made bearable by their intermissions. The very intensity of agonizing pain brings it to an end, since no one can endure extreme pain for long. Nature in her kindness has so made us that pain is either bearable or

8. aut brevem faceret. Maximi dolores consistunt in macerrimis corporis
    partibus: nervi articulique et quidquid aliud exile est acerrime saevit
    cum in arto vitia concepit. Sed cito hae partes obstupescunt et ipso
    dolore sensum doloris amittunt, sive quia spiritus naturali prohibitus
    cursu et mutatus in peius vim suam qua viget admonetque nos perdit,
    sive quia corruptus umor, cum desiit habere quo confluat, ipse se
9. elidit et iis quae nimis implevit excutit sensum. Sic podagra et
    cheragra et omnis vertebrarum dolor nervorumque interquiescit cum illa
    quae torquebat hebetavit; omnium istorum prima verminatio vexat,
    impetus mora extinguitur et finis dolendi est optorpuisse. Dentium,
    oculorum, aurium dolor ob hoc ipsum acutissimus est quod inter
    angusta corporis nascitur, non minus, mehercule, quam capitis ipsius;
10. sed si incitatior est, in alienationem soporemque convertitur. Hoc
    itaque solacium vasti doloris est, quod necesse est desinas illum sentire
    si nimis senseris. Illud autem est quod inperitos in vexatione corporis
    male habet: non adsueverunt animo esse contenti; multum illis cum
    corpore fuit. Ideo vir magnus ac prudens animum diducit a corpore
    et multum cum meliore ac divina parte versatur, cum hac querula et
11. fragili quantum necesse est. 'Sed molestum est' inquit 'carere adsuetis
    voluptatibus, abstinere cibo, sitire, esurire.' Haec prima abstinentia
    gravia sunt, deinde cupiditas relanguescit ipsis per [se] quae cupimus
    fatigatis ac deficientibus; inde morosus est stomachus, inde quibus fuit
    aviditas cibi odium est. Desideria ipsa moriuntur; non est autem
12. acerbum carere eo quod cupere desieris. Adice quod nullus non
    intermittitur dolor aut certe remittitur. Adice quod licet cavere
    venturum et obsistere inminenti remediis; nullus enim non signa
    praemittit, utique qui ex solito revertitur. Tolerabilis est morbi
    patientia, si contempseris id quod extremum minatur.
13. Noli mala tua facere tibi ipse graviora et te querelis onerare:
    levis est dolor si nihil illi opinio adiecerit. Contra si exhortari te
    coeperis ac dicere 'nihil est aut certe exiguum est; duremus; iam
    desinet', levem illum, dum putas, facies. Omnia ex opinione suspensa
    sunt; non ambitio tantum ad illam respicit et luxuria et avaritia: ad
14. opinionem dolemus. Tam miser est quisque quam credidit.
    Detrahendas praeteritorum dolorum conquestiones puto et illa verba:

8.   brief. The acutest pains arise in the most attenuated regions of our body, like tendons, joints and all the other physically tiny organs which cause us appalling suffering when disorders occur in a confined area. But these parts quickly become numb, and the pain itself makes them lose the sense of pain, either because the vital force is blocked in its natural channel, and being thus impaired it loses its effective power to warn us of pain, or because diseased discharges, when they can no longer find an outlet, eliminate themselves and

9.   deprive of sensation the parts they have flooded. Thus gout in the feet and hands and any pains in the spine or tendons have intermissions when they have numbed the areas they were afflicting. In all these cases we are first attacked by a sharp pain the violence of which gradually ceases, and the suffering finally ends in a total loss of feeling. Pain in the teeth, eyes or ears is particularly severe just because it arises in confined parts of the body, and this indeed is just as true of the head; yet if it gets even more acute it becomes a

10.   deadened numbness. So there is this relief for extreme pain that you must cease to feel it if you feel it too much. But the disadvantage which the unphilosophical have in experiencing physical suffering is that they have not acquired mental tranquillity and are preoccupied by their bodies. For this reason a man of high character and good sense separates his mind from his body, concentrates his attention on the former superior and divine part, and has only the minimum to do

11.   with the latter frail and querulous part. 'But', objects somebody, 'it is tiresome to go without our usual pleasures, to give up food, to be hungry and thirsty.' These things are hard to bear in the first stage of deprivation, but then our cravings decline as the organs of our appetites become weak and feeble. Then the stomach becomes hard to please, loathing what it used to crave. The desires themselves pass away and there is no ache in doing without what you no longer want.

12.   Don't forget too that every pain has intervals of remission, or at any rate eases in intensity, and that you can watch out for its arrival and counter its onslaught with drugs. For every pain gives us advance warning — or at least every recurrent pain does so. You can grit your teeth and bear illness if you aren't bothered by its final threat.

13.   Don't yourself make your own troubles worse than necessary and burden yourself with complaints. Pain is trivial if you don't increase it by thinking about it. If on the other hand you start to encourage yourself by saying 'It is nothing, or anyway nothing much; let us put up with it and it will soon pass', by thinking it trivial you will make it so. Everything depends on our mental attitude. Not only are ambition, luxury and greed regulated by it, but even the way

14.   we feel pain. Everyone is as wretched as he thinks he is. We ought to banish complaints about past sufferings and remarks like 'No

'nulli umquam fuit peius. Quos cruciatus, quanta mala pertuli! Nemo me surrecturum putavit. Quotiens deploratus sum a meis, quotiens a medicis relictus! In eculeum inpositi non sic distrahuntur.' Etiam si sunt vera ista, transierunt: quid iuvat praeteritos dolores retractare et miserum esse quia fueris? Quid quod nemo non multum malis suis adicit et sibi ipse mentitur? Deinde quod acerbum fuit ferre, tulisse iucundum est: naturale est mali sui fine gaudere. Circumcidenda ergo duo sunt, et futuri timor et veteris incommodi

15. memoria: hoc ad me iam non pertinet, illud nondum. In ipsis positus difficultatibus dicat,

> forsan et haec olim meminisse iuvabit.

Toto contra ille pugnet animo; vincetur si cesserit, vincet si se contra dolorem suum intenderit: nunc hoc plerique faciunt, adtrahunt in se ruinam cui obstandum est. Istud quod premit, quod inpendet, quod urguet, si subducere te coeperis, sequetur et gravius incumbet; si

16. contra steteris et obniti volueris, repelletur. Athletae quantum plagarum ore, quantum toto corpore excipiunt! ferunt tamen omne tormentum gloriae cupiditate nec tantum quia pugnant ista patiuntur, sed ut pugnent: exercitatio ipsa tormentum est. Nos quoque evincamus omnia, quorum praemium non corona nec palma est nec tubicen praedicationi nominis nostri silentium faciens, sed virtus et firmitas animi et pax in ceterum parta, si semel in aliquo certamine

17. debellata fortuna est. 'Dolorem gravem sentio.' Quid ergo? non sentis si illum muliebriter tuleris? Quemadmodum perniciosior est hostis fugientibus, sic omne fortuitum incommodum magis instat cedenti et averso. 'Sed grave est.' Quid? nos ad hoc fortes sumus, ut levia portemus? Utrum vis longum esse morbum an concitatum et brevem? Si longus est, habet intercapedinem, dat refectioni locum, multum temporis donat, necesse est, ut exsurgat, et desinat: brevis morbus ac praeceps alterutrum facient, aut extinguetur aut extinguet. Quid autem interest, non sit an non sim? in utroque finis dolendi est.

18. Illud quoque proderit, ad alias cogitationes avertere animum et a dolore discedere. Cogita quid honeste, quid fortiter feceris; bonas partes tecum ipse tracta; memoriam in ea quae maxime miratus es

one ever suffered as I did. What torture, what agony I endured! Nobody thought I would recover. The number of times I was given up by my family and despaired of by the doctors! Victims on the rack aren't torn apart as I was.' Even if all that is true, it is over. What is the point of rehearsing past pains and being wretched now because you once were? Don't forget too that everyone embroiders his troubles and deceives himself too. Besides, what was bitter to bear is pleasant to have borne, for it is natural to delight in the cessation of one's troubles. So there are two states of mind which I should prune away, fear of future afflictions and memory of past ones: the latter matter no longer to me, and the former not yet.

15. And when one is caught in the midst of troubles then he should say
'Even these things one day may be pleasant to recall'.
Let him fight back with all his heart. If he gives way he will lose the battle; if he exerts himself against his affliction he will win. As it is, most people simply pull down upon themselves the ruin which they should be withstanding. If you start to withdraw from something which is pressing upon you and threatening you with its weight, it will follow and lie more heavily upon you. But if you stand firm and

16. make yourself resist it, it will be forced back. Consider the quantity of blows that athletes receive on their faces and all over their bodies. But they endure every kind of suffering in their desire for glory, and they undergo all this not just while fighting but while practising for the fight: their training itself causes them anguish. Let us too overcome all things, though our reward is not the victor's wreath and palm, nor the trumpeter calling for silence for the announcement of our name, but virtue, strength of mind and a lasting tranquillity achieved once we have fought and routed fortune.

17. 'I feel an awful pain', you might say. Well, do you stop feeling it if you bear it in an effeminate way? Just as the enemy inflicts more damage on an army in retreat, so all our chance afflictions bear more heavily on us if we yield and turn our backs to them. 'But it really is awful.' Well, are we given strength just to carry light loads? Would you prefer an illness to be long or short and sharp? If it is long, it has intermissions, gives us a chance to rally, lets us off its attacks for long periods, these intervals being essential to its renewed attacks. A short, swift illness will have one or other outcome: it will quench itself or quench us. And what's the difference whether it ceases or I cease? In either case the pain is over.

18. It will also help if you turn your mind to other thoughts and distance yourself from your suffering. Reflect on the things you have done which were honourable and brave; relive the noble rôles you played in your life; direct your memory to the things you have most

sparge; tunc tibi fortissimus quisque et victor doloris occurrat: ille qui dum varices exsecandas praeberet legere librum perseveravit, ille qui non desiit ridere cum hoc ipsum irati tortores omnia instrumenta crudelitatis suae experirentur. Non vincetur dolor ratione, qui victus

19. est risu? Quidquid vis nunc licet dicas, destillationes et vim continuae tussis egerentem viscerum partes et febrem praecordia ipsa torrentem et sitim et artus in diversum articulis exeuntibus tortos: plus est flamma et eculeus et lamina et vulneribus ipsis intumescentibus quod illa renovaret et altius urgueret inpressum. Inter haec tamen aliquis non gemuit. Parum est: non rogavit. Parum est: non respondit. Parum est: risit et quidem ex animo. Vis tu post hoc dolorem deridere?

20. 'Sed nihil' inquit 'agere sinit morbus, qui me omnibus abduxit officiis.' Corpus tuum valetudo tenet, non et animum. Itaque cursoris moratur pedes, sutoris aut fabri manus inpedit: si animus tibi esse in usu solet, suadebis docebis, audies disces, quaeres recordaberis. Quid porro? nihil agere te credis si temperans aeger sis? ostendes

21. morbum posse superari vel certe sustineri. Est, mihi crede, virtuti etiam in lectulo locus. Non tantum arma et acies dant argumenta alacris animi indomitique terroribus: et in vestimentis vir fortis apparet. Habes quod agas: bene luctare cum morbo. Si nihil te coegerit, si nihil exoraverit, insigne prodis exemplum. O quam magna erat gloriae materia, si spectaremur aegri! ipse te specta, ipse te lauda.

22. Praeterea duo genera sunt voluptatum. Corporales morbus inhibet, non tamen tollit; immo, si verum aestimes, incitat. Magis iuvat bibere sitientem, gratior est esurienti cibus; quidquid ex abstinentia contingit avidius excipitur. Illas vero animi voluptates, quae maiores certioresque sunt, nemo medicus aegro negat. Has quisquis sequitur et bene intellegit omnia sensuum blandimenta

23. contemnit. 'O infelicem aegrum!' Quare! quia non vino nivem diluit? quia non rigorem potionis suae, quam capaci scypho miscuit, renovat fracta insuper glacie? quia non ostrea illi Lucrina in ipsa mensa aperiuntur? quia non circa cenationem eius tumultus cocorum est ipsos cum opsoniis focos transferentium? Hoc enim iam luxuria

admired.   Conjure up all the outstandingly brave men who have triumphed over pain: the man who carried on reading a book while he was having his varicose veins cut out; the man who persisted in smiling at his torturers when this was the very thing which angered them into trying every instrument of cruelty upon him.   Won't pain be conquered by reason if it has been conquered by a smile?

19. Mention anything you like: catarrh, chronic coughing so violent it brings up parts of your insides, fever that sears your very vitals, thirst, limbs twisted by dislocated joints; or worse, being burnt, stretched on the rack, suffering red—hot plates and instruments pressed into your swelling wounds to re—open and deepen them.   Yet even under these sufferings some men have not been heard to groan. 'Give him more: he hasn't appealed for mercy.'   'Give him more: he hasn't given us the answer.'   'Give him more: he has smiled — and he meant it.'   Surely you can smile at pain after this?

20.   'But I can't do anything as my illness has kept me from all my duties.'   It is your body which is ill, not your mind too.   So illness slows down a sprinter's feet and hampers a cobbler's or a blacksmith's hands; but if your mind is habitually active you can advise and teach, listen and learn, inquire and remember.   What's more, do you think you are achieving nothing if you suffer illness with self—control?   You

21. will prove that it can be overcome or at least endured.   Believe me, there is a place for courage even in the sick—bed.   You don't find proof of a keen and fearless spirit only in battle and warfare: a man can show bravery under the bedclothes.   You have the chance of achievement: put up a good fight with your illness.   If it cannot threaten or prevail over you then you are setting us a noble example. What an opportunity there would be to win fame if we had an audience at our illnesses!   Be your own audience and give yourself applause.

22.   Another point is that there are two kinds of pleasures.   Physical ones are restricted but not banished by illness: in fact, if you consider this realistically, it stimulates them.   There is more enjoyment in drinking when you are thirsty, and food is more welcome when you are hungry: after a period of abstinence we devour what we can more greedily.   But no doctor denies his patient those greater and more genuine pleasures of the mind.   Whoever follows these and really understands them can look down upon all the

23. enticements of the senses.   'What a pity he is ill', someone says. Why?   Because he can't melt snow into his wine and break ice into a massive goblet to keep his drink cold?   Because Lucrine oysters are not being opened for him at his table?   Because cooks aren't bustling around his dining—room and bringing in the cooking—stoves as well as the food?   For luxury has now devised this refinement of having

commenta est: ne quis intepescat cibus, ne quid palato iam calloso
24. parum ferveat, cenam culina prosequitur. 'O infelicem aegrum!'
Edet quantum concoquat; non iacebit in conspectu aper ut vilis caro a
mensa relegatus, nec in repositorio eius pectora avium (totas enim
videre fastidium est) congesta ponentur. Quid tibi mali factum est?
cenabis tamquam aeger, immo aliquando tamquam sanus.

25.   Sed omnia ista facile perferemus, sorbitionem, aquam calidam,
et quidquid aliud intolerabile videtur delicatis et luxu fluentibus
magisque animo quam corpore morbidis: tantum mortem desinamus
horrere.   Desinemus autem, si fines bonorum ac malorum
26. cognoverimus; ita demum nec vita taedio erit nec mors timori. Vitam
enim occupare satietas sui non potest tot res varias, magnas, divinas
percensentem: in odium illam sui adducere solet iners otium. Rerum
naturam peragranti numquam in fastidium veritas veniet: falsa
27. satiabunt.   Rursus si mors accedit et vocat, licet inmatura sit, licet
mediam praecidat aetatem, perceptus longissimae fructus est. Cognita
est illi ex magna parte natura; scit tempore honesta non crescere: iis
necesse est videri omnem vitam brevem qui illam voluptatibus vanis et
ideo infinitis metiuntur.

28.   His te cogitationibus recrea et interim epistulis nostris vaca.
Veniet aliquando tempus quod nos iterum iungat ac misceat;
quantulumlibet sit illud, longum faciet scientia utendi. Nam, ut
Posidonius ait, 'unus dies hominum eruditorum plus patet quam
29. inperitis longissima aetas'. Interim hoc tene, hoc morde: adversis non
succumbere, laetis non credere, omnem fortunae licentiam in oculis
habere, tamquam quidquid potest facere factura sit. Quidquid
expectatum est diu, levius accedit. Vale.

LETTER 79

1.   Expecto epistulas tuas quibus mihi indices circuitus Siciliae totius
quid tibi novi ostenderit, et omnia de ipsa Charybdi certiora. Nam
Scyllam saxum esse et quidem non terribile navigantibus optime scio:

the kitchen escort the meal in, to prevent the food getting cooler than the boiling temperature our leathery palates now demand.

24. 'What a pity he is ill.' He'll eat as much as he can digest, and there won't be a boar lying in view of the table but banished from it as being too ordinary a meat, nor will he have a trolley piled up with birds' breasts (whole birds are now considered a vulgar sight). So what are you suffering? You will be eating like a sick man, but at last you will be eating as a healthy man should.

25. However, we can easily endure all these things — broths, warm water, everything considered intolerable by self—indulgent people who have become soft through easy living and are diseased more in their minds than in their bodies — provided only we stop dreading death. And we shall stop if we come to recognize the boundaries between good and bad things: only then will life cease to be a burden and

26. death a source of fear. For life cannot suffer from boredom if it keeps in review the variety, the greatness and the sublimity of the world; it is the emptiness of an idle existence that makes life tired of itself. A man will never grow weary of exploring the truth of the

27. natural world; it is the false things that will sicken him. Moreover, if death comes and summons him, even if it is premature and cuts him off in the prime of life, he has already gained the reward of even the longest life. He has acquired a wide knowledge of the world and he knows that worthwhile things do not grow with the passage of time. On the other hand, any life must seem short to those who measure it by pleasures which are empty and therefore cannot be completed.

28. Let these thoughts help to cure you, and meanwhile keep in touch with me. The time will come when we shall be together again, and however short that reunion will be, we shall prolong it by knowing how to make the most of it. As Posidonius says, 'For enlightened men one day is longer than the most extended lifetime for

29. the unphilosophical'. In the meantime grasp this rule and hang on to it: don't give way to adversity, don't trust prosperity, remember that fortune is a law unto herself, assuming that she will do anything that she can do. Whatever you have expected for a long time is easier to deal with when it comes.

LETTER 79

1. I am looking forward to your letter in which you will tell me what you discovered in your trip around the whole of Sicily, with full and reliable details about Charybdis in particular. For I am well aware that Scylla is a rock and not in fact dangerous to sailors, but I

Charybdis an respondeat fabulis perscribi mihi desidero et, si forte observaveris (dignum est autem quod observes), fac nos certiores utrum uno tantum vento agatur in vertices an omnis tempestas aeque mare illud contorqueat, et an verum sit quidquid illo freti turbine abreptum

2. est per multa milia trahi conditum et circa Tauromenitanum litus emergere. Si haec mihi perscripseris, tunc tibi audebo mandare ut in honorem meum Aetnam quoque ascendas, quam consumi et sensim subsidere ex hoc colligunt quidam, quod aliquanto longius navigantibus solebat ostendi. Potest hoc accidere non quia montis altitudo descendit, sed quia ignis evanuit et minus vehemens ac largus effertur, ob eandem causam fumo quoque per diem segniore. Neutrum autem incredibile est, nec montem qui devoretur cotidie minui, nec manere eundem, quia non ipsum <ignis> exest sed in aliqua inferna valle conceptus exaestuat et aliis pascitur, in ipso monte non alimentum

3. habet sed viam. In Lycia regio notissima est (Hephaestion incolae vocant), foratum pluribus locis solum, quod sine ullo nascentium damno ignis innoxius circumit. Laeta itaque regio est et herbida, nihil flammis adurentibus sed tantum vi remissa ac languida refulgentibus.

4. Sed reservemus ista, tunc quaesituri cum tu mihi scripseris quantum ab ipso ore montis nives absint, quas ne aestas quidem solvit; adeo tutae sunt ab igne vicino. Non est autem quod istam curam inputes mihi; morbo enim tuo daturus eras, etiam si nemo mandaret.

5. Quid tibi do ne Aetnam describas in tuo carmine, ne hunc sollemnem omnibus poetis locum adtingas? Quem quominus Ovidius tractaret, nihil obstitit quod iam Vergilius impleverat; ne Severum quidem Cornelium uterque deterruit. Omnibus praeterea feliciter hic locus se dedit, et qui praecesserant non praeripuisse mihi videntur quae dici

6. poterant, sed aperuisse. [Sed] Multum interest utrum ad consumptam materiam an ad subactam accedas: crescit in dies, et inventuris inventa non obstant. Praeterea condicio optima est ultimi: parata verba invenit, quae aliter instructa novam faciem habent. Nec illis manus inicit tamquam alienis; sunt enim publica. [Iurisconsulti negant

7. quicquam publicum usu capi.] Aut ego te non novi aut Aetna tibi salivam movet; iam cupis grande aliquid et par prioribus scribere.

want you to tell me whether Charybdis matches up to the tales about it. Also, if you happen to notice (which is well worth noticing), do inform me whether it is lashed into whirlpools by only one wind, or any storm at all stirs up that sea, and whether it is true that anything caught up by that whirling eddy is dragged under water for many miles and does not surface till it reaches the shore of

2. Tauromenium. If you write and tell me these details I'll venture to commission you to climb Etna too for my sake. Some people judge that it is being worn away and is gradually sinking from the fact that sailors used to be able to see it from further away. This might happen not because the mountain is getting lower, but because its fire has declined and is ejected with less force and volume, causing the smoke too to appear more sluggishly during the day. Neither possibility can be ruled out, that the mountain is daily diminished by being consumed, or that it remains unchanged because the fire is not actually devouring it, but, starting in some subterranean hollow, blazes away there, feeding on other material and using the mountain itself

3. not as food but as a way out. There is a well known region of Lycia (the local name is Hephaestion), where the ground is perforated in several places, and a harmless fire plays around the area without doing the least damage to the local plant life. In fact the region is lush and rich in vegetation, as the flames do not scorch anything, but simply cause a glow without any strength in their heat.

4. But let us defer these questions for consideration when you've written to tell me how far away from the crater are the snows, which do not melt even in summer, so safe are they from the nearby fire. However, there is no question of your doing this investigation as a favour to me: you were going to indulge your obsession anyway,

5. even if nobody asked you to. What could I give you *not* to describe Etna in your poem and handle this theme so well—worn by every poet? Ovid was in no way prevented from treating it by the fact that Virgil had previously dealt with it fully; and neither of them deterred Cornelius Severus from doing the same. Besides, this subject is a rich field for all writers, and those who have gone before do not seem to me to have pre—empted what can be said about it, but

6. rather to have shown the way. There is a great difference between taking on a topic which is exhausted and one which is well prepared for you. The latter is always expanding, and previous treatments of it do not preclude later ones. What is more, the latest writer is in the best position: he finds words ready to hand which he can re—arrange to produce a new effect. And since they are public property he cannot be said to be doing violence to the words of

7. others. If I know you, Etna is making your mouth water: you've been longing to tackle some lofty theme in a way to rival your

Plus enim sperare modestia tibi tua non permittit, quae tanta in te est
ut videaris mihi retracturus ingenii tui vires, si vincendi periculum sit:
tanta tibi priorum reverentia est.

8.   Inter cetera hoc habet boni sapientia: nemo ab altero potest
vinci nisi dum ascenditur.   Cum ad summum perveneris, paria sunt;
non est incremento locus, statur.   Numquid sol magnitudini suae
adicit? numquid ultra quam solet luna procedit?   Maria non crescunt;

9.   mundus eundem habitum ac modum servat.   Extollere se quae iustam
magnitudinem implevere non possunt: quicumque fuerint sapientes,
pares erunt et aequales.   Habebit unusquisque ex iis proprias dotes:
alius erit affabilior, alius expeditior, alius promptior in eloquendo, alius
facundior: illud de quo agitur, quod beatum facit, aequalest in

10.   omnibus.   An Aetna tua possit sublabi et in se ruere, an hoc
excelsum cacumen et conspicuum per vasti maris spatia detrahat
adsidua vis ignium, nescio: virtutem non flamma, non ruina inferius
adducet; haec una maiestas deprimi nescit.   Nec proferri ultra nec
referri potest; sic huius, ut caelestium, stata magnitudo est.   Ad hanc

11.   nos conemur educere.   Iam multum operis effecti est; immo, si verum
fateri volo, non multum.   Nec enim bonitas est pessimis esse
meliorem: quis oculis glorietur qui suspicetur diem?   Cui sol per
caliginem splendet, licet contentus interim sit effugisse tenebras, adhuc

12.   non fruitur bono lucis.   Tunc animus noster habebit quod gratuletur
sibi cum emissus his tenebris in quibus volutatur non tenui visu clara
prospexerit, sed totum diem admiserit et redditus caelo suo fuerit, cum
receperit locum quem occupavit sorte nascendi.   Sursum illum vocant
initia sua; erit autem illic etiam antequam hac custodia exsolvatur,
cum vitia disiecerit purusque ac levis in cogitationes divinas emicuerit.

13.   Hoc nos agere, Lucili carissime, in hoc ire impetu toto, licet
pauci sciant, licet nemo, iuvat.   Gloria umbra virtutis est: etiam
invitam comitabitur.   Sed quemadmodum aliquando umbra antecedit,
aliquando sequitur vel a tergo est, ita gloria aliquando ante nos est
visendamque se praebet, aliquando in averso est maiorque quo serior,

14.   ubi invidia secessit.   Quamdiu videbatur furere Democritus!   Vix
recepit Socraten fama.   Quamdiu Catonem civitas ignoravit! respuit

predecessors. Your modesty does not allow you to hope for more, and it is so excessive that you actually seem to me to curtail your mental powers if there's any risk of your outdoing another writer: so greatly do you respect your predecessors.

8.   Wisdom has this among its other advantages, that no one can be outdone by another except in the act of rising to achieve it. When you have come to the top everything is equal: they have come to a halt and there is no room for further development. Can the sun add to its bulk or the moon exceed its normal fulness? The seas do not increase; the world preserves the same physical form and

9. limits. Things which have arrived at their prescribed bulk cannot extend themselves: all men who have achieved wisdom are equal and on a level. Each individual among them will have his own natural gifts: one will be more genial than the others, another more quick−witted, another swifter in repartee, another more eloquent. But the quality we are concerned with, the one that brings them bliss,

10. is equal in all of them. I don't know whether this Etna of yours can collapse and fall on itself, and whether the unrelenting force of its fires is demolishing that lofty peak which is visible over vast tracks of ocean. But I do know that no fire or collapse will bring down virtue: this is one grandeur that cannot be humbled. It cannot be raised or lowered as its stature is fixed, like that of the heavenly

11. bodies: let us try to raise ourselves to this height. By now much of the task has been accomplished − no, if I am to be honest with you, not much of it. For goodness does not consist in being better than the worst. Who would boast about his eyesight if he had only a hazy view of daylight? If the sun shines on a man through the mist, he can be glad that for a while he has escaped the darkness, but he

12. is not yet enjoying the blessing of light. Our mind will only have grounds for self−congratulation when it has emerged from this darkness which enfolds it and sees clearly with no restricted vision, when it absorbs the full light of day and is restored to the heavens where it belongs, recovering the place allotted to it at birth. Its own origins summon it upwards, and it will get there even before its bodily prison disssolves, when it has shaken off its faults and being pure and unburdened it darts upwards to divine reflections.

13.   This activity, this whole−hearted journey of ours, is a joy, dear Lucilius, even if few or none know about it. Fame is the shadow of virtue and attends virtue even against its will. But just as you'll see a shadow sometimes preceding, sometimes following behind, so fame sometimes goes ahead of us, visible to all, and sometimes follows us,

14. and is all the greater for coming late when envy has departed. What a long time did Democritus seem to be mad! Socrates scarcely achieved fame in the end. What a long time was Cato ignored by

nec intellexit nisi cum perdidit. Rutili innocentia ac virtus lateret, nisi accepisset iniuriam: dum violatur, effulsit. Numquid non sorti suae gratias egit et exilium suum complexus est? De his loquor quos inlustravit fortuna dum vexat: quam multorum profectus in notitiam

15. evasere post ipsos! quam multos fama non excepit sed eruit! Vides Epicurum quantopere non tantum eruditiores sed haec quoque inperitorum turba miretur: hic ignotus ipsis Athenis fuit, circa quas delituerat. Multis itaque iam annis Metrodoro suo superstes in quadam epistula, cum amicitiam suam et Metrodori grata commemoratione cecinisset, hoc novissime adiecit, nihil sibi et Metrodoro inter bona tanta nocuisse quod ipsos illa nobilis Graecia non ignotos solum

16. habuisset sed paene inauditos. Numquid ergo non postea quam esse desierat inventus est? numquid non opinio eius enituit? Hoc Metrodorus quoque in quadam epistula confitetur, se et Epicurum non satis enotuisse; sed post se et Epicurum magnum paratumque nomen

17. habituros qui voluissent per eadem ire vestigia. Nulla virtus latet, et latuisse non ipsius est damnum: veniet qui conditam et saeculi sui malignitate conpressam dies publicet. Paucis natus est qui populum aetatis suae cogitat. Multa annorum milia, multa populorum supervenient: ad illa respice. Etiam si omnibus tecum viventibus silentium livor indixerit, venient qui sine offensa, sine gratia iudicent. Si quod est pretium virtutis ex fama, nec hoc interit. Ad nos quidem nihil pertinebit posterorum sermo; tamen etiam non sentientes colet ac

18. frequentabit. Nulli non virtus et vivo et mortuo rettulit gratiam, si modo illam bona secutus est fide, si se non exornavit et pinxit, sed idem fuit sive ex denuntiato videbatur sive inparatus ac subito. Nihil simulatio proficit; paucis inponit leviter extrinsecus inducta facies: veritas in omnem partem sui eadem est. Quae decipiunt nihil habent solidi. Tenue est mendacium: perlucet si diligenter inspexeris. Vale.

his country! It disdained him and did not realize its mistake until it lost him. Rutilius' innocence and virtue would have escaped notice had he not been wronged; but when violated they shone forth in glory. Did he not give thanks to his fortune and welcome his exile with open arms? I am talking about those whom fortune glorified while she afflicted them. But how many are there whose enlightened conduct achieved celebrity only after their death, whose fame did not

15. attend their lives but restored them later to renown. Look at how greatly Epicurus is admired not only by the learned but by crowds of unphilosophical men everywhere: yet he was unknown even in Athens, near which he had 'lived unnoticed'. That was why many years after his pupil Metrodorus' death he wrote a letter in which, having extolled their friendship with grateful reminiscences, he added at the end that he and Metrodorus had enjoyed so many blessings that they had suffered no hurt from the fact that Greece with all its fair fame had not only not known them, but had scarcely heard of

16. them. Well, did not men discover him after he died, and did he not then acquire a shining reputation? Metrodorus too admits in a letter that he and Epicurus had scarcely become known, but that after his and Epicurus' death anyone who wanted to follow in their footsteps

17. would find a great and ready—made name. No virtue remains concealed, and to have been concealed does it no damage, for time will bring it to light though it was suppressed in obscurity by the spite of its own contemporaries. The man who has in mind only his own generation is born for few people. Thousands of years and many generations will follow: these are what you must consider. Even if malice produces silence about you during the lifetime of your contemporaries, others will come who will judge you without animosity and without favour. Whatever reward virtue enjoys from fame is not lost. Certainly we will not be affected by what later generations say about us, but even though we shall feel nothing they will cherish our

18. memory with affection. Virtue rewards everyone both in his life and after his death, provided he has sincerely cultivated it, and provided he has not tricked himself out with adornments, but has remained the same individual, whether warned in advance of your seeing him or caught unaware. Pretence achieves nothing. A mask that is easily slipped on doesn't fool many people: truth is the same through and through. Things that deceive have no substance. Falsehood is a flimsy thing, and if you look hard you can see through it.

LETTER 83

1.   Singulos dies tibi meos et quidem totos indicari iubes: bene de me iudicas si nihil esse in illis putas quod abscondam. Sic certe vivendum est tamquam in conspectu vivamus, sic cogitandum tamquam aliquis in pectus intimum introspicere possit: et potest. Quid enim prodest ab homine aliquid esse secretum? nihil deo clusum est; interest animis nostris et cogitationibus medius intervenit — sic 'intervenit' dico

2. tamquam aliquando discedat. Faciam ergo quod iubes, et quid agam et quo ordine libenter tibi scribam. Observabo me protinus et, quod est utilissimum, diem meum recognoscam. Hoc nos pessimos facit, quod nemo vitam suam respicit; quid facturi simus cogitamus, et id raro, quid fecerimus non cogitamus; atqui consilium futuri ex praeterito venit.

3.   Hodiernus dies solidus est, nemo ex illo quicquam mihi eripuit; totus inter stratum lectionemque divisus est; minimum exercitationi corporis datum, et hoc nomine ago gratias senectuti: non magno mihi constat. Cum me movi, lassus sum; hic autem est exercitationis etiam

4. fortissimis finis. Progymnastas meos quaeris? unus mihi sufficit Pharius, puer, ut scis, amabilis, sed mutabitur: iam aliquem teneriorem quaero. Hic quidem ait nos eandem crisin habere, quia utrique dentes cadunt. Sed iam vix illum adsequor currentem et intra paucissimos dies non potero: vide quid exercitatio cotidiana proficiat. Cito magnum intervallum fit inter duos in diversum euntes: eodem tempore ille ascendit, ego descendo, nec ignoras quanto ex his velocius alterum fiat. Mentitus sum; iam enim aetas nostra non descendit sed cadit.

5. Quomodo tamen hodiernum certamen nobis cesserit quaeris? quod raro cursoribus evenit, hieran fecimus. Ab hac fatigatione magis quam exercitatione in frigidam descendi: hoc apud me vocatur parum calda. Ille tantus psychrolutes, qui kalendis Ianuariis euripum salutabam, qui anno novo quemadmodum legere, scribere, dicere aliquid, sic auspicabar in Virginem desilire, primum ad Tiberim transtuli castra, deinde ad hoc solium quod, cum fortissimus sum et omnia bona fide

6. fiunt, sol temperat: non multum mihi ad balneum superest. Panis deinde siccus et sine mensa prandium, post quod non sunt lavandae manus. Dormio minimum. Consuetudinem meam nosti: brevissimo

LETTER 83

1.   You ask me to tell you about my days, individually and in general, and you judge well of me if you think I have nothing to hide in them. We should certainly live as if we lived in full view, and we should think as if someone could gaze right into our hearts — and someone can do just that. For what is the good of keeping anything secret from man? Nothing is barred to god: he is present in our minds and attends in the midst of our thoughts — I say

2. 'attends' as if he could sometimes be absent! So I'll do as you ask and willingly write you an account of my doings and my routine. I shall at once take note of myself and (a most useful procedure) review my day. What most harms our characters is the fact that no one looks back over his life. We think about what we are going to do, and we only rarely do that; but we don't think about what we've done. Yet plans for the future are based on the past.

3.   To−day has been uninterrupted: nobody has stolen any of it from me, and it has all been divided between bed and reading. I've taken a very little exercise, and on this account I am grateful to old age that exercise doesn't cost me much effort. Just moving myself tires me out, and that is the limit of exercise even for the most

4. vigorous people. Do you want to know my trainers? One is enough for me, Pharius, a pleasant lad, as you know, but I'll be changing him, as I now want someone more youthful. Actually, he says that we are at the same stage of life because we are both losing our teeth. But now I can scarcely keep up with him when we are running, and in a very few days I won't be able to at all — see what daily exercise does for you. A wide gap soon develops between two people going in opposite directions: at the same time that he is going up I am going down, and you well know how much quicker the latter journey is. But I'm lying, for my age is not 'going down' but collapsing.

5.   However, you'd like to know how our race to−day turned out? We had a dead heat, a rare occurrence with runners. Exhausted rather than exercised I had a cold bath — which is what I call a lukewarm one. Here am I, your stalwart cold bath enthusiast, who used to salute the canal on the first of January, and inaugurated the New Year by jumping into the Maiden Aqueduct just as I did by reading, writing and saying something or other. Now I have shifted my activities first to the Tiber, and then to the pool here which, even when I'm feeling brave and don't cheat, is warmed by the sun.

6. Soon it will be the hot bath for me! Next I have some dry bread — not a meal at table and no need to wash my hands afterwards. Then a short nap: you know my habit of just unharnessing myself,

somno utor et quasi interiungo; satis est mihi vigilare desisse;
7. aliquando dormisse me scio, aliquando suspicor. Ecce circensium
obstrepit clamor; subita aliqua et universa voce feriuntur aures meae,
nec cogitationem meam excutiunt, ne interrumpunt quidem. Fremitum
patientissime fero; multae voces et in unum confusae pro fluctu mihi
sunt aut vento silvam verberante et ceteris sine intellectu sonantibus.

8. Quid ergo est nunc cui animum adiecerim? dicam. Superest ex
hesterno mihi cogitatio quid sibi voluerint prudentissimi viri qui rerum
maximarum probationes levissimas et perplexas fecerint, quae ut sint
9. verae, tamen mendacio similes sunt. Vult nos ab ebrietate deterrere
Zenon, vir maximus, huius sectae fortissimae ac sanctissimae conditor.
Audi ergo quemadmodum colligat virum bonum non futurum ebrium:
'ebrio secretum sermonem nemo committit, viro autem bono committit;
ergo vir bonus ebrius non erit'. Quemadmodum opposita
interrogatione simili derideatur adtende (satis enim est unam ponere ex
multis): 'dormienti nemo secretum sermonem committit, viro autem
10. bono committit; vir bonus ergo non dormit'. Quo uno modo potest
Posidonius Zenonis nostri causam agit, sed ne sic quidem, ut existimo,
agi potest. Ait enim 'ebrium' duobus modis dici, altero cum aliquis
vino gravis est et inpos sui, altero si solet ebrius fieri et huic
obnoxius vitio est; hunc a Zenone dici qui soleat fieri ebrius, non qui
sit; huic autem neminem commissurum arcana quae per vinum eloqui
11. possit. Quod est falsum; prima enim illa interrogatio conplectitur eum
qui est ebrius, non eum qui futurus est. Plurimum enim interesse
concedes et inter ebrium et ebriosum: potest et qui ebrius est tunc
primum esse nec habere hoc vitium, et qui ebriosus est saepe extra
ebrietatem esse; itaque id intellego quod significari verbo isto solet,
praesertim cum ab homine diligentiam professo ponatur et verba
examinante. Adice nunc quod, si hoc intellexit Zenon et nos
intellegere noluit, ambiguitate verbi quaesiit locum fraudi, quod
12. faciendum non est ubi veritas quaeritur. Sed sane hoc senserit: quod
sequitur falsum est, ei qui soleat ebrius fieri non committi sermonem
secretum. Cogita enim quam multis militibus non semper sobriis et
imperator et tribunus et centurio tacenda mandaverint. De illa C.
Caesaris caede, illius dico qui superato Pompeio rem publicam tenuit,
tam creditum est Tillio Cimbro quam C. Cassio. Cassius tota vita

as it were, for a cat—nap. All I need is to have stopped being awake: sometimes I know I've slept, sometimes I only suspect it.

7. Here I have the uproar of the Circus games assailing me: my ears are smitten by some sudden widespread shouting, but without scattering my thoughts — without even interrupting them. A loud commotion doesn't bother me, and a multitude of voices merging into one are like sea—waves to me, or trees battered by a wind, and all other meaningless sounds.

8. So, what have I now been turning my thoughts to? I'll tell you. Since yesterday I've been reflecting on what those sagacious individuals were up to who have offered the most trivial and muddled proofs about vital matters — proofs which, though true, yet give a

9. false impression. Zeno, that great man who founded our stalwart and saintly school of philosophy, seeks to warn us against drunkenness. Well, listen to his proof that the good man will not get drunk: 'Nobody entrusts a secret to a man who is drunk, but he does to a good man: therefore a good man will not get drunk.' Consider how you can make fun of this by a similar counter—argument (I need only adduce one out of many possibilities): 'Nobody entrusts a secret to a sleeping person, but he does to a good man: therefore a good man

10. does not sleep.' Posidonius supports Zeno's argument in the only way possible, but I don't think even in his formulation it can be supported. For he says that 'drunk' can be used in two senses: when someone succumbs to wine and loses control of himself, and when someone is habitually drunk and liable to this failing. He supposes Zeno to refer to the habitual drunkard, not the man who happens to be drunk, meaning that no one would share secrets with

11. the drunkard which he could reveal in his cups. This is wrong, for the original argument concerns a man who is actually drunk, not one who will be in the future. You will agree that there is a big difference between being drunk and being addicted to drink. A man who is drunk might be drunk for the first time on that occasion and not have the addiction, while a drunkard is often not drunk. So I understand that word 'drunk' to have its conventional meaning, especially when used by a man who claimed to be careful in weighing his words. Furthermore, if Zeno understood it in this (Posidonius') sense and did not want us to do so, he was deliberately deceptive in

12. speaking ambiguously, and this is no way to discover the truth. But granted this was his meaning, the conclusion is false that a habitual drunkard is not entrusted with a secret. Consider how many soldiers not always sober have been given secret orders by a general, tribune or centurion. Regarding Gaius Caesar's murder (I mean the Caesar who controlled the state after Pompey's overthrow), Tillius Cimber was as much in the secret as Gaius Cassius. Cassius was teetotal all his

aquam bibit, Tillius Cimber et nimius erat in vino et scordalus.   In
hanc rem iocatus est ipse: 'ego' inquit 'quemquam feram, qui vinum
ferre non possum?'

13.   Sibi quisque nunc nominet eos quibus scit et vinum male credi
et sermonem bene; unum tamen exemplum quod occurrit mihi
referam, ne intercidat.   Instruenda est enim vita exemplis inlustribus,
14. nec semper confugiamus ad vetera.   L. Piso, urbis custos, ebrius ex
quo semel factus est fuit.   Maiorem noctis partem in convivio
exigebat; usque in horam sextam fere dormiebat: hoc eius erat
matutinum.   Officium tamen suum, quo tutela urbis continebatur,
diligentissime administravit.   Huic et divus Augustus dedit secreta
mandata, cum illum praeponeret Thraciae, quam perdomuit, et
Tiberius proficiscens in Campaniam, cum multa in urbe et suspecta
15. relinqueret et invisa.   Puto, quia bene illi cesserat Pisonis ebrietas,
postea Cossum fecit urbis praefectum, virum gravem, moderatum, sed
mersum vino et madentem, adeo ut ex senatu aliquando, in quem e
convivio venerat, oppressus inexcitabili somno tolleretur.   Huic tamen
Tiberius multa sua manu scripsit quae committenda ne ministris
quidem suis iudicabat: nullum Cosso aut privatum secretum aut
publicum elapsum est.

16.   Itaque declamationes istas de medio removeamus: 'non est
animus in sua potestate ebrietate devinctus: quemadmodum musto dolia
ipsa rumpuntur et omne quod in imo iacet in summam partem vis
caloris eiectat, sic vino exaestuante quidquid in imo iacet abditum
effertur et prodit in medium.   Onerati mero quemadmodum non
continent cibum vino redundante, ita ne secretum quidem; quod suum
17. alienumque est pariter effundunt.'   Sed quamvis hoc soleat accidere,
ita et illud solet, ut cum iis quos sciamus libentius bibere de rebus
necessariis deliberemus; falsum ergo est hoc quod patrocinii loco
ponitur, ei qui soleat ebrius fieri non dari tacitum.

      Quanto satius est aperte accusare ebrietatem et vitia eius
exponere, quae etiam tolerabilis homo vitaverit, nedum perfectus ac
sapiens, cui satis est sitim extinguere, qui, etiam si quando hortata est
hilaritas aliena causa producta longius, tamen citra ebrietatem resistit.
18. Nam de illo videbimus, an sapientis animus nimio vino turbetur et
faciat ebriis solita: interim, si hoc colligere vis, virum bonum non

life, while Tillius Cimber was notorious for drinking and brawling: hence his own quip 'How can I carry anyone if I can't even carry my wine?'

13.   Let each of us now name for himself those who he knows could be trusted to hold a secret but not to hold their liquor. I will give one example which occurs to me, so it doesn't get lost from memory. Life should be furnished with notable examples and we

14. need not always look to antiquity for them. Lucius Piso was drunk from the time of his appointment as warden of Rome. He spent most of the night carousing, and then slept till around midday: this was early morning to him. But he was extremely conscientious in carrying out his job of looking after the city. He received confidential instructions from the deified Augustus when he made him governor of Thrace (which he thoroughly subjugated), and also from Tiberius, when the latter was setting out for Campania and leaving

15. behind him in the city many dangerous objects of suspicion. I suppose it was because Piso's drunken ways had worked well for Tiberius that he later appointed Cossus prefect of Rome, a man of dignity and moderation, except that he steeped and soaked himself in wine so much that on one occasion, when he had gone to the Senate from a party, he had to be carried out because he was so fast asleep he could not be roused. Yet Tiberius personally wrote to him many things which he did not think it wise to entrust even to his own ministers, and Cossus never let out a secret, private or public.

16.   So let us put out of sight those set speeches, like: 'When it is gripped by drunkenness the mind is not under its own control. Just as wine vats are actually cracked by the unfermented grape juice, and all the sediment is thrown up to the surface by the boiling heat, so when we are heated with excess of wine everything lying hidden within us is cast forth and comes into the open. Steeped in liquor men can keep down neither their food, because of the excess of wine, nor even a secret, and they pour out equally their own and other

17. people's private concerns.' But although this commonly happens, it is also common for us to discuss matters of vital importance with those we know drink too freely. So it is a false plea that you don't tell a secret to a man who is habitually drunk.

It is much better to censure drunkenness openly and expose its vices. These even a moderately good man would avoid, let alone the ideal sage, for whom it is enough to satisfy his thirst, and who stops well short of drunkenness even when tempted by some festive occasion

18. which for the sake of another has been excessively prolonged. We shall see later whether the wise man's mind is disturbed by over—indulgence and acts as drunkards normally do. Meanwhile, if you want to prove that the good man should not get drunk why do it

debere ebrium fieri, cur syllogismis agis? Dic quam turpe sit plus sibi ingerere quam capiat et stomachi sui non nosse mensuram, quam multa ebrii faciant quibus sobrii erubescant, nihil aliud esse ebrietatem quam voluntariam insaniam. Extende in plures dies illum ebrii habitum: numquid de furore dubitabis? nunc quoque non est minor sed

19. brevior. Refer Alexandri Macedonis exemplum, qui Clitum carissimum sibi ac fidelissimum inter epulas transfodit et intellecto facinore mori voluit, certe debuit. Omne vitium ebrietas et incendit et detegit, obstantem malis conatibus verecundiam removet; plures enim pudore

20. peccandi quam bona voluntate prohibitis abstinent. Ubi possedit animum nimia vis vini, quidquid mali latebat emergit. Non facit ebrietas vitia sed protrahit: tunc libidinosus ne cubiculum quidem expectat, sed cupiditatibus suis quantum petierunt sine dilatione permittit; tunc inpudicus morbum profitetur ac publicat; tunc petulans non linguam, non manum continet. Crescit insolenti superbia, crudelitas saevo, malignitas livido; omne vitium laxatur et prodit.

21. Adice illam ignorationem sui, dubia et parum explanata verba, incertos oculos, gradum errantem, vertiginem capitis, tecta ipsa mobilia velut aliquo turbine circumagente totam domum, stomachi tormenta cum effervescit merum ac viscera ipsa distendit. Tunc tamen utcumque tolerabile est, dum illi vis sua est: quid cum somno vitiatur et quae

22. ebrietas fuit cruditas facta est? Cogita quas clades ediderit publica ebrietas: haec acerrimas gentes bellicosasque hostibus tradidit, haec multorum annorum pertinaci bello defensa moenia patefecit, haec contumacissimos et iugum recusantes in alienum egit arbitrium, haec

23. invictos acie mero domuit. Alexandrum, cuius modo feci mentionem, tot itinera, tot proelia, tot hiemes per quas victa temporum locorumque difficultate transierat, tot flumina ex ignoto cadentia, tot maria tutum dimiserunt: intemperantia bibendi et ille Herculaneus ac

24. fatalis scyphus condidit. Quae gloria est capere multum? cum penes te palma fuerit et propinationes tuas strati somno ac vomitantes recusaverint, cum superstes toti convivio fueris, cum omnes viceris

25. virtute magnifica et nemo vini tam capax fuerit, vinceris a dolio. M. Antonium, magnum virum et ingeni nobilis, quae alia res perdidit et

with syllogisms? Rather say how disgusting it is to pack more into yourself than you can hold and not to know the limits of your stomach; how drunks do many things which sober men would blush at; and that drunkenness is nothing else than self—induced madness. If you prolonged the condition of the drunkard over several days would you have any doubts of his lunacy? At the moment the lunacy

19. is not less but shorter. Consider the example of Alexander of Macedon, who during a banquet stabbed Clitus, a very dear and faithful friend, and then realizing the outrage he had committed wished to die himself — as he certainly deserved to. Drunkenness inflames and exposes all our faults by removing the sense of shame which inhibits our baser urges. For more people abstain from forbidden actions through shame at the crime than because they have

20. made a morally good decision. But when the mind is overpowered by too much wine all its latent wickedness appears. Drunkenness does not create vices: it just brings them to light. Then the lecher does not even wait to find a bedroom, but straightway indulges his lusts to the full; then the pervert openly acknowledges his weakness; then the wanton controls neither his tongue nor his hand. The overbearing show more pride, the cruel more savagery, the spiteful more malice:

21. every vice appears freed from restraint. Note too the familiar forgetfulness of our own identity, the hesitant incoherent words, wandering eyes, uncertain gait, dizziness, when the very ceiling seems to be moving as if a whirlwind were spinning the whole house round, agonizing stomach ache, as the wine ferments and distends the bowels. Yet all that can at any rate be endured as long as one's natural strength remains. But when this gives way in sleep and drunkenness

22. has become indigestion, what then? Consider what disasters have resulted from drunkenness in a nation. This has betrayed the fiercest and most warlike nations to their enemies, breached city walls which had been defended for many years of stubborn warfare, driven the most defiant and unyielding men into the power of others, tamed

23. through wine those who were unconquered in battle. Alexander, whom I have just mentioned, survived unscathed all those marches, battles and winters, when he came through all difficulties of weather and terrain, all those rivers of unknown source and all those seas: it was unrestrained drinking that finished him off, and that fatal goblet

24. of Hercules. What is so glorious in being able to hold a lot? When the victory is yours and the others, stretched out asleep or vomiting, have declined your toasts, when you alone survive the banquet, when you have defeated everyone by your noble prowess and nobody can

25. match your capacity, you will still be beaten by the wine jar. What else than a passion equally for wine and for Cleopatra destroyed that great and noble man Marcus Antonius, and drove him to foreign

in externos mores ac vitia non Romana traiecit quam ebrietas nec minor vino Cleopatrae amor? Haec illum res hostem rei publicae, haec hostibus suis inparem reddidit; haec crudelem fecit, cum capita principum civitatis cenanti referrentur, cum inter apparatissimas epulas luxusque regales ora ac manus proscriptorum recognosceret, cum vino gravis sitiret tamen sanguinem. Intolerabile erat quod ebrius fiebat cum haec faceret: quanto intolerabilius quod haec in ipsa ebrietate faciebat! Fere vinolentiam crudelitas sequitur; vitiatur enim exasperaturque sanitas mentis. Quemadmodum < morosos> difficilesque faciunt diutini morbi et ad minimam rabidos offensionem, ita ebrietates continuae efferant animos; nam cum saepe apud se non sint, consuetudo insaniae durat et vitia vino concepta etiam sine illo valent.

26.

27. Dic ergo quare sapiens non debeat ebrius fieri; deformitatem rei et inportunitatem ostende rebus, non verbis. Quod facillimum est, proba istas quae voluptates vocantur, ubi transcenderunt modum, poenas esse. Nam si illud argumentaberis, sapientem multo vino non inebriari et retinere rectum tenorem etiam si temulentus sit, licet colligas nec veneno poto moriturum nec sopore sumpto dormiturum nec elleboro accepto quidquid in visceribus haerebit eiecturum deiecturumque. Sed si temptantur pedes, lingua non constat, quid est quare illum existimes in parte sobrium esse, in parte ebrium? Vale.

LETTER 88

1. De liberalibus studiis quid sentiam scire desideras: nullum suspicio, nullum in bonis numero quod ad aes exit. Meritoria artificia sunt, hactenus utilia si praeparant ingenium, non detinent. Tamdiu enim istis inmorandum est quamdiu nihil animus agere maius potest;

2. rudimenta sunt nostra, non opera. Quare liberalia studia dicta sint vides: quia homine libero digna sunt. Ceterum unum studium vere liberale est quod liberum facit, hoc est sapientiae, sublime, forte, magnanimum: cetera pusilla et puerilia sunt. An tu quicquam in istis esse credis boni quorum professores turpissimos omnium ac flagitiosissimos cernis? Non discere debemus ista, sed didicisse.

Quidam illud de liberalibus studiis quaerendum iudicaverunt, an

habits and un—Roman vices? This was what made him an enemy of the state and unable to match his own enemies. This made him cruel, when he had the heads of the country's leading men brought to him as he dined, identifying the faces and hands of his condemned enemies in the midst of a luxurious and royally splendid banquet, and though full of wine still thirsting for blood. It was intolerable that he was getting drunk when he did this, but how much more intolerable

26. that he did it in the depths of his drunkenness! Cruelty usually attends intoxication, as the sound health of the mind is corrupted and roughened. Just as protracted illnesses make people peevish, bad—tempered and violent at the slightest provocation, so continued bouts of drunkenness brutalize the mind. For when people are frequently deprived of their senses, the condition of frenzy becomes lasting, and the vices that originally derived from drinking flourish even without it.

27. So, explain why the wise man should not become drunk, and show by means of facts, not words, how unsightly and offensive is the habit. The easiest thing you can prove is that what are called pleasures become punishments when they exceed a reasonable limit. For if you try to argue that the wise man does not get drunk after taking much wine, and can walk a straight path even if he is tipsy, then you can also deduce that he will not die after drinking poison, nor fall asleep after taking an opiate, nor after a dose of hellebore vomit or evacuate anything that is troubling his bowels. But if his footsteps are unsteady and his speech not under his control, why should you think him partly sober and only partly drunk?

LETTER 88

1. You want to know what I feel about liberal studies. I don't admire or count as worthwhile any study which aims at making money. Such studies are just hiring out our talents and are only of value if they train the mind and do not pre—occupy it. We should only spend time on them as long as the mind has nothing better to

2. do, as they form our apprenticeship, not our proper work. You can see why liberal studies are so called: they are worthy of a free man. But only one study is truly liberal in making a man free, and that is the study of wisdom, with its strength of purpose and its noble and exalted ideals. All the others are trivial and childish. Do you think there can be anything of value in those subjects which are expounded by the most disgraceful and outrageous teachers you could find? We should have finished learning such things, not still be learning them.

Some people have thought it worth asking whether liberal

virum bonum facerent: ne promittunt quidem nec huius rei scientiam
3.   adfectant.   Grammatice circa curam sermonis versatur et, si latius
evagari vult, circa historias, iam ut longissime fines suos proferat,
circa carmina.   Quid horum ad virtutem viam sternit?   Syllabarum
enarratio et verborum diligentia et fabularum memoria et versuum lex
ac modificatio — quid ex his metum demit, cupiditatem eximit,
4.   libidinem frenat?   Ad geometriam transeamus et ad musicen: nihil
apud illas invenies quod vetet timere, vetet cupere.   Quae quisquis
ignorat, alia frustra scit.

     *** utrum doceant isti virtutem an non: si non docent, ne
tradunt quidem; si docent, philosophi sunt.   Vis scire quam non ad
docendam   virtutem   consederint?   aspice   quam   dissimilia   inter   se
5.   omnium studia sint: atqui similitudo esset idem docentium.   Nisi forte
tibi Homerum philosophum fuisse persuadent, cum his ipsis quibus
colligunt negent; nam modo Stoicum illum faciunt, virtutem solam
probantem et voluptates refugientem et ab honesto ne immortalitatis
quidem pretio recedentem, modo Epicureum, laudantem statum quietae
civitatis   et   inter   convivia   cantusque   vitam   exigentis,   modo
Peripateticum, tria bonorum genera inducentem, modo Academicum,
omnia incerta dicentem.   Apparet nihil horum esse in illo, quia omnia
sunt; ista enim inter se dissident.   Demus illis Homerum philosophum
fuisse: nempe sapiens factus est antequam carmina ulla cognosceret;
6.   ergo illa discamus quae Homerum fecere sapientem.   Hoc quidem me
quaerere, uter maior aetate fuerit, Homerus an Hesiodus, non magis
ad rem pertinet quam scire, cum minor Hecuba fuerit quam Helena,
quare tam male tulerit aetatem.   Quid, inquam, annos Patrocli et
7.   Achillis inquirere ad rem existimas pertinere?   Quaeris Ulixes ubi
erraverit potius quam efficias ne nos semper erremus?   Non vacat
audire utrum inter Italiam et Siciliam iactatus sit an extra notum nobis
orbem (neque enim potuit in tam angusto error esse tam longus):
tempestates nos animi cotidie iactant et nequitia in omnia Ulixis mala
inpellit.   Non deest forma quae sollicitet oculos, non hostis; hinc
monstra effera et humano cruore gaudentia, hinc insidiosa blandimenta
aurium, hinc naufragia et tot varietates malorum.   Hoc me doce,
quomodo patriam amem, quomodo uxorem, quomodo patrem, quomodo
8.   ad haec tam honesta vel naufragus navigem.   Quid inquiris an

3. studies create the good man. Well, they do not even undertake to do this and they do not claim the requisite knowledge. The study of literature is concerned with the correct use of language; if it branches out a bit it deals with points of subject matter; at its widest range, the rules governing poetry. Which of these topics paves the way to virtue? Analysis of syllables, careful attention to words, the recording of stories, the laws of scansion — which of these banishes fear, gets

4. rid of desire, or curbs passion? Let us turn to geometry and music: you'll find nothing in them to bid us stop being afraid and stop being covetous. And if a man doesn't know these things all his other knowledge is useless. The point is whether or not these scholars are teaching us virtue. If they are not teaching it they are not even imparting it indirectly; if they are teaching it, they are philosophers. If you want to know how far they are from formally teaching virtue consider how very disparate are all the things they study: yet if they were teaching the same thing they would show some shared

5. characteristic. Unless perhaps they persuade you that Homer was a philosopher, although they deny this conclusion by the very passages from which they derive it. For at one time they make him out to have been a Stoic, approving of virtue alone, rejecting pleasures and refusing even immortality if the price was dishonourable. At other times they claim him as an Epicurean, praising the condition of tranquillity in a state which spends its days in banqueting and song. Now he is a Peripatetic, dividing benefits into three classes; now an Academic, stating that nothing is certain. It is quite clear that none of these doctrines is in Homer because they all are, and they are mutually incompatible. Even granting that Homer was a philosopher, he surely acquired his wisdom before he mastered any of his songs.

6. So let us learn those things which made Homer wise. For me to investigate who was earlier, Homer or Hesiod, is as irrelevant as knowing why Hecuba, though younger than Helen, seemed so much older. What, I repeat, is the point of trying to establish the ages of

7. Patroclus and Achilles? Would you rather know where Ulysses wandered than find a way of stopping our own everlasting wanderings? We have no time to hear whether he was storm—tossed between Italy and Sicily, or outside of the known world (since such extensive wanderings could not have taken place in such a confined area). It's the storms of the soul which daily harry us, and our wickedness drives us into all the troubles Ulysses suffered. There's always some beauty to distract us, some enemy to face; here savage monsters rejoicing in human blood; here seductive sounds to beguile our ears, here shipwrecks and every kind of disaster. Teach me how to love my country, my wife, my father, and how to keep on these honourable

8. courses even after suffering shipwreck. Why enquire whether

Penelopa inpudica fuerit, an verba saeculo suo dederit? an Ulixem illum esse quem videbat, antequam sciret, suspicata sit? Doce me quid sit pudicitia et quantum in ea bonum, in corpore an in animo posita sit.

9.   Ad musicum transeo. Doces me quomodo inter se acutae ac graves consonent, quomodo nervorum disparem reddentium sonum fiat concordia: fac potius quomodo animus secum meus consonet nec consilia mea discrepent. Monstras mihi qui sint modi flebiles: monstra potius quomodo inter adversa non emittam flebilem vocem.

10.   Metiri me geometres docet latifundia potius quam doceat quomodo metiar quantum homini satis sit; numerare docet me et avaritiae commodat digitos potius quam doceat nihil ad rem pertinere istas conputationes, non esse feliciorem cuius patrimonium tabularios lassat, immo quam supervacua possideat qui infelicissimus futurus est si

11.   quantum habeat per se conputare cogetur. Quid mihi prodest scire agellum in partes dividere, si nescio cum fratre dividere? Quid prodest colligere subtiliter pedes iugeri et conprendere etiam si quid decempedam effugit, si tristem me facit vicinus inpotens et aliquid ex meo abradens? Docet quomodo nihil perdam ex finibus meis: et ego discere volo quomodo totos hilaris amittam. 'Paterno agro et avito'

12.   inquit 'expellor.' Quid? ante avum tuum quis istum agrum tenuit? cuius, non dico hominis, sed populi fuerit potes expedire? Non dominus isto, sed colonus intrasti. Cuius colonus es? si bene tecum agitur, heredis. Negant iurisconsulti quicquam usu capi publicum: hoc quod tenes, quod tuum dicis, publicum est et quidem generis humani.

13.   O egregiam artem! scis rotunda metiri, in quadratum redigis quamcumque acceperis formam, intervalla siderum dicis, nihil est quod in mensuram tuam non cadat: si artifex es, metire hominis animum, dic quam magnus sit, dic quam pusillus sit. Scis quae recta sit linea: quid tibi prodest, si quid in vita rectum sit ignoras?

14.   Venio nunc ad illum qui caelestium notitia gloriatur:

    frigida Saturni sese quo stella receptet,
    quos ignis caeli Cyllenius erret in orbes.

Hoc scire quid proderit? ut sollicitus sim cum Saturnus et Mars ex contrario stabunt aut cum Mercurius vespertinum faciet occasum vidente Saturno, potius quam hoc discam, ubicumque sunt ista, propitia

Penelope was an unchaste hussy who deceived her contemporaries? Whether she suspected the man she saw was Ulysses before she was sure of it? Teach me rather what chastity is, how much goodness there is in it, and whether it lies in the body or in the mind.

9.   Turning to music, I say that you teach me how treble and bass notes harmonize, and how a concord is produced from strings that give dissimilar sounds. I would rather learn how to harmonize my mind and stop my purposes being out of tune. You show me which are the plaintive melodies: show me instead how not to utter a plaintive cry in times of trouble.

10.   A geometrician teaches me to measure my estates rather than how to measure the amount that is enough for a man. He teaches me to do sums and put my fingers to the service of greed, instead of teaching me that those calculations have no importance, that a man is not the happier for having properties which tire out his accountants — in fact that possessions are superfluous if the owner is plunged in misery at the thought of having to calculate them all by himself.

11. What's the good of my knowing how to divide a plot of land into sections if I don't know how to divide it with my brother? What's the good of carefully computing the units of an acre, including even the bits which have escaped the measuring rod, if I get upset by an arrogant neighbour who encroaches on my land? The geometrician teaches me how to keep my boundaries intact, but what I want to

12. learn is how to lose the whole lot cheerfully. Someone says 'I'm being driven out of the land of my father and grandfather'. So what? Who held that land before your grandfather? Can you identify even the community, let alone the individual, who owned it? You came into it not as an owner, but as a tenant. Whose tenant? If things go well for you, your heir's. The lawyers state that public property cannot be acquired by prescription. What you hold and call

13. your own is public property, and indeed belongs to all mankind. O noble art of geometry! You can measure circles, reduce any given shape to a square, tell us the distances between the stars: there is nothing which is outside your scope in measurement. Well, if such is your skill, measure a man's soul and say how large or small it is. You can tell a straight line: what good is that to you if you don't know what a straight life is?

14.   I come now to the man who prides himself on his knowledge of astrology:

> 'On which side Saturn's icy star retreats,
>   And in what orbits blazing Mercury roams.'

What will be the benefit of this knowledge? To make me feel worried when Saturn and Mars are in opposition, or when Mercury sets in the evening in view of Saturn, rather than helping me to learn

15. esse nec posse mutari? Agit illa continuus ordo fatorum et inevitabilis cursus; per statas vices remeant et effectus rerum omnium aut movent aut notant. Sed sive quidquid evenit faciunt, quid inmutabilis rei notitia proficiet? sive significant, quid refert providere quod effugere non possis? Scias ista, nescias: fient.

16.
>   Si vero solem ad rapidum stellasque sequentes
>   ordine respicies, numquam te crastina fallet
>   hora, nec insidiis noctis capiere serenae.

17. Satis abundeque provisum est ut ab insidiis tutus essem. 'Numquid me crastina non fallit hora? fallit enim quod nescienti evenit.' Ego quid futurum sit nescio: quid fieri possit scio. Ex hoc nihil deprecabor, totum expecto: si quid remittitur, boni consulo. Fallit me hora si parcit, sed ne sic quidem fallit. Nam quemadmodum scio omnia accidere posse, sic scio et non utique casura; itaque secunda expecto, malis paratus sum.

18. In illo feras me necesse est non per praescriptum euntem; non enim adducor ut in numerum liberalium artium pictores recipiam, non magis quam statuarios aut marmorarios aut ceteros luxuriae ministros. Aeque luctatores et totam oleo ac luto constantem scientiam expello ex his studiis liberalibus; aut et unguentarios recipiam et cocos et

19. ceteros voluptatibus nostris ingenia accommodantes sua. Quid enim, oro te, liberale habent isti ieiuni vomitores, quorum corpora in sagina, animi in macie et veterno sunt? An liberale studium istuc esse iuventuti nostrae credimus, quam maiores nostri rectam exercuerunt hastilia iacere, sudem torquere, equum agitare, arma tractare? Nihil liberos suos docebant quod discendum esset iacentibus. Sed nec hae nec illae docent aluntve virtutem; quid enim prodest equum regere et cursum eius freno temperare, adfectibus effrenatissimis abstrahi? quid prodest multos vincere luctatione vel caestu, ab iracundia vinci?

20. 'Quid ergo? nihil nobis liberalia conferunt studia?' Ad alia multum, ad virtutem nihil; nam et hae viles ex professo artes quae manu constant ad instrumenta vitae plurimum conferunt, tamen ad virtutem non pertinent. 'Quare ergo liberalibus studiis filios

15. that these planets are propitious whatever their position and cannot change? They are driven on in unalterable courses by a fixed sequence of destined events; they reappear in established cycles and they either cause or signalize all the operations of the universe. But if they bring about everything that happens what will be the use of knowing about an unchangeable process? And if they indicate events what is the point of foreseeing what you cannot avoid? They will happen whether you know about them or not.

16.   'Observe the burning sun and coursing stars:
         The morrow's coming ne'er will prove you wrong
         Nor cloudless nights deceive you with their wiles.'

17. I have taken enough and more than enough care to be safe from nature's wiles. You retort 'Does the morrow's coming really not prove you wrong? Surely whatever happens which you did not foresee proves you wrong?' I do not know what will happen, but I do know what can happen, and none of it will I pray to avoid since I am ready for anything. If I am let off anything I am grateful. The morrow proves me wrong if it spares me something — but not actually wrong even so. For just as I know that everything can happen, I know too that it is not bound to happen. So, I hope for the best and I'm ready for trouble.

18.   You must bear with me if I do not stick to the regular programme of studies. I refuse utterly to include painters in the list of liberal arts any more than sculptors or marble—masons or the other panders to luxury. Equally I reject wrestlers and the oil—and—mud artists from our liberal studies, or else I must accept perfumers and cooks and all the others who devote their skills to our

19. pleasures. What, I ask you, is liberal about those people who vomit after drinking on an empty stomach, whose bodies are stuffed while their minds are starved and sluggish? Can we think of that as a liberal study for our youth — the youth whom our ancestors trained to stand up straight and throw javelins, hurl staves, manage horses and handle weapons? They taught their children nothing which had to be learned lying down. But neither these nor the other forms of training teach or foster virtue. For how does it benefit you to control a horse and restrain him with a bridle, if you yourself are swept away by unbridled emotions? How does it benefit you to overcome lots of opponents in wrestling or boxing, if you are overcome by your own temper?

20.   'Well, then,' you say, 'do we gain nothing at all from liberal studies?' Regarding other things we gain a lot; regarding virtue, nothing. So too, those admittedly inferior manual skills contribute a great deal to life's amenities but have no relevance to virtue. 'Why then do we educate our sons in liberal studies?' Not because they

erudimus?' Non quia virtutem dare possunt; sed quia animum ad accipiendam virtutem praeparant. Quemadmodum prima illa, ut antiqui vocabant, litteratura, per quam pueris elementa traduntur, non docet liberales artes sed mox percipiendis locum parat, sic liberales artes non perducunt animum ad virtutem sed expediunt.

21.   Quattuor ait esse artium Posidonius genera: sunt vulgares et sordidae, sunt ludicrae, sunt pueriles, sunt liberales.   Vulgares opificum, quae manu constant et ad instruendam vitam occupatae sunt,

22. in quibus nulla decoris, nulla honesti simulatio est.   Ludicrae sunt quae ad voluptatem oculorum atque aurium tendunt; his adnumeres licet machinatores qui pegmata per se surgentia excogitant et tabulata tacite in sublime crescentia et alias ex inopinato varietates, aut dehiscentibus quae cohaerebant aut his quae distabant sua sponte coeuntibus aut his quae eminebant paulatim in se residentibus.   His inperitorum feriuntur oculi, omnia subita quia causas non novere

23. mirantium.   Pueriles sunt et aliquid habentes liberalibus simile hae artes quas ἐγκυκλίους Graeci, nostri autem liberales vocant.   Solae autem liberales sunt, immo, ut dicam verius, liberae, quibus curae virtus est.

24.   'Quemadmodum' inquit 'est aliqua pars philosophiae naturalis, est aliqua moralis, est aliqua rationalis, sic et haec quoque liberalium artium turba locum sibi in philosophia vindicat.   Cum ventum est ad naturales quaestiones, geometriae testimonio statur; ergo eius quam

25. adiuvat pars est.'   Multa adiuvant nos nec ideo partes nostri sunt; immo si partes essent, non adiuvarent.   Cibus adiutorium corporis nec tamen pars est.   Aliquod nobis praestat geometria ministerium: sic philosophiae necessaria est quomodo ipsi faber, sed nec

26. his geometriae pars est nec illa philosophiae.   Praeterea utraque fines suos habet; sapiens enim causas naturalium et quaerit et novit, quorum numeros mensurasque geometres persequitur et supputat.   Qua ratione constent caelestia, quae illis sit vis quaeve natura sapiens scit: cursus et recursus et quasdam obversationes per quas descendunt et adlevantur ac speciem interdum stantium praebent, cum caelestibus

27. stare non liceat, colligit mathematicus.   Quae causa in speculo imagines exprimat sciet sapiens: illud tibi geometres potest dicere, quantum abesse debeat corpus ab imagine et qualis forma speculi

can confer virtue but because they prepare the mind to receive it. Just as what long ago used to be called basic grammar, by which children acquire the rudiments of their education, does not teach the liberal arts but prepares the ground for them to be acquired in due course, so the liberal arts themselves do not lead the mind to virtue but clear the way for it.

21.   According to Posidonius there are four kinds of arts: the common and unrefined type; the theatrical type; those centred on children; the liberal arts.   The common arts are those of the craftsman: they are manual and concerned with fitting out our lives

22. materially, and they make no pretence of dignity or grace.   Theatrical arts aim at giving pleasure to the eyes and ears.   Herein you would class the engineers who devise platforms which go upwards of their own accord, floors that rise into the air silently, and other kinds of unexpected and inconsistent effects, when things which were joined together begin to gape, or those which were separated join together spontaneously, or things which formerly projected gradually subside into themselves.   These effects look impressive to the eyes of the naïve, who marvel at any sudden phenomena they cannot explain.

23. The arts relating to children, which are somewhat like the liberal arts, are those which the Greeks call 'encyclic' and we call 'liberal'.   But the only liberal arts — or, to speak more accurately, the only ones worthy of free men — are those whose concern is virtue.

24.   Someone objects: 'Just as one area of philosophy is devoted to physics, one to ethics, and one to dialectic, so this throng of the liberal arts also claims for itself a place within philosophy.   For example, when dealing with problems in physics we resort to geometrical proofs.   Therefore geometry is a part of the study which

25. it assists.'   But many things assist us without thereby being parts of us: in fact, if they were they wouldn't assist us.   Food is an assistance to the body but not part of it.   Geometry offers us some service: it is a requisite of philosophy in the same sense that the craftsman is a requisite of itself; but neither is the craftsman a part

26. of geometry nor geometry a part of philosophy.   Moreover each of these activities has its set limits: the philosopher learns by investigation the causes of the natural phenomena which the

27. geometrician counts and measures by his assiduous calculations.   The philosopher knows the principles underlying the existence of the heavenly bodies, and what is their nature and their vital energy.   The mathematician works out their courses to and fro, and the sort of movements which make them travel higher and lower and sometimes appear to be motionless, though this is not possible for heavenly bodies.   The philosopher will know the cause of reflections in a mirror.   The geometrician can tell you how far a body should be

quales imagines reddat.   Magnum esse solem philosophus probabit, quantus sit mathematicus, qui usu quodam et exercitatione procedit. Sed ut procedat, inpetranda illi quaedam principia sunt; non est autem

28. ars sui iuris cui precarium fundamentum est.   Philosophia nil ab alio petit, totum opus a solo excitat: mathematice, ut ita dicam, superficiaria est, in alieno aedificat; accipit prima, quorum beneficio ad ulteriora perveniat.   Si per se iret ad verum, si totius mundi naturam posset conprendere, dicerem multum conlaturam mentibus nostris, quae tractatu caelestium crescunt trahuntque aliquid ex alto.

    Una re consummatur animus, scientia bonorum ac malorum inmutabili; nihil autem ulla ars alia de bonis ac malis quaerit.

29. Singulas lubet circumire virtutes.   Fortitudo contemptrix timendorum est; terribilia et sub iugum libertatem nostram mittentia despicit, provocat, frangit: numquid ergo hanc liberalia studia corroborant? Fides sanctissimum humani pectoris bonum est, nulla necessitate ad fallendum cogitur, nullo corrumpitur praemio: 'ure', inquit 'caede, occide: non prodam, sed quo magis secreta quaeret dolor, hoc illa altius condam'.   Numquid liberalia studia hos animos facere possunt? Temperantia voluptatibus imperat, alias odit atque abigit, alias dispensat et ad sanum modum redigit nec umquam ad illas propter ipsas venit; scit optimum esse modum cupitorum non quantum velis,

30. sed quantum debeas sumere.   Humanitas vetat superbum esse adversus socios, vetat amarum; verbis, rebus, adfectibus comem se facilemque omnibus praestat; nullum alienum malum putat, bonum autem suum ideo maxime quod alicui bono futurum est amat.   Numquid liberalia studia hos mores praecipiunt? non magis quam simplicitatem, quam modestiam ac moderationem, non magis quam frugalitatem ac parsimoniam, non magis quam clementiam, quae alieno sanguini tamquam suo parcit et scit homini non esse homine prodige utendum.

31.   'Cum dicatis' inquit 'sine liberalibus studiis ad virtutem non perveniri, quemadmodum negatis illa nihil conferre virtuti?' Quia nec sine cibo ad virtutem pervenitur, cibus tamen ad virtutem non pertinet; ligna navi nihil conferunt, quamvis non fiat navis nisi ex lignis: non est, inquam, cur aliquid putes eius adiutorio fieri sine quo

from its reflection, and what shape of mirror gives what shape of reflections. The philosopher will prove that the sun is large; the mathematician with the practical procedures of his skill will prove how large it is. But these procedures depend on his acquiring certain first principles, and no skill is independent if its foundation is borrowed

28. from elsewhere. Philosophy seeks nothing from any other source and builds up its whole structure from the ground. Mathematics is a lease—holder, so to speak, building on someone else's land: it is given its first principles, by virtue of which it arrives at further conclusions. If by itself it could arrive at the truth and grasp the nature of the universe, I would admit that it would greatly benefit our minds, which expand through considering celestial phenomena and do derive something from the heavens.

The mind achieves its highest excellence in one sphere only, the unalterable knowledge of good and evil, and no other art shows any

29. interest in good and evil. I would like to take a look at individual virtues. Bravery treats with contempt things that fill us with dread, despising and challenging and destroying all that makes us slaves to terror. Can we then say that bravery is strengthened by liberal stuides? Loyalty is the most sacred virtue of the human heart, never forced to deceive by any compulsion, never corrupted by a bribe. 'Burn, beat, kill me,' it says, 'I shall not betray. The more the agony searches out my secrets, the deeper I shall hide them.' Can we say that liberal studies create this sort of courage? Moderation controls our pleasures, hating and banishing some, regulating others and reducing them to healthy limits, and never approaching them for their own sake: she knows that the best limit for our desires is not

30. how much you want but how much you ought to have. Kindness stops us being arrogant towards our fellows, or bad—tempered. In words, deeds and feelings she shows herself obliging and good—natured to all, regarding other people's troubles as her own and valuing her own blessings in particular because they can be blessings to somebody else. Can we say that liberal studies teach these attitudes? Not any more than they teach candour, or modesty and self—control, or thrift and frugality, or mercy that spares another's blood as if it were its own, and knows that no human being should make wasteful use of another human being.

31. Some may object here: 'When you people say that virtue cannot be attained without liberal studies how can you also say that they offer no assistance to virtue?' The answer is that virtue cannot be attained without food either, but there is no connection between virtue and food. Timbers offer no assistance to a ship even though a ship cannot be created without them. I repeat that you must not think that anything comes into being through the assistance of

32. non potest fieri.   Potet quidem etiam illud dici, sine liberalibus studiis
veniri ad sapientiam posse; quamvis enim virtus discenda sit, tamen
non per haec discitur.   Quid est autem quare existimem non futurum
sapientem eum qui litteras nescit, cum sapientia non sit in litteris?
Res tradit, non verba, et nescio an certior memoria sit quae nullum

33. extra se subsidium habet.   Magna et spatiosa res est sapientia; vacuo
illi loco opus est; de divinis humanisque discendum est, de praeteritis
de futuris, de caducis de aeternis, de tempore.   De quo uno vide
quam multa quaerantur: primum an per se sit aliquid; deinde an
aliquid ante tempus sit sine tempore; cum mundo coeperit an etiam

34. ante mundum quia fuerit aliquid, fuerit et tempus.   Innumerabiles
quaestiones sunt de animo tantum: unde sit, qualis sit, quando esse
incipiat, quamdiu sit, aliunde alio transeat et domicilia mutet in alias
animalium formas aliasque coniectus, an non amplius quam semel
serviat et emissus vagetur in toto; utrum corpus sit an non sit; quid
sit facturus cum per nos aliquid facere desierit, quomodo libertate sua
usurus cum ex hac effugerit cavea; an obliviscatur priorum et illinc
nosse se incipiat unde corpori abductus in sublime secessit.

35. Quamcumque partem rerum humanarum divinarumque conprenderis,
ingenti copia quaerendorum ac discendorum fatigaberis.   Haec tam
multa, tam magna ut habere possint liberum hospitium, supervacua ex
animo tollenda sunt.   Non dabit se in has angustias virtus; laxum
spatium res magna desiderat.   Expellantur omnia, totum pectus illi
vacet.

36.   'At enim delectat artium notitia multarum.'   Tantum itaque ex
illis retineamus quantum necessarium est.   An tu existimas
reprendendum qui supervacua usibus comparat et pretiosarum rerum
pompam in domo explicat, non putas eum qui occupatus est in

37. supervacua litterarum supellectile?   Plus scire velle quam sit satis
intemperantiae genus est.   Quid quod ista liberalium artium consectatio
molestos, verbosos, intempestivos, sibi placentes facit et ideo non
discentes necessaria quia supervacua didicerunt?   Quattuor milia
librorum Didymus grammaticus scripsit: misererer si tam multa
supervacua legisset.   In his libris de patria · Homeri quaeritur, in his
de Aeneae matre vera, in his libidinosior Anacreon an ebriosior
vixerit, in his an Sappho publica fuerit, et alia quae erant dediscenda

32. something without which it cannot come into being. Indeed you can even argue that wisdom can be achieved without liberal studies: for although virtue has to be learnt, it is not learnt through these. Anyway, why should I imagine that a man who is ignorant of books will not become wise, seeing that wisdom does not lie in books? Wisdom hands down deeds, not words, and I rather think that the memory is more reliable when it has nothing external to help it.

33. Wisdom is extensive, and as it covers a lot of ground it needs room to move in. It has to learn about matters divine and human, about the past and the future, about the transitory and the eternal, about the nature of time. On this one topic of time look how many questions are asked. First, does it have an independent existence? Then, does anything exist before time and outside of it? Did it begin with the world, or before then, given that something existed before

34. the world? There are countless questions about the soul alone: its origin, its nature, when it begins to exist and for how long; whether it moves from one place to another and changes its abode, as it passes into different forms of living creatures, or it does service only once and when released it wanders about the universe; whether it is corporeal or not; what it will do when it has ceased to act through us, and how it will use its freedom when it has escaped its cage here; whether it will forget its past and begin to learn its true nature from the moment it leaves the body and departs up and away.

35. Whatever sphere of human and divine matters you deal with, you will be worn out by the huge mass of facts to be looked into and learnt. So in order that material of this size and scope should find an unrestrained welcome, everything superfluous must be banished from the mind. Virtue will not venture into the present cramped quarters: an important activity needs a lot of room. Let all else be turned out and the whole heart opened to her.

36. 'But knowledge of many subjects is a real source of pleasure.' In that case let us only retain as much of them as we need. Do you regard one man as blameworthy who equates superfluous things with useful ones and sets out a display of costly objects in his house, and not another one who is engrossed in a superfluous quantity of the furniture of learning? To wish to know more than is sufficient is a

37. kind of extravagance. Observe too how that obsession with the liberal arts makes people tiresome, long—winded, tactless and self—satisfied, not learning what they need to because they have spent their time learning what is useless. The grammarian Didymus wrote four thousand books: I would be sorry for him if he had only read so many useless works. In these books he discusses Homer's birthplace, who was Aeneas' real mother, whether Anacreon lived the life of a lecher or of a drunkard, whether Sappho was a whore, and other

si scires. I nunc et longam esse vitam nega!

38.   Sed ad nostros quoque cum perveneris, ostendam multa securibus recidenda.   Magno inpendio temporum, magna alienarum aurium molestia laudatio haec constat: 'o hominem litteratum!'   Simus hoc

39. titulo rusticiore contenti: 'o virum bonum!'   Itane est? annales evolvam omnium gentium et quis primus carmina scripserit quaeram? quantum temporis inter Orphea intersit et Homerum, cum fastos non habeam, conputabo? et Aristarchi notas quibus aliena carmina conpunxit recognoscam, et aetatem in syllabis conteram?   Itane in geometriae pulvere haerebo? adeo mihi praeceptum illud salutare

40. excidit: 'tempori parce'?   Haec sciam? et quid ignorem?   Apion grammaticus, qui sub C. Caesare tota circulatus est Graecia et in nomen Homeri ab omnibus civitatibus adoptatus, aiebat Homerum utraque materia consummata, et Odyssia et Iliade, principium adiecisse operi suo quo bellum Troianum conplexus est.   Huius rei argumentum adferebat quod duas litteras in primo versu posuisset ex industria

41. librorum suorum numerum continentes.   Talia sciat oportet qui multa vult scire.

      Non vis cogitare quantum temporis tibi auferat mala valetudo, quantum occupatio publica, quantum occupatio privata, quantum

42. occupatio cotidiana, quantum somnus?   Metire aetatem tuam: tam multa non capit.   De liberalibus studiis loquor: philosophi quantum habent supervacui, quantum ab usu recedentis!   Ipsi quoque ad syllabarum distinctiones et coniunctionum ac praepositionum proprietates descenderunt et invidere grammaticis, invidere geometris; quidquid in illorum artibus supervacuum erat transtulere in suam.   Sic

43. effectum est ut diligentius loqui scirent quam vivere.   Audi quantum mali faciat nimia subtilitas et quam infesta veritati sit.   Protagoras ait de omni re in utramque partem disputari posse ex aequo et de hac ipsa, an omnis res in utramque partem disputabilis sit.   Nausiphanes ait ex his quae videntur esse nihil magis esse quam non esse.

44. Parmenides ait ex his quae videntur nihil esse †universo†.   Zenon Eleates omnia negotia de negotio deiecit: ait nihil esse.   Circa eadem fere Pyrrhonei versantur et Megarici et Eretrici et Academici, qui

45. novam induxerunt scientiam, nihil scire.   Haec omnia in illum

things you would want to unlearn if you knew them.   Go on, tell me
life isn't long enough!

38.   But when you come to our own writers too I'll show you many
candidates for severe pruning.   It costs a great deal of time — and a
great deal of annoyance to other people's ears — to win the
compliment 'What a learned man!'   Let us be satisfied with the
39.   humbler title 'What a good man!'   Really, then, am I to go through
histories of every race to discover who was the earliest poet?   Am I
to calculate how much time elapsed between Orpheus and Homer,
though I have no records to work on?   Am I to pore over
Aristarchus' critical symbols with which he tattooed other people's
poetry, and waste my life dealing with syllables?   Shall I spend all
my time drawing geometric diagrams in the dust?   Have I really
forgotten that wholesome precept 'Don't waste time'?   Am I to learn
all these things?   And what may I be allowed not to know?   The
40.   grammarian Apion, who travelled all around Greece giving lectures in
the time of Gaius Caesar, and was acclaimed by all the states as a
second Homer, used to say that Homer, after finishing both the
Odyssey and the *Iliad*, had added an opening passage to the work in
which he took in the whole Trojan War.   He claimed to prove this
by the fact that Homer had deliberately put two letters into the
41.   opening verse which stated the number of his books.   That's the sort
of thing you should know if you have a thirst for knowledge!

        Shouldn't you reflect on how much time you lose through ill
health, official business, private business, ordinary everyday business,
42.   sleep?   Measure your life: it simply has no room for all that.   I am
talking about liberal studies.   Yet what a deal of superfluous, useless
stuff you will find in the philosophers!   They too have descended to
discussing distinctions in the use of syllables and the proper meanings
of conjunctions and prefixes, and envying the grammarians and the
geometricians they have taken over all the superfluous elements of
these studies.   The result is that they know more about speaking with
43.   care than living with care.   Consider the mischievous consequences of
over—subtlety and how damaging it is to truth.   Protagoras declares
that it is possible to argue with equal cogency for either side of any
question — even the very question whether you can argue for either
side of any question.   Nausiphanes declares that of the things that
seem to us to exist nothing exists any more than it does not exist.
44.   Parmenides declares that of all that seems to exist nothing exists
except the whole.   Zeno of Elea has removed the debatables from
the debate: he declares that nothing exists.   This is more or less the
view of the Pyrrhonians, the Megarians, the Eretrians and the
Academics: this last school has introduced a new type of knowledge
45.   — knowing nothing.   Just chuck all these theories onto that useless

supervacuum studiorum liberalium gregem coice; illi mihi non profuturam scientiam tradunt, hi spem omnis scientiae eripiunt. Satius est supervacua scire quam nihil. Illi non praeferunt lumen per quod acies derigatur ad verum, hi oculos mihi effodiunt. Si Protagorae credo, nihil in rerum natura est nisi dubium; si Nausiphani, hoc unum certum est, nihil esse certi; si Parmenidi, nihil est praeter unum; si

46. Zenoni, ne unum quidem. Quid ergo nos sumus? quid ista quae nos circumstant, alunt, sustinent? Tota rerum natura umbra est aut inanis aut fallax. Non facile dixerim utris magis irascar, illis qui nos nihil scire voluerunt, an illis qui ne hoc quidem nobis reliquerunt, nihil scire. Vale.

LETTER 90

1.   Quis dubitare, mi Lucili, potest quin deorum inmortalium munus sit quod vivimus, philosophiae quod bene vivimus? Itaque tanto plus huic nos debere quam dis quanto maius beneficium est bona vita quam vita pro certo haberetur, nisi ipsam philosophiam di tribuissent; cuius

2. scientiam nulli dederunt, facultatem omnibus. Nam si hanc quoque bonum vulgare fecissent et prudentes nasceremur, sapientia quod in se optimum habet perdidisset, inter fortuita non esse. Nunc enim hoc in illa pretiosum atque magnificum est, quod non obvenit, quod illam sibi quisque debet, quod non ab alio petitur. Quid haberes quod in

3. philosophia suspiceres si beneficiaria res esset? Huius opus unum est de divinis humanisque verum invenire; ab hac numquam recedit religio, pietas, iustitia et omnis alius comitatus virtutum consertarum et inter se cohaerentium. Haec docuit colere divina, humana diligere, et penes deos imperium esse, inter homines consortium. Quod aliquamdiu inviolatum mansit, antequam societatem avaritia distraxit et paupertatis causa etiam iis quos fecit locupletissimos fuit; desierunt

4. enim omnia possidere, dum volunt propria. Sed primi mortalium quique ex his geniti naturam incorrupti sequebantur eundem habebant et ducem et legem, commissi melioris arbitrio; naturaest enim potioribus deteriora summittere. Mutis quidem gregibus aut maxima

heap of liberal studies. Some offer me knowledge which is no use to me, and others deprive me of the hope of any knowledge at all. Even superfluous knowledge is better than no knowledge. That group holds out no light to guide my eyes to the truth; this one deprives me altogether of my eyes. If I believe Pythagoras there is nothing certain in the world. If I believe Nausiphanes, the only certainty is that there is no certainty. If I believe Parmenides, only one thing

46. exists. If I believe Zeno, not even one thing. What then are we? What are these things which surround and nourish and sustain us? The whole world is a shadow, whether calculated to deceive us or totally without substance. I would find it hard to say which school makes me more angry, those who would have us know nothing or those who don't even leave us the privilege of knowing nothing.

LETTER 90

1.   My dear Lucilius, who can doubt that life is a gift from the immortal gods, but that the good life is the gift of philosophy? And so our debt to philosophy would undoubtedly seem to be greater than our debt to the gods by the same degree that the good life is a greater blessing than life, were it not that philosophy itself was bestowed on us by the gods. They have given to no one the knowledge of philosophy, but to everyone the faculty of acquiring it.

2. For if they had caused philosophy to be a blessing shared by all and we were born wise, wisdom would have lost its finest quality — the fact that it is not one of the things that happen by chance. As it is, there is this noble and valuable element in wisdom that it doesn't just fall to one's lot, that each man has to find it for himself and not seek it from another. What would you see in philosophy to admire if she were a free gift?

3.   The single task of philosophy is to discover the truth about things divine and human. She is attended constantly by religious feeling, sense of duty, justice and all the rest of the virtues joined together in a closely knit association. Philosophy has taught us to worship what is divine and cherish what is human, and that authority is in the hands of the gods and fellowship is the way for men. This fellowship lasted for a long time unspoiled, until greed tore society apart and impoverished even those it had most enriched: for men cease to possess everything once they want it all for themselves.

4.   But the first and second generation of men followed nature uncorrupted and chose one individual to act as their leader and their law, submitting themselves to the will of a superior person, since it is the law of nature that the worse give way to the better. With dumb

corpora praesunt aut vehementissima: non praecedit armenta degener taurus, sed qui magnitudine ac toris ceteros mares vicit; elephantorum gregem excelsissimus ducit: inter homines pro maximo est optimum. Animo itaque rector eligebatur, ideoque summa felicitas erat gentium in quibus non poterat potentior esse nisi melior; tuto enim quantum vult potest qui se nisi quod debet non putat posse.

5.   Illo ergo saeculo quod aureum perhibent penes sapientes fuisse regnum Posidonius iudicat.   Hi continebant manus et infirmiorem a validioribus tuebantur, suadebant dissuadebantque et utilia atque inutilia monstrabant; horum prudentia ne quid deesset suis providebat, fortitudo pericula arcebat, beneficentia augebat ornabatque subiectos. Officium erat imperare, non regnum.   Nemo quantum posset adversus eos experiebatur per quos coeperat posse, nec erat cuiquam aut animus in iniuriam aut causa, cum bene imperanti bene pareretur, nihilque rex maius minari male parentibus posset quam ut abiret e

6. regno.   Sed postquam subrepentibus vitiis in tyrannidem regna conversa sunt, opus esse legibus coepit, quas et ipsas inter initia tulere sapientes.   Solon, qui Athenas aequo iure fundavit, inter septem fuit sapientia notos; Lycurgum si eadem aetas tulisset, sacro illi numero accessisset octavus.   Zaleuci leges Charondaeque laudantur; hi non in foro nec in consultorum atrio, sed in Pythagorae tacito illo sanctoque secessu didicerunt iura quae florenti tunc Siciliae et per Italiam Graeciae ponerent.

7.   Hactenus Posidonio adsentior: artes quidem a philosophia inventas quibus in cotidiano vita utitur non concesserim, nec illi fabricae adseram gloriam.   'Illa' inquit 'sparsos et aut casis tectos aut aliqua rupe suffossa aut exesae arboris trunco docuit tecta moliri.' Ego vero philosophiam iudico non magis excogitasse has machinationes tectorum supra tecta surgentium et urbium urbes prementium quam vivaria piscium in hoc clausa ut tempestatum periculum non adiret gula et quamvis acerrime pelago saeviente haberet luxuria portus suos

8. in quibus distinctos piscium greges saginaret.   Quid ais? philosophia homines docuit habere clavem et seram?   Quid aliud erat avaritiae signum dare?   Philosophia haec cum tanto habitantium periculo

animals it is the largest or the fiercest who dominate. It is not a degenerate bull that leads the herd, but the one which has defeated the other males by its size and muscular power. The tallest elephant leads the herd: among men 'biggest' is replaced by 'best' as the criterion. So the leader was chosen for his mental qualities, with the result that those races enjoyed the highest good fortune in which no one could acquire superior power unless he was a better man. For a man can safely have all the power he wants if he limits his ideas of power only to what he ought to do.

5.   Well, then, in what is commonly called the Golden Age Posidonius claims that power was in the hands of the wise. They kept violence in check, protected the weak from the strong, made speeches for and against courses of action, pointing out advantages and disadvantages. Their forethought ensured that their people did not lack essentials; their courage averted dangers; their kindliness brought success and prosperity. To rule was a duty, not an enjoyment of power. No one tried out the extent of his power over those who had first given him that power; and no one had either inclination or pretext to commit injustice, since good ruling elicited good obedience, and a king's worst threat to his disobedient people

6.   was to give up his office. But after vices stole in and kingships turned into tyrannies, laws became necessary, which themselves in the early days were introduced by the wise. Solon, who established Athens as a democracy, was one of the celebrated Seven Wise Men. Had Lycurgus lived in the same age an eighth would have joined that reverend number. The laws of Zaleucus and Charondas are still admired, and the constitutions which they were to establish for Sicily, then enjoying its period of glory, and through Italy for Greece, were not learnt in public life or in the consulting—rooms of lawyers, but in the hallowed privacy of Pythagoras' school.

7.   Up to this point I agree with Posidonius; but I would not concede that philosophy discovered the techniques which life makes daily use of, nor would I claim for her the honour of an artisan. 'Philosophy', says Posidonius, 'taught men to construct buildings at a time when they were living in scattered communities, sheltered by huts, rock—caves or hollowed—out tree trunks.' No, I really cannot believe that philosophy devised our complex multi—storey buildings and our cities built in uncomfortable proximity to each other, any more than our fish—tanks, enclosed to ensure that our gluttony is not threatened by storms, and that however fiercely the sea is raging we have the luxury of our own harbours in which to fatten different

8.   kinds of fish. Surely you don't really think philosophy taught men the use of keys and bolts? What else was that but a signal for greed? Did philosophy raise up our towering blocks that cause such

inminentia tecta suspendit? Parum enim erat fortuitis tegi et sine arte
9. et sine difficultate naturale invenire sibi aliquod receptaculum. Mihi
crede, felix illud saeculum ante architectos fuit, ante tectores. Ista
nata sunt iam nascente luxuria, in quadratum tigna decidere et serra
per designata currente certa manu trabem scindere;
> nam primi cuneis scindebant fissile lignum.

Non enim tecta cenationi epulum recepturae parabantur, nec in hunc
usum pinus aut abies deferebatur longo vehiculorum ordine vicis
10. intrementibus, ut ex illa lacunaria auro gravia penderent. Furcae
utrimque suspensae fulciebant casam; spissatis ramalibus ac fronde
congesta et in proclive disposita decursus imbribus quamvis magnis
erat. Sub his tectis habitavere [sed] securi: culmus liberos texit, sub
marmore atque auro servitus habitat.

11. In illo quoque dissentio a Posidonio, quod ferramenta fabrilia
excogitata a sapientibus viris iudicat; isto enim modo dicat licet
sapientes fuisse per quos
> tunc laqueis captare feras et fallere visco
> inventum et magnos canibus circumdare saltus.

12. Omnia enim ista sagacitas hominum, non sapientia invenit. In hoc
quoque dissentio, sapientes fuisse qui ferri metalla et aeris invenerint,
cum incendio silvarum adusta tellus in summo venas iacentis liquefacta
13. fudisset: ista tales inveniunt quales colunt. Ne illa quidem. tam subtilis
mihi quaestio videtur quam Posidonio, utrum malleus in usu esse prius
an forcipes coeperint. Utraque invenit aliquis excitati ingenii, acuti,
non magni nec elati, et quidquid aliud corpore incurvato et animo
humum spectante quaerendum est. Sapiens facilis victu fuit. Quidni?
14. cum hoc quoque saeculo esse quam expeditissimus cupiat. Quomodo,
oro te, convenit ut et Diogenen mireris et Daedalum? Uter ex his
sapiens tibi videtur? qui serram commentus est, an ille qui, cum
vidisset puerum cava manu bibentem aquam, fregit protinus exemptum
e perula calicem <cum> hac obiurgatione sui: 'quamdiu homo stultus
supervacuas sarcinas habui!', qui se conplicuit in dolio et in eo
15. cubitavit? Hodie utrum tandem sapientiorem putas qui invenit
quemadmodum in immensam altitudinem crocum latentibus fistulis
exprimat, qui euripos subito aquarum impetu implet aut siccat et
versatilia cenationum laquearia ita coagmentat ut subinde alia facies
atque alia succedat et totiens tecta quotiens fericula mutentur, an eum

danger to the inhabitants? I suppose it wasn't enough for men to depend on chance for their shelter, and to find without trouble some

9.   natural refuge which did not require technical skill! Believe me, that age before architects and builders appeared was a happy one. The rise of luxury saw the rise too of the skill to square off timbers and to cut planks accurately by following a line marked out for the saw.

        'For early men with wedges split their wood.'

Yes, since they were not building a public banqueting—hall, nor were pine and fir trees being carried on a long procession of vehicles through trembling streets in order to support ceilings heavy with gold

10.   panels. Their huts were propped up by forked poles set up at either side, and by densely packed branches and sloping piles of leaves they contrived escape channels for even heavy showers of rain. In such dwellings they lived, and their minds were free from care. Free men had roofs of thatch; slaves now dwell beneath marble and gold.

11.   I also disagree with Posidonius in his belief that iron tools were invented by wise men; for on that principle he could say that through wise men

        'Then learnt they game to snare and trap with lime,
        And woodlands wide to ring with hunting—dogs.'

12.   No, all those skills were discovered by human ingenuity, not by wisdom. I disagree too with the theory that wise men discovered iron and copper mining, after forest fires had caused the scorched earth to melt and produce liquid veins of ore on its surface. Such things are

13.   discovered by the sort of people who are interested in them. I don't even share Posidonius' interest in the nice problem whether the hammer or the tongs first came into use. Both were invented by someone of an alert and sagacious intellect, but not an elevated and inspired one — as was anything else which has to be discovered by a bent back and a mind contemplating the ground.

     The wise man lived a simple life, — not surprising, since even

14.   in our times he wishes to be as unencumbered as possible. How, pray, can you consistently admire both Diogenes and Daedalus? Which of these two seems to you the wise man? — the one who invented the saw, or the one who, when he had seen a boy drinking water from his cupped hands, straightway took a cup from his knapsack and broke it, scolding himself with these words, 'What a fool I've been to carry around superfluous baggage all this time!', and

15.   who curled up and went to sleep in a jar. And to—day I'd like to know which you consider the wiser, the man who discovers how to spray jets of saffron to an enormous height from hidden pipes, who fills or empties channels by a sudden rush of water, who constructs revolving panelled ceilings for dining—rooms, which produce a succession of different designs that change with every course; or the

qui et aliis et sibi hoc monstrat, quam nihil nobis natura durum ac
difficile imperaverit, posse nos habitare sine marmorario ac fabro,
posse nos vestitos esse sine commercio sericorum, posse nos habere
usibus nostris necessaria si contenti fuerimus iis quae terra posuit in
summo?   Quem si audire humanum genus voluerit, tam supervacuum
sciet sibi cocum esse quam militem.

16.   Illi sapientes fuerunt aut certe sapientibus similes quibus expedita
erat tutela corporis.   Simplici cura constant necessaria: in delicias
laboratur.   Non desiderabis artifices: sequere naturam.   Illa noluit esse
districtos; ad quaecumque nos cogebat instruxit.   'Frigus intolerabilest
corpori nudo.'   Quid ergo? non pelles ferarum et aliorum animalium
a frigore satis abundeque defendere queunt? non corticibus arborum
pleraeque gentes tegunt corpora? non avium plumae in usum vestis
conseruntur? non hodieque magna Scytharum pars tergis vulpium
induitur ac murum, quae tactu mollia et inpenetrabilia ventis sunt?
Quid ergo? non quilibet virgeam cratem texuerunt manu et vili
obliverunt luto, deinde [de] stipula aliisque silvestribus operuere
fastigium et pluviis per devexa labentibus hiemem transiere securi?

17. 'Opus est tamen calorem solis aestivi umbra crassiore propellere.'
Quid ergo? non vetustas multa abdidit loca quae vel iniuria temporis
vel alio quolibet casu excavata in specum recesserunt?   Quid ergo?
non in defosso latent Syrticae gentes quibusque propter nimios solis
ardores nullum tegimentum satis repellendis caloribus solidum est nisi

18. ipsa arens humus?   Non fuit tam iniqua natura ut, cum omnibus aliis
animalibus facilem actum vitae daret, homo solus non posset sine tot
artibus vivere; nihil durum ab illa nobis imperatum est, nihil aegre
quaerendum, ut possit vita produci.   Ad parata nati sumus: nos omnia
nobis difficilia facilium fastidio fecimus.   Tecta tegimentaque et
fomenta corporum et cibi et quae nunc ingens negotium facta sunt
obvia erant et gratuita et opera levi parabilia; modus enim omnium
prout necessitas erat: nos ista pretiosa, nos mira, nos magnis multisque

19. conquirenda artibus fecimus.   Sufficit ad id natura quod poscit.   A
natura luxuria descivit, quae cotidie se ipsa incitat et tot saeculis
crescit et ingenio adiuvat vitia.   Primo supervacua coepit concupiscere,
inde contraria, novissime animum corpori addixit et illius deservire

man who proves to others as well as himself that nature gives us no tough or difficult orders, that we can live without the marble—mason and the carpenter, and clothe ourselves without imported silks, and that we can have the essentials for our needs if we content ourselves with what the earth supplies on its surface. If mankind would listen to this man it would realize that the cook is as superfluous as the soldier.

16.   Those who regarded the care of the body as a simple matter were wise men, or at any rate very like them. Life's essentials do not cost us much effort: it is the luxuries that we toil after. Follow nature and you won't need craftsmen. She did not wish us to be too preoccupied, and she equipped us to deal with anything she made us cope with. 'The naked body cannot stand cold.' So what? Cannot the skins of wild beasts and other animals give us ample protection from the cold? Don't many races cover their bodies with the bark of trees? Are there not garments made of bird feathers sewn together? Even to—day don't the majority of the Scythians wear the skins of foxes and mice, which are soft to the touch and keep out the wind? Again, have not some people you can think of woven by hand a latticework of wattles, smeared it over with ordinary mud, then covered the roof with straw and other wild vegetation, and spent the winter unconcerned by the rain which ran off along the slopes of this

17.   roof? 'But we need fairly dense shade to ward off the heat of the sun in summer.' So what? Have not past ages given us lots of sheltered places, which either the ravages of time or some other chance occurrence have hollowed out to form caves? Again, don't the Syrtic tribes shelter themselves in trenches, like other races, who because of the fierceness of the sun's heat have no covering strong

18.   enough to ward it off but the parched earth itself? Nature was not so unfair as to give all the other animals an easy passage through life, and to make it impossible for man alone to survive without all these skills. She has made no harsh demands on us; we need no laborious discoveries to be able to keep on living. We were born to a supply of things easily obtained: we have made everything difficult for ourselves because we scorn what is easily had. Shelter, clothes, warm wrappings for the body, food, all the things that involve huge trouble to us, were ready to hand, free and obtainable with very little effort. In all things the limit was in proportion to the need. It is we who have made those things costly, remarkable and obtainable only by many elaborate skills.

19.   Nature suffices for all her demands on us. Luxury has abandoned nature, daily urging herself on, increasing through many ages, and using her ingenuity to stimulate vices. First she began to hanker after superfluities, then things that were injurious, and finally

libidini iussit.   Omnes istae artes quibus aut circitatur civitas aut strepit corpori negotium gerunt, cui omnia olim tamquam servo praestabantur, nunc tamquam domino parantur.   Itaque hinc textorum, hinc fabrorum officinae sunt, hinc odores coquentium, hinc molles corporis motus docentium mollesque cantus et infractos.   Recessit enim ille naturalis modus desideria ope necessaria finiens; iam rusticitatis et miseriae est velle quantum sat est.

20.   Incredibilest, mi Lucili, quam facile etiam magnos viros dulcedo orationis abducat a vero.   Ecce Posidonius, ut mea fert opinio, ex iis qui plurimum philosophiae contulerunt, dum vult describere primum quemadmodum alia torqueantur fila, alia ex molli solutoque ducantur, deinde   quemadmodum   tela   suspensis   ponderibus   rectum   stamen extendat, quemadmodum subtemen insertum, quod duritiam utrimque conprimentis tramae remolliat, spatha coire cogatur et iungi, textrini quoque artem a sapientibus dixit inventam, oblitus postea repertum hoc subtilius genus in quo

> tela iugo vincta est, stamen secernit harundo,
> inseritur medium radiis subtemen acutis,
> quod lato paviunt insecti pectine dentes.

Quid si contigisset illi videre has nostri temporis telas, in quibus vestis nihil celatura conficitur, in qua non dico nullum corpori auxilium, sed
21. nullum pudori est?   Transit deinde ad agricolas nec minus facunde describit proscissum aratro solum et iteratum quo solutior terra facilius pateat radicibus, tunc sparsa semina et collectas manu herbas ne quid fortuitum et agreste succrescat quod necet segetem.   Hoc quoque opus ait esse sapientium, tamquam non nunc quoque plurima cultores
22. agrorum nova inveniant per quae fertilitas augeatur.   Deinde non est contentus his artibus, sed in pistrinum sapientem summittit; narrat enim quemadmodum rerum naturam imitatus panem coeperit facere. 'Receptas' inquit 'in os fruges concurrens inter se duritia dentium frangit, et quidquid excidit ad eosdem dentes lingua refertur; tunc umore miscetur ut facilius per fauces lubricas transeat; cum pervenit in ventrem, aequali eius fervore concoquitur; tunc demum corpori
23. accedit.   Hoc aliquis secutus exemplar lapidem asperum aspero inposuit ad similitudinem dentium, quorum pars immobilis motum alterius expectat;   deinde   utriusque   adtritu   grana   franguntur   et   saepius

she assigned the mind as a slave to the body with orders to obey its lusts. All those skills that are noisily paraded around a city are doing business for the body, which at one time had everything handed out to it as to a slave, but now has everything procured for it as for a master. Hence arise shops for weavers and carpenters and perfume—extractors, and salons for those who teach sensual dances and mincing, effeminate songs. The reason is that we have lost sight of our natural limits, which used to restrict our wants to those which need essential relief: nowadays to want only what is enough marks you out as unsophisticated and pitiful.

20.   It is astonishing, Lucilius, how easily even great men can be distracted from the truth by indulging in the charms of persuasive argument. Look at Posidonius — in my view one of those who have contributed most to philosophy — when he wants to describe, firstly how some threads are twisted and others drawn out softly and loosely; then how the threads of the warp are stretched straight up and down by means of hanging weights, and how the weft, worked in to soften the warp threads which grip it on either side, is pressed close together by means of the batten; he says that the weaver's art too was invented by philosophers, forgetting that it was in a later age that this more sophisticated technique was devised in which

'The warp is bound to the beam; the rod then parts
Its threads, while pointed shuttles insert the weft
And the wide comb's notched teeth strike it home.'

Suppose he had been able to see the looms of our day which produce clothes which conceal nothing and are no help to modesty,

21.   let alone the body! He next turns to farmers and with equal eloquence describes the initial ploughing of the land, and the second ploughing which further breaks up the soil for the benefit of the roots of plants; then sowing the seed, and weeding by hand to prevent the growth of stray weeds which would ruin the crop. This work too, he says, is derived from philosophers, as though even now agriculturalists are not discovering many new techniques to increase land fertility.

22.   Then not content with these skills he relegates the philosopher to the bakery, describing how by imitating nature he first produced bread. To quote Posidonius: 'The grain is taken into the mouth and broken up by the coming together of hard teeth, and whatever escapes is taken back to the teeth by the tongue. Then it is mixed with saliva to enable it to pass through the moistened throat; on arrival into the stomach it is digested in an even heat, and so finally absorbed into

23.   the body. Following this model somebody placed one rough stone on top of another like teeth, one set of which is motionless and awaits the movement of the other. Then by the friction caused by the two stones the grains are broken up in a frequently repeated process, until

regeruntur donec ad minutiam frequenter trita redigantur: tum farinam aqua sparsit et adsidua tractatione perdomuit finxitque panem, quem primo cinis calidus et fervens testa percoxit, deinde furni paulatim reperti et alia genera quorum fervor serviret arbitrio.' Non multum afuit quin sutrinum quoque inventum a sapientibus diceret.

24.   Omnia ista ratio quidem, sed non recta ratio commenta est. Hominis enim, non sapientis inventa sunt, tam mehercules quam navigia quibus amnes quibusque maria transimus, aptatis ad excipiendum ventorum impetum velis et additis a tergo gubernaculis quae huc atque illuc cursum navigii torqueant. Exemplum a piscibus tractum est, qui cauda reguntur et levi eius in utrumque momento

25. velocitatem suam flectunt.   'Omnia' inquit 'haec sapiens quidem invenit, sed minora quam ut ipse tractaret sordidioribus ministris dedit.' Immo non aliis excogitata ista sunt quam quibus hodieque curantur. Quaedam nostra demum prodisse memoria scimus, ut speculariorum usum perlucente testa clarum transmittentium lumen, ut suspensuras balneorum et inpressos parietibus tubos per quos circumfunderetur calor qui ima simul ac summa foveret aequaliter. Quid loquar marmora quibus templa, quibus domus fulgent? quid lapideas moles in rotundum ac leve formatas quibus porticus et capacia populorum tecta suscipimus? quid verborum notas quibus quamvis citata excipitur oratio et celeritatem linguae manus sequitur? Vilissimorum

26. mancipiorum ista commenta sunt: sapientia altius sedet nec manus edocet: animorum magistra est.   Vis scire quid illa eruerit, quid effecerit? Non decoros corporis motus nec varios per tubam ac tibiam cantus, quibus exceptus spiritus aut in exitu aut in transitu formatur in vocem. Non arma nec muros nec bello utilia molitur: paci favet et

27. genus humanum ad concordiam vocat.   Non est, inquam, instrumentorum ad usus necessarios opifex. Quid illi tam parvola adsignas? artificem vides vitae. Alias quidem artes sub dominio habet; nam cui vita, illi vitae quoque ornantia serviunt: ceterum ad beatum

28. statum tendit, illo ducit, illo vias aperit. Quae sint mala, quae videantur ostendit; vanitatem exuit mentibus, dat magnitudinem solidam, inflatam vero et ex inani speciosam reprimit, nec ignorari

the constant grinding reduces them to a powder. This meal he then sprinkled with water and by a long process of kneading with his hands he moulded it into the form of a loaf. At first this was baked in a hot earthenware pot standing in glowing ashes; then gradually ovens were invented, and other devices in which you could regulate the heat.' Posidonius came close to claiming that even shoemaking was invented by philosophers!

24.   Now all these things were indeed invented by reason, but not by reason in its perfect form. They were discoveries of men, not of philosophical men, as were, to be sure, the vessels in which we cross rivers and seas, fitted with sails to catch the winds and rudders at the stern to guide the vessel's course. Fish provided the model for this, for they steer with their tail which alters their swift course by a slight

25.   impulse in either direction. 'The philosopher,' says Posidonius, 'invented all these things, but as they were too trivial for him to deal with personally he passed them over to his more unrefined assistants.' No, these things were not thought up by anyone other than those who even to—day are concerned with them. Certain devices we know have only appeared within living memory, like the use of windows which let the light in fully through transparent glass; or raised bathrooms heated by means of pipes set into the walls so as to diffuse the warmth evenly from top to bottom of the rooms. And what about the marble which gleams in our temples and our homes? Or the smooth round stone blocks on which we support colonnades and buildings big enough to hold huge crowds? Or our system of shorthand, by which the quickest speech can be taken down as the hand can keep up with the speed of the tongue? These are the

26.   inventions of common slaves. Philosophy occupies a higher seat and does not teach men's hands: she is the instructress of our minds.

You would like to know what she has unearthed and what she has achieved? Not graceful dance movements, nor the range of musical notes produced by horns and pipes, which take in the human breath and transform it as it passes through or out of them into tunes. She does not devise arms or walls or things useful in war: she is on the side of peace and she summons humanity to live in

27.   concord. She is not, I tell you, the creator of equipment for our daily needs. Why assign such trivialities to her? You can see that her speciality is the art of living. Certainly her authority extends to other arts, for the equipment that serves life also serves life's own mistress. But her aim is the state of happiness: that is the goal to

28.   which she is leading us and opening up the way. She shows us what are real and what are apparent evils; she strips our minds of trivial thinking; she grants the greatness which is genuine and checks the sort which is puffed up and just an empty show; she makes sure we can

sinit inter magna quid intersit et tumida; totius naturae notitiam ac sui tradit. Quid sint di qualesque declarat, quid inferi, quid lares et genii, quid in secundam numinum formam animae perpetitae, ubi consistant, quid agant, quid possint, quid velint. Haec eius initiamenta sunt, per quae non municipale sacrum sed ingens deorum omnium templum, mundus ipse, reseratur, cuius vera simulacra verasque facies cernendas mentibus protulit; nam ad spectacula tam magna hebes visus

29. est. Ad initia deinde rerum redit aeternamque rationem toti inditam et vim omnium seminum singula proprie figurantem. Tum de animo coepit inquirere, unde esset, ubi, quamdiu, in quot membra divisus. Deinde a corporibus se ad incorporalia transtulit veritatemque et argumenta eius excussit; post haec quemadmodum discernerentur vitae aut vocis ambigua; in utraque enim falsa veris inmixta sunt.

30. Non abduxit, inquam, se (ut Posidonio videtur) ab istis artibus sapiens, sed ad illas omnino non venit. Nihil enim dignum inventu iudicasset quod non erat dignum perpetuo usu iudicaturus; ponenda

31. non sumeret. 'Anacharsis' inquit 'invenit rotam figuli, cuius circuitu vasa formantur.' Deinde quia apud Homerum invenitur figuli rota, maluit videri versus falsos esse quam fabulam. Ego nec Anacharsim auctorem huius rei fuisse contendo et, si fuit, sapiens quidem hoc invenit, sed non tamquam sapiens, sicut multa sapientes faciunt qua homines sunt, non qua sapientes. Puta velocissimum esse sapientem: cursu omnis anteibit qua velox est, non qua sapiens. Cuperem Posidonio aliquem vitrearium ostendere, qui spiritu vitrum in habitus plurimos format qui vix diligenti manu effingerentur. Haec inventa

32. sunt postquam sapientem invenire desimus. 'Democritus' inquit 'invenisse dicitur fornicem, ut lapidum curvatura paulatim inclinatorum medio saxo alligaretur.' Hoc dicam falsum esse; necesse est enim ante Democritum et pontes et portas fuisse, quarum fere summa

33. curvantur. Excidit porro vobis eundem Democritum invenisse quemadmodum ebur molliretur, quemadmodum decoctus calculus in zmaragdum converteretur, qua hodieque coctura inventi lapides < in>

distinguish between what is great and what is pretentious; she imparts knowledge of herself and of the whole of nature. She explains the gods and their natures, the underworld deities, the spirits that protect us and the spirits of our families, the souls brought through to a secondary form of divinity — where they abide and what are their activities, powers and wishes. These are her initiation rites, through which is opened to us not some provincial shrine, but the great temple of all the gods, the world itself, whose genuine images and genuine aspects she has offered to our mental vision — for our

29. physical eyesight is too weak for so great a sight. Then she returns to the beginnings of things, and the everlasting reason implanted in the universe, and the force within all seeds which gives their own shape to individual things. Then she begins to investigate the soul — whence it comes, where it is located, how long it remains there, how many component parts it is divided into. Then she turns her attention from material to immaterial things and scrutinizes the nature of truth and the proofs required to establish it. Finally she shows us how to see through the ambiguities in our life and our language: for in both the false is mingled with the true.

30.   The philosopher has not divorced himself (as Posidonius thinks) from those skills: rather he has nothing whatever to do with them. For he would not have judged anything worth inventing if he did not judge it worthy of lasting use: he would not take up things he would

31. then have to lay aside. 'Anacharsis,' says Posidonius, 'invented the potter's wheel on which earthenware vessels are shaped by turning.' Then, because the potter's wheel is found in Homer he prefers to regard these verses as spurious than his own account of the matter. I maintain that it was not Anacharsis who should be credited with this invention, or if it was he, he was indeed a philosopher when he invented it but he did not do so by virtue of being a philosopher, just as philosophers do many things as men, but not as philosophers. Imagine a philosopher who is a champion runner: he will outstrip everyone in a race by virtue of his speed, not by virtue of his philosophy. I'd like to show Posidonius some glass—blower, using his breath to fashion the glass into a multitude of shapes which could scarcely be formed even by a skilful hand: these skills came in after

32. the philosophers disappeared. To quote Posidonius again: 'Democritus is said to have devised the arch, the principle by which a curving line of gradually sloping stones is held together by a keystone.' This is nonsense, for before the time of Democritus there must have been bridges and gateways, the tops of which are usually

33. curved. And haven't you and your friends forgotten to mention too that the same Democritus discovered how to soften ivory, and how to convert a pebble by boiling into an emerald — the kind of boiling

hoc utiles colorantur. Ista sapiens licet invenerit, non qua sapiens erat invenit; multa enim facit quae ab inprudentissimis aut aeque fieri videmus aut peritius atque exercitatius.

34.   Quid sapiens investigaverit, quid in lucem protraxerit quaeris? Primum verum naturamque, quam non ut cetera animalia oculis secutus est, tardis ad divina; deinde vitae legem, quam ad universa derexit, nec nosse tantum sed sequi deos docuit et accidentia non aliter excipere quam imperata. Vetuit parere opinionibus falsis et quanti quidque esset vera aestimatione perpendit; damnavit mixtas paenitentia voluptates et bona semper placitura laudavit et palam fecit felicissimum esse cui felicitate non opus est, potentissimum esse qui se

35. habet in potestate. Non de ea philosophia loquor quae civem extra patriam posuit, extra mundum deos, quae virtutem donavit voluptati, sed < de> illa quae nullum bonum putat nisi quod honestum est, quae nec hominis nec fortunae muneribus deleniri potest, cuius hoc pretium est, non posse pretio capi.

        Hanc philosophiam fuisse illo rudi saeculo quo adhuc artificia

36. deerant et ipso usu discebantur utilia non credo.   †Sicut aut† fortunata tempora, cum in medio iacerent beneficia naturae promiscue utenda, antequam avaritia atque luxuria dissociavere mortales et ad rapinam ex consortio < docuere> discurrere: non erant illi sapientes

37. viri, etiam si faciebant facienda sapientibus. Statum quidem generis humani non alium quisquam suspexerit magis, nec si cui permittat deus terrena formare et dare gentibus mores, aliud probaverit quam quod apud illos fuisse memoratur apud quos

        nulli subigebant arva coloni;
    ne signare quidem aut partiri limite campum
    fas erat: in medium quaerebant, ipsaque tellus
    omnia liberius nullo poscente ferebat.

38. Quid hominum illo genere felicius? In commune rerum natura fruebantur; sufficiebat illa ut parens in tutelam omnium; haec erat publicarum opum secura possessio. Quidni ego illud locupletissimum mortalium genus dixerim in quo pauperem invenire non posses? Inrupit in res optime positas avaritia et, dum seducere aliquid cupit

used even to—day for colouring stones found suitable for this process? Even granted that a philosopher discovered these techniques, he did not do so by virtue of being a philosopher. For he does lots of things which we see being done just as well, or in fact more skilfully and dexterously, by the most unphilosophical people.

34. What, you want to know, has the philosopher searched out and brought to light? First of all, truth and nature, having followed nature not, as all other animals do, just with his eyes (which are slow to grasp divine things); then a rule of life by which he has steered life towards the universal, teaching us not merely to recognize but to obey the gods, and to accept all that happens to us as divinely decreed. He has forbidden us to follow false opinions and has weighed all things according to a true valuation. He has condemned pleasures which bring repentance in their wake, praised the good things which will always give satisfaction, and openly decreed that the most fortunate man is the man who does not need good fortune, and

35. the most powerful man is the man who has power over himself. I am not talking about that philosophy which removes the citizen from public life and the gods from the world, and which hands over virtue to pleasure; but about the one which considers that only the honourable is good, which cannot be cajoled by the gifts of men or fortune, whose value consists in the fact that no valuation can buy it.

I do not believe that this philosophy existed in that primitive age when technical skills were still unknown and practical knowledge

36. was acquired by actual experience; nor in those happy times when nature's gifts were freely available for all and sundry to use, before greed and luxury set men at variance and taught them to abandon partnership and go for plunder. Those men were not philosophers even if they were doing what philosophers are supposed to do.

37. Assuredly no other condition of mankind could evoke greater admiration, and if anyone was allowed by god to fashion earthly matters and to allocate their customs to the various peoples, he would not sanction any other system than what we are told prevailed among those men where

'no farmers tilled the fields;
Even a boundary—line between their lands was wrong;
Their gains they used to swell the common store,
And earth unasked her produce freely gave.'

38. Could any race of men be more fortunate than that? They enjoyed nature as a joint possession, and everyone was maintained by her bounty as by a parent: this was undisturbed possession of resources which everyone owned. Am I not justified in calling that the richest of all races of men in which you could not discover a poor man? Then greed burst into this ideal world, and in its desire to set things

atque in suum vertere, omnia fecit aliena et in angustum se ex inmenso redegit. Avaritia paupertatem intulit et multa concupiscendo
39. omnia amisit. Licet itaque nunc conetur reparare quod perdidit, licet agros agris adiciat vicinum vel pretio pellens vel iniuria, licet in provinciarum spatium rura dilatet et possessionem vocet per sua longam peregrinationem: nulla nos finium propagatio eo reducet unde discessimus. Cum omnia fecerimus, multum habebimus: universum
40. habebamus. Terra ipsa fertilior erat inlaborata et in usus populorum non diripientium larga. Quidquid natura protulerat, id non minus invenisse quam inventum monstrare alteri voluptas erat; nec ulli aut superesse poterat aut deesse: inter concordes dividebatur. Nondum valentior inposuerat infirmiori manum, nondum avarus abscondendo quod sibi iaceret alium necessariis quoque excluserat: par erat alterius
41. ac sui cura. Arma cessabant incruentaeque humano sanguine manus odium omne in feras verterant. Illi quos aliquod nemus densum a sole protexerat, qui adversus saevitiam hiemis aut imbris vili receptaculo tuti sub fronde vivebant, placidas transigebant sine suspirio noctes. Sollicitudo nos in nostra purpura versat et acerrimis excitat
42. stimulis: at quam mollem somnum illis dura tellus dabat! Non inpendebant caelata laquearia, sed in aperto iacentis sidera superlabebantur et, insigne spectaculum noctium, mundus in praeceps agebatur, silentio tantum opus ducens. Tam interdiu illis quam nocte patebant prospectus huius pulcherrimae domus; libebat intueri signa ex
43. media caeli parte vergentia, rursus ex occulto alia surgentia. Quidni iuvaret vagari inter tam late sparsa miracula? At vos ad omnem tectorum pavetis sonum et inter picturas vestras, si quid increpuit, fugitis attoniti. Non habebant domos instar urbium: spiritus ac liber inter aperta perflatus et levis umbra rupis aut arboris et perlucidi fontes rivique non opere nec fistula nec ullo coacto itinere obsolefacti sed sponte currentes et prata sine arte formosa, inter haec agreste domicilium rustica politum manu — haec erat secundum naturam domus, in qua libebat habitare nec ipsam nec pro ipsa timentem: nunc magna pars nostri metus tecta sunt.
44. Sed quamvis egregia illis vita fuerit et carens fraude, non fuere

apart and appropriate them for its own use it caused everything to belong to someone else and reduced its previously huge stock to very little. It was greed which introduced poverty since by coveting much

39. it lost all. So even if it now tries to make up what it has lost, acquiring farm after farm by means of buying up or driving out its neighbours, extending its estates to the dimensions of provinces, and only regarding itself as a property−owner if it can travel extensively abroad without leaving its own land, no extension of our boundaries will bring us back to the condition we started from. When we have done all we can we shall have a lot, but once we had everything.

40. The earth herself, though untilled, was more fertile, and generous enough for the needs of people who did not rob each other. As nature produced her offerings they were just as pleased to tell others of their discoveries as to make the discoveries. No one could surpass or be surpassed by another: they divided their stock in harmony. The stronger had not yet laid a hand on the weaker; the miser had not yet hidden away a private store for himself, thus depriving someone else even of essentials. Everyone was as concerned for the

41. next man as for himself. Arms were unused, and hands unstained with human blood had turned all their hostility against wild animals. Protected from the sun by some thick wood, living safely in a humble shelter of leaves to fend off the rigours of storm or rain, they passed peaceful nights without a sigh. Anxiety harries us in our purple, and goads us with stinging cares: what soft sleep the hard ground gave

42. them! No engraved and panelled ceilings hung over them, but the stars glided over them as they lay in the open, and they had the glorious spectacle of the night sky, as the firmament hurried down to the horizon taking with it silently all that mighty creation. By day, too, as well as by night they had open views of that most beautiful mansion, and they enjoyed watching constellations sinking away from

43. the zenith and others rising again to view from the horizon. Surely it was delightful to roam the earth with such marvellous sights all around them? Whereas you tremble at every sound in your houses, and surrounded by your painted walls at the slightest creak you take to your heels in a panic. They did not have houses to match towns in size. Fresh air and breezes blowing unobstructed through open spaces, the gentle shade of a rock or tree, springs of clear water, streams which were not spoiled by artificial works or pipes or forced diversion of their natural channels, meadows lovely without the aid of man — these were the surroundings of their rural dwellings built with simple rustic neatness; this was a home in conformity with nature, where you could enjoy living without fearing the house itself or on its behalf. Now our very homes cause a great part of our fears.

44. However, no matter how excellent and guileless their lives were,

sapientes, quando hoc iam in opere maximo nomen est. Non tamen negaverim fuisse alti spiritus viros et, ut ita dicam, a dis recentes; neque enim dubium est quin meliora mundus nondum effetus ediderit. Quemadmodum autem omnibus indoles fortior fuit et ad labores paratior, ita non erant ingenia omnibus consummata. Non enim dat
45. natura virtutem: ars est bonum fieri. Illi quidem non aurum nec argentum nec perlucidos <lapides in> ima terrarum faece quaerebant parcebantque adhuc etiam mutis animalibus: tantum aberat ut homo hominem non iratus, non timens, tantum spectaturus occideret. Nondum vestis illis erat picta, nondum texebatur aurum, adhuc nec
46. eruebatur. Quid ergo <est>? Ignorantia rerum innocentes erant; multum autem interest utrum peccare aliquis nolit an nesciat. Deerat illis iustitia, deerat prudentia, deerat temperantia ac fortitudo. Omnibus his virtutibus habebat similia quaedam rudis vita: virtus non contingit animo nisi instituto et edocto et ad summum adsidua exercitatione perducto. Ad hoc quidem, sed sine hoc nascimur, et in optimis quoque, antequam erudias, virtutis materia, non virtus est. Vale.

LETTER 92

1.   Puto, inter me teque conveniet externa corpori adquiri, corpus in honorem animi coli, in animo esse partes ministras, per quas movemur alimurque, propter ipsum principale nobis datas. In hoc principali est aliquid inrationale, est et rationale; illud huic servit, hoc unum est quod alio non refertur sed omnia ad se refert. Nam illa quoque divina ratio omnibus praeposita est, ipsa sub nullo est; et haec autem nostra eadem est, quae ex illa est.
2.   Si de hoc inter nos convenit, sequitur ut de illo quoque conveniat, in hoc uno positam esse beatam vitam, ut in nobis ratio perfecta sit. Haec enim sola non summittit animum, stat ˙ contra fortunam; in quolibet rerum habitu †servitus† servat. Id autem unum bonum est quod numquam defringitur. Is est, inquam, beatus quem nulla res minorem facit; tenet summa, et ne ulli quidem nisi sibi

they were not wise men, for this title is really reserved for the most distinguished achievements. Not that I would deny that they were men of profound spirit and, so to speak, fresh from the gods; for there is no doubt that the earth produced superior offspring in the days before it was worn out. But though they all had characters which were tougher and more fitted for hard work, still their intellects lacked the highest endowments. For nature does not give virtue: to
45. become a good man is a practical art. Certainly they did not go looking for gold or silver or gleaming stones in the depths of the earth. They still showed mercy even to dumb animals, so far were they from killing their fellow—men not from anger or fear, but simply to provide a spectacle. They did not yet wear embroidered clothes and these were not yet interwoven with gold — which was not yet
46. even mined. So what? Their innocence was due only to ignorance, and there is an enormous difference between not wanting to do wrong and simply not knowing how to. They lacked a sense of justice, practical wisdom, self—control and courage. Their primitive life did have certain qualities which resembled all these virtues, but virtue only reaches a mind which has been trained and schooled and brought to its highest state by ceaseless practice. We are born for this perfection but not with it, and even in the best people, until you cultivate them, there is only the raw material for virtue, not virtue itself.

LETTER 92

1. I think you and I will agree that we acquire external goods for the body; that the body is looked after for the sake of the soul; that the soul has subordinate parts, through which we achieve movement and nourishment and which are given to us for the sake of the ruling element of the soul. This ruling element is partly rational and partly irrational: the irrational part serves the rational, which alone is subordinate to nothing else but has everything subordinate to itself. For the divine reason has authority over all and is subject to none; so our human reason must have the same quality as the divine, since it derives from it.

2. If we are agreed on this point, it follows that we shall agree also that the happy life depends solely on our possession of reason in its perfect form. For this alone keeps our courage from failing, standing firm against fortune and guarding us whatever the state of our circumstances. Now the one good is that which never suffers damage. That man, I say, is happy whom nothing can diminish: he occupies the heights, supported by himself alone; for he who is held

innixus; nam qui aliquo auxilio sustinetur potest cadere. Si aliter est, incipient multum in nobis valere non nostra. Quis autem vult

3. constare fortuna aut quis se prudens ob aliena miratur? Quid est beata vita? securitas et perpetua tranquillitas. Hanc dabit animi magnitudo, dabit constantia bene iudicati tenax. Ad haec quomodo pervenitur? si veritas tota perspecta est; si servatus est in rebus agendis ordo, modus, decor, innoxia voluntas ac benigna, intenta rationi nec umquam ab illa recedens, amabilis simul mirabilisque. Denique ut breviter tibi formulam scribam, talis animus esse sapientis

4. viri debet qualis deum deceat. Quid potest desiderare is cui omnia honesta contingunt? Nam si possunt aliquid non honesta conferre ad optimum statum, in his erit beata vita sine quibus non est. Et quid turpius stultiusve quam bonum rationalis animi ex inrationalibus nectere?

5. Quidam tamen augeri summum bonum iudicant, quia parum plenum sit fortuitis repugnantibus. Antipater quoque inter magnos sectae huius auctores aliquid se tribuere dicit externis, sed exiguum admodum. Vides autem quale sit die non esse contentum nisi aliquis igniculus adluxerit: quod potest in hac claritate solis habere scintilla

6. momentum? Si non es sola honestate contentus, necesse est aut quietem adici velis, quam Graeci ἀοχλησίαν vocant, aut voluptatem. Horum alterum utcumque recipi potest; vacat enim animus molestia liber ad inspectum universi, nihilque illum avocat a contemplatione naturae. Alterum illud, voluptas, bonum pecoris est: adicimus rationali inrationale, honesto inhonestum, magno *** vitam facit titillatio

7. corporis? Quid ergo dubitatis dicere bene esse homini, si palato bene est? Et hunc tu, non dico inter viros numeras, sed inter homines, cuius summum bonum saporibus et coloribus et sonis constat? Excedat ex hoc animalium numero pulcherrimo ac dis secundo; mutis

8. adgregetur animal pabulo laetum. Inrationalis pars animi duas habet partes, alteram animosam, ambitiosam, inpotentem, positam in adfectionibus, alteram humilem, languidam, voluptatibus deditam: illam effrenatam, meliorem tamen, certe fortiorem ac digniorem viro, reliquerunt, hanc necessariam beatae vitae putaverunt, enervem et

up by another's help is capable of falling. Otherwise, things outside ourselves will begin to extend their power over us. But who wants to
3. be dependent on fortune? What man of sense glories in what is not his own? What is a happy life? Freedom from care and unbroken tranquillity, which will be acquired by nobility of soul and sticking firmly to wise judgments. But how does one acquire these qualities? If truth has been grasped in its entirety; if in our actions we have observed regularity, moderation, seemliness, and have revealed intentions which are inoffensive and kindly, which strictly observe reason and never depart from it, and which inspire admiration as well as affection. In fact, to give you the rule in a nutshell: the soul of the wise man should be such as would befit a god.

4. What can be lacking to the man who has all the honourable qualities? For if dishonourable qualities can contribute anything to the highest state of being, the happy life will depend on those things which are inseparable from it. And what is more shameful and senseless than for the virtue of a rational soul to be composed of
5. irrational elements? Yet some claim that the highest good can be increased because it is not fully developed as long as it faces the hostility of chance occurrences. Even Antipater, one of the most distinguished of the Stoic school, says that he allows some importance to externals, but not much. You see what it is not to be satisfied with daylight without a bit of lamplight as well. But what effect has
6. a spark with bright sunlight around you? If you are not satisfied with moral integrity alone you must be willing to add to it the tranquillity which the Greeks call ἀοχλησία, or pleasure. The first of these at any rate can be allowed, for the mind when free from turmoil has time to contemplate the universe, since nothing distracts it from studying nature. But the other one, pleasure, is a benefit for animals: this is to link the irrational to the rational, the disreputable to the reputable, the trivial to the great. Is the quality of our life to
7. depend on the titillation of our senses? Why then do you hesitate to say that all is well with a man if all is well with his palate? And do you class, I won't say among men of worth, but even among human beings, the man whose highest good lies in tastes and colours and sounds? Let him rather be banished from this noble class of creatures holding second place to the gods, and join the dumb brutes as a creature whose joy lies in his food.

8. The irrational part of the soul has itself two parts, one being spirited, ambitious, headstrong, committed to passions, and the other drooping, inert, addicted to pleasures. People have ignored the former which, though unrestrained, is however superior, and at any rate bolder and more worthy of a man; whereas they have considered
9. the latter feeble and listless part as essential to the good life. They

9. abiectam. Huic rationem servire iusserunt, et fecerunt animalis generosissimi summum bonum demissum et ignobile, praeterea mixtum portentosumque et ex diversis ac male congruentibus membris. Nam ut ait Vergilius noster in Scylla,

> prima hominis facies et pulchro pectore virgo
> pube tenus, postrema inmani corpore pistrix
> delphinum caudas utero commissa luporum.

Huic tamen Scyllae fera animalia adiuncta sunt, horrenda, velocia: at

10. isti sapientiam ex quibus composuere portentis? Prima pars hominis est ipsa virtus; huic committitur inutilis caro et fluida, receptandis tantum cibis habilis, ut ait Posidonius. Virtus illa divina in lubricum desinit et superioribus eius partibus venerandis atque caelestibus animal iners ac marcidum adtexitur. Illa utcumque altera quies nihil quidem ipsa praestabat animo, sed inpedimenta removebat: voluptas ultro dissolvit et omne robur emollit. Quae invenietur tam discors inter se iunctura corporum? Fortissimae rei inertissima adstruitur, severissimae parum seria, sanctissimae intemperans usque ad incesta.

11. 'Quid ergo?' inquit 'si virtutem nihil inpeditura sit bona valetudo et quies et dolorum vacatio, non petes illas?' Quidni petam? non quia bona sunt, sed quia secundum naturam sunt, et quia bono a me iudicio sumentur. Quid erit tunc in illis bonum? hoc unum, bene eligi. Nam cum vestem qualem decet sumo, cum ambulo ut oportet, cum ceno quemadmodum debeo, non cena aut ambulatio aut vestis bona sunt, sed meum in iis propositum servantis in quaque re rationi

12. convenientem modum. Etiamnunc adiciam: mundae vestis electio adpetenda est homini; natura enim homo mundum et elegans animal est. Itaque non est bonum per se munda vestis sed mundae vestis electio, quia non in re bonum est sed in electione quali;

13. actiones nostrae honestae sunt, non ipsa quae aguntur. Quod de veste dixi, idem me dicere de corpore existima. Nam hoc quoque natura ut quandam vestem animo circumdedit; velamentum eius est. Quis autem umquam vestimenta aestimavit arcula? nec bonum nec malum vagina gladium facit. Ergo de corpore quoque idem tibi respondeo: sumpturum quidem me, si detur electio, et sanitatem et vires, bonum autem futurum iudicium de illis meum, non ipsa.

14. 'Est quidem' inquit 'sapiens beatus; summum tamen illud bonum non consequitur nisi illi et naturalia instrumenta respondeant. Ita miser quidem esse qui virtutem habet non potest, beatissimus autem non est qui naturalibus bonis destituitur, ut valetudine, ut membrorum

have subordinated reason to it and made the highest good of the noblest of creatures something ignoble and mean, and what is more, a monstrous hybrid of opposing and ill—fitting elements. As our Virgil says of Scylla:

'A human face above and a girl's lovely bosom
To the waist; below she's a monstrous sea—creature,
With dolphins' tails joined to a belly of wolves.'

At least to this Scylla wild creatures are attached which are fearful and energetic; but of what monstrosities have these people composed

10. wisdom? The upper part of mankind is virtue itself, and to this is joined the worthless, flabby flesh, serving only, to quote Posidonius, as a receptacle for food. That divine virtue passes into a sticky mire, and to its venerable and heavenly upper parts is linked a torpid and apathetic animal. That other condition, tranquillity, at any rate, though it did not offer anything to the soul did at least remove obstacles from its way. Pleasure positively enervates and saps all its strength. Can you imagine a more incongruous union of elements — the most spiritless joined to the most stouthearted, the trivial to the most serious, the licentious (even incestuous) to the most hallowed?

11. 'Well, then', someone says, 'if good health, tranquillity and freedom from pains do not stand in the way of virtue, will you not seek them?' Of course I shall, not because they are goods, but because they are in accord with nature and because I shall make use of them sensibly. What will then be good in these conditions? This alone, that they are chosen well. For when I dress in suitable clothes, when I walk or eat in a suitably decorous way, it is not the meal or the walking or the clothes which are good, but my firm resolution to preserve in each a way of behaviour which conforms to

12. reason. Let me add yet again: a man ought to choose clean clothes because man is naturally a clean and fastidious creature. So the good lies not in clean clothes themselves but in choosing them, since it is not the thing which is good but the nature of the choice. Our

13. actions are honourable, not the objects of them. What I have said about clothes applies also to the body. For nature has enveloped the soul with the body as with a garment: it is the soul's wrapping. But who ever judged the value of clothes from the chest which contains them? The scabbard does not make a sword good or bad. So, regarding the body I give you the same reply: if I have the choice I will opt for health and strength; but the good will lie not in these qualities themselves but in my choice of them.

14. 'The wise man', we are told, 'is indeed happy, but he does not achieve the supreme good unless he also has the appropriate natural means to achieve it. Thus, a man of virtue cannot be wretched, but one cannot achieve supreme happiness who lacks natural goods, like

15. integritate.' Quod incredibilius videtur, id concedis, aliquem in maximis et continuis doloribus non esse miserum, esse etiam beatum: quod levius si negas, beatissimum esse. Atqui si potest virtus efficere ne miser aliquis sit, facilius efficiet ut beatissimus sit; minus enim intervalli a beato ad beatissimum restat quam a misero ad beatum. An quae res tantum valet ut ereptum calamitatibus inter beatos locet non potest adicere quod superest, ut beatissimum faciat? in summo

16. deficit clivo? Commoda sunt in vita et incommoda, utraque extra nos. Si non est miser vir bonus quamvis omnibus prematur incommodis, quomodo non est beatissimus si aliquibus commodis deficitur? Nam quemadmodum incommodorum onere usque ad miserum non deprimitur, sic commodorum inopia non deducitur a beatissimo, sed tam sine commodis beatissimus est quam non est sub incommodis miser; aut potest illi eripi bonum suum, si potest minui.

17. Paulo ante dicebam igniculum nihil conferre lumini solis; claritate enim eius quidquid sine illo luceret absconditur. 'Sed quaedam' inquit 'soli quoque opstant.' At sol integer est etiam inter opposita, et quamvis aliquid interiacet quod nos prohibeat eius aspectu, in opere est, cursu suo fertur; quotiens inter nubila eluxit, non est sereno minor, ne tardior quidem, quoniam multum interest utrum aliquid obstet tantum

18. an inpediat. Eodem modo virtuti opposita nihil detrahunt: non est minor, sed minus fulget. Nobis forsitan non aeque apparet ac nitet, sibi eadem est et more solis obscuri in occulto vim suam exercet. Hoc itaque adversus virtutem possunt calamitates et damna et iniuriae quod adversus solem potest nebula.

19. Invenitur qui dicat sapientem corpore parum prospero usum nec miserum esse nec beatum. Hic quoque fallitur; exaequat enim fortuita virtutibus et tantundem tribuit honestis quantum honestate carentibus. Quid autem foedius, quid indignius quam comparari veneranda contemptis? Veneranda enim sunt iustitia, pietas, fides, fortitudo, prudentia: e contrario vilia sunt quae saepe contingunt pleniora vilissimis, crus solidum et lacertus et dentes et horum sanitas

20. firmitasque. Deinde si sapiens cui corpus molestum est nec miser habebitur nec beatus, sed < in> medio relinquetur, vita quoque eius

15. health and sound limbs.' You admit what is harder to believe, that someone in extreme and continual suffering is not wretched, and is even happy; but you deny the lesser inference, that he can be supremely happy. Yet if virtue can prevent someone being wretched, it will the more easily make him supremely happy, for there is a smaller gap between the happy man and the supremely happy man than between the wretched man and the happy man. What power strong enough to snatch a man from disaster and place him among the happy could not manage the extra bit and make him supremely

16. happy? Is it going to fail as it reaches the summit of its task? Life has its advantages and its disadvantages, both outside ourselves. If a good man is not wretched even when afflicted by every kind of disadvantage, how can he not be supremely happy if he is merely short of some advantages? For just as the weight of the former does not reduce him to wretchedness, so the lack of the latter does not withdraw him from beatitude: he is as supremely happy without advantages as he is not wretched when suffering from disadvantages. Otherwise, if his happiness can be diminished, it can be taken from

17. him altogether. A while ago I was saying that a lamp adds nothing to the light of the sun, for the sun's brilliance dims whatever would shine in its absence. 'But', objects someone, 'even the sun is blocked by some things.' Yet the sun remains unaffected by obstacles, and even if some intervening object prevents our seeing it, it remains at work and pursues its course. When shining through clouds its own power is not less than in clear weather nor its course more slow, since it is important to distinguish what just stands in the

18. way and what hampers the force of something. In the same way, the things that oppose virtue do not at all detract from it: it is not lessened but shines forth less. To us perhaps its glow is less clear, but it remains unchanged in itself, and like the sun when hidden it wields its power in obscurity. Thus disasters, losses and injuries have as little power against virtue as clouds against the sun.

19. You'll find people who say that a wise man who is physically afflicted is neither wretched nor happy. This view too is fallacious, for it puts accidentals on the same level as virtues, and attributes the same importance to honourable qualities as to those with no title to respect. What could be more revolting and unworthy than to compare the praiseworthy with the contemptible? Praiseworthy things include justice, piety, loyalty, bravery, commonsense; on the other side stand the trivial qualities with which worthless people are often lavishly endowed: a sturdy leg and arm, and teeth all healthy and

20. strong. Furthermore, if a wise man with physical problems is to be considered neither wretched nor happy, but classed somewhere in between, then his life too will neither be desirable nor to be avoided.

nec adpetenda erit nec fugienda. Quid autem tam absurdum quam sapientis vitam adpetendam non esse? aut quid tam extra fidem quam esse aliquam vitam nec adpetendam nec fugiendam? Deinde si damna corporis miserum non faciunt, beatum esse patiuntur; nam quibus potentia non est in peiorem transferendi statum, ne interpellandi quidem optimum.

21.   'Frigidum' inquit 'aliquid et calidum novimus, inter utrumque tepidum est; sic aliquis beatus est, aliquis miser, aliquis nec beatus nec miser.' Volo hanc contra nos positam imaginem excutere. Si tepido illi plus frigidi ingessero, fiet frigidum; si plus calidi adfudero, fiet novissime calidum. At huic nec misero nec beato quantumcumque ad miserias adiecero, miser non erit, quemadmodum dicitis; ergo
22. imago ista dissimilis est. Deinde trado tibi hominem nec miserum nec beatum. Huic adicio caecitatem: non fit miser; adicio debilitatem: non fit miser; adicio dolores continuos et graves: miser non fit. Quem tam multa mala in miseram vitam non transferunt ne ex beata
23. quidem educunt. Si non potest, ut dicitis, sapiens ex beato in miserum decidere, non potest in non beatum. Quare enim qui labi coepit alicubi subsistat? quae res illum non patitur ad imum devolvi retinet in summo. Quidni non possit beata vita rescindi? ne remitti quidem potest, et ideo virtus ad illam per se ipsa satis est.

24.   'Quid ergo?' inquit 'sapiens non est beatior qui diutius vixit, quem nullus avocavit dolor, quam ille qui cum mala fortuna semper luctatus est?' Responde mihi: numquid et melior est et honestior? Si haec non sunt, ne beatior quidem est. Rectius vivat oportet ut beatius vivat: si rectius non potest, ne beatius quidem. Non intenditur virtus, ergo ne beata quidem vita, quae ex virtute est. Virtus enim tantum bonum est ut istas accessiones minutas non sentiat, brevitatem aevi et dolorem et corporum varias offensiones; nam voluptas non est
25. digna ad quam respiciat. Quid est in virtute praecipuum? futuro non indigere nec dies suos conputare. In quantulo libet tempore bona aeterna consummat. Incredibilia nobis haec videntur et supra humanam naturam excurrentia; maiestatem enim eius ex nostra inbecillitate metimur et vitiis nostris nomen virtutis inponimus. Quid porro? non aeque incredibile videtur aliquem in summis cruciatibus positum dicere 'beatus sum'? Atqui haec vox in ipsa officina voluptatis audita est. 'Beatissimum' inquit 'hunc et ultimum diem ago' Epicurus, cum illum hinc urinae difficultas torqueret, hinc

But what is so absurd as to regard the wise man's life as undesirable? What so beyond belief as that a life should be neither desirable nor to be avoided? Again, if bodily defects do not make a man wretched they allow him to be happy; for what cannot force us into a worse condition cannot prevent us achieving the best one.

21.   'We recognize', comes the objection, 'states of hot and of cold and of tepid between them. Similarly, one man is happy, one is wretched, and one is neither happy nor wretched.' I'd like to examine this comparison offered against us. If I add more cold to what is tepid, it will become cold; if I add more hot, it will finally become hot. But however much misery I pile onto that man who is neither wretched nor happy, he will not become wretched, as you say.

22. So your comparison does not apply. Now, take the man who is neither wretched nor happy. On him I inflict blindness: he does not become wretched. I inflict infirmity: he does not become wretched. I inflict continual wearisome pains: he does not become wretched. If all such afflictions do not bring a man's life into wretchedness,

23. they cannot either debar him from a happy life. If, as you say, the wise man cannot fall from happiness into wretchedness, he cannot fall into non—happiness. For having begun to slide why should he halt at any particular point? Whatever prevents him from rolling to the bottom keeps him at the top. How could the happy life not be indestructible? It cannot even lose intensity, and that is because virtue alone suffices to produce it.

24.   'Well, then', someone asks, 'is not the wise man happier who has lived longer and been undistracted by any suffering, than the man who has struggled everlastingly with ill—fortune?' Answer me this: is he a better or more honourable man? If not, he is not happier either. One must live a more morally upright life for it to be a happier life: if not more morally upright, it cannot be happier either. Virtue does not have degrees of intensity, so the happy life does not either, since it is compounded of virtue. For virtue is so great a good that it does not feel those trivial accessories, shortness of life and suffering and the host of bodily discomforts, since pleasure

25. is not an end worthy of its consideration. What is the paramount quality of virtue? The fact that it does not need the future nor count up its days. The smallest instant of time is enough for it to perfect blessings that last for ever. These appear unbelievable to us and surpassing human nature, because we measure virtue's grandeur by our own feebleness and apply its name to our vices. Well, then: does it not seem equally unbelievable that someone subjected to extreme torture should say 'I am happy'? And yet these words were heard in the very studio of pleasure. 'This is the last and happiest day of my life', said Epicurus, at a time when he was in agony from

26. insanabilis exulcerati dolor ventris.   Quare ergo incredibilia ista sint apud eos qui virtutem colunt, cum apud eos quoque reperiantur apud quos voluptas imperavit?   Hi quoque degeneres et humillimae mentis aiunt in summis doloribus, in summis calamitatibus sapientem nec miserum futurum nec beatum.   Atqui hoc quoque incredibile est, immo incredibilius; non video enim quomodo лоn in imum agatur e fastigio suo deiecta virtus.   Aut beatum praestare debet aut, si ab hoc depulsa est, non prohibebit fieri miserum.   Stans non potest mitti: aut vincatur oportet aut vincat.

27.   'Dis' inquit 'inmortalibus solis et virtus et beata vita contigit, nobis umbra quaedam illorum bonorum et similitudo; accedimus ad illa, non pervenimus.'   Ratio vero dis hominibusque communis est:

28. haec in illis consummata est, in nobis consummabilis.   Sed ad desperationem nos vitia nostra perducunt.   Nam ille alter secundus est ut aliquis parum constans ad custodienda optima, cuius iudicium labat etiamnunc et incertum est.   Desideret oculorum atque aurium sensum, bonam valetudinem et non foedum aspectum corporis et habitu

29. manente suo aetatis praeterea longius spatium.   Per haec potest non paenitenda agi vita, at inperfecto viro huic malitiae vis quaedam inest, quia animum habet mobilem ad prava, illa †aitarens malitia et ea agitata† abest [de bono].   Non est adhuc bonus, sed in bonum

30. fingitur; cuicumque autem deest aliquid ad bonum, malus est.   Sed
              si cui virtus animusque in corpore praesens,
hic deos aequat, illo tendit originis suae memor.   Nemo inprobe eo conatur ascendere unde descenderat.   Quid est autem cur non existimes in eo divini aliquid existere qui dei pars est?   Totum hoc quo continemur et unum est et deus; et socii sumus eius et membra.   Capax est noster animus, perfertur illo si vitia non deprimant.   Quemadmodum corporum nostrorum habitus erigitur et spectat in caelum, ita animus, cui in quantum vult licet porrigi, in hoc a natura rerum formatus est, ut paria dis vellet; et si utatur suis viribus ac se in spatium suum extendat, non aliena via ad summa nititur.   Magnus

31. erat labor ire in caelum: redit.   Cum hoc iter nactus est, vadit audaciter contemptor omnium nec ad pecuniam respicit aurumque et argentum, illis in quibus iacuere tenebris dignissima, non ab hoc aestimat splendore quo inperitorum verberant oculos, sed a vetere

the double afflictions of strangury and an incurably ulcerated stomach.

26. So why should those reactions among people who cultivate virtue be unbelievable when we find them also displayed by those who are governed by pleasure? These degenerate and petty—minded people also assert that in the most extreme sufferings and disasters the wise man will be neither wretched nor happy. Yet this too is unbelievable, in fact more unbelievable: for I can't see how, once virtue has been dislodged from its pinnacle, it will not fall to the lowest point. Either it ought to make a man happy or, if it is freed from this task, it will not prevent him from being wretched. Once virtue has taken its stand it is allowed no discharge: it must either be conquered or conquer.

27.   'The immortal gods alone', we are told, 'enjoy both virtue and the happy life; we have but a semblance and a shadow of these blessings, approaching them without achieving them.' In fact, reason is common to gods and men, perfected in them, perfectible in us.

28. But our vices lead us to abandon hope. For that second type (man) is of a lower order, like one not resolute enough to preserve the highest qualities, whose judgment even now is tottering and uncertain. He may long to enjoy the use of his eyes and his ears, to have good health and a not unattractive body, and to stay physically well—

29. preserved to the end of a long life. With these endowments he can lead a life he won't regret, but in this imperfect individual there abides some potency for wickedness, because his mind is easily swayed towards what is corrupt, though he is free from wickedness of a more violent and deep—rooted kind. He is not yet a good man though he is being moulded to become one. However, anyone who lacks some

30. quality which makes up the good man is a bad man. But
        'Whoever has physical courage and valour'
equals the gods, and aspires thereto conscious of his origins. There is no presumption in trying to climb up to the point from which one has descended. And why should you not believe that there is some element of the divine in one who is a part of god? All you see that surrounds us is one and is god: we share in it as component members. Our soul is capable of understanding and reaches out thither unless clogged by its own vices. As our bodies go upright and we gaze at the sky, so our soul, whose range can extend as widely as it likes, has been formed by nature to match its wishes with those of the gods; and if it uses its powers and stretches out to its own

31. domain, it pushes its own way up to the heights. It would be a mighty toil to go to heaven: the soul is simply returning there. When it has found this path it journeys boldly, despising all else, with no regard for wealth, and valuing gold and silver (full worthy of the darkness in which they once lay) not according to the glitter with

caeno ex quo illa secrevit cupiditas nostra et effodit. Scit, inquam,
aliubi positas esse divitias quam quo congeruntur; animum impleri
32. debere, non arcam. Hunc inponere dominio rerum omnium licet,
hunc in possessionem rerum naturae inducere, ut sua orientis
occidentisque terminis finiat, deorumque ritu cuncta possideat, cum
opibus suis divites superne despiciat, quorum nemo tam suo laetus est
33. quam tristis alieno. Cum se in hanc sublimitatem tulit, corporis
quoque ut oneris necessarii non amator sed procurator est, nec se illi
cui inpositus est subicit. Nemo liber est qui corpori servit; nam ut
alios dominos quos nimia pro illo sollicitudo invenit transeas, ipsius
34. morosum imperium delicatumque est. Ab hoc modo aequo animo
exit, modo magno prosilit, nec quis deinde relicti eius futurus sit
exitus quaerit; sed ut ex barba capilloque tonsa neglegimus, ita ille
divinus animus egressurus hominem, quo receptaculum suum conferatur,
ignis illud †excludat† an terra contegat an ferae distrahant, non magis
ad se iudicat pertinere quam secundas ad editum infantem. Utrum
proiectum aves differant an consumatur

        canibus data praeda marinis,

35. quid ad illum qui nullus < est>? Sed tunc quoque cum inter homines
est, < non> timet ullas post mortem minas eorum quibus usque ad
mortem timeri parum est. 'Non conterret' inquit 'me nec uncus nec
proiecti ad contumeliam cadaveris laceratio foeda visuris. Neminem de
supremo officio rogo, nulli reliquias meas commendo. Ne quis
insepultus esset rerum natura prospexit: quem saevitia proiecerit dies
condet.' Diserte Maecenas ait,

        nec tumulum curo: sepelit natura relictos.

Alte cinctum putes dixisse; habuit enim ingenium et grande et virile,
nisi illud secunda discinxissent. Vale.

LETTER 104

1.   In Nomentanum meum fugi — quid putas? urbem? immo febrem
et quidem subrepentem; iam manum mihi iniecerat. Medicus initia
esse dicebat motis venis et incertis et naturalem turbantibus modum.

which they dazzle the ignorant, but the ancient slime from which our
greed has separated and dug them up. It knows, I say, that riches
are to be found elsewhere than where we pile them up; that we

32. ought to stock our souls, not our money–boxes. We can give the
soul supreme power over all things and possession of the world, so
that its territory stretches to the limits of east and west, and like the
gods it owns everything and looks down in contempt on the rich with
their wealth, who are less pleased with their own possessions than

33. distressed by another's. When it has reached these heights, it acts as
a guardian rather than a lover to the body, regarding this too as a
necessary burden and not subjecting itself to what was put under its
own authority. No one is free who is a servant of the body, for not
to mention other masters we acquire through too much concern for its
welfare, the body itself exercises a peevish and fastidious tyranny over

34. us. At times the soul leaves the body with equanimity, at times it
rushes forth courageously, and it does not bother to enquire about the
subsequent fate of the abandoned body. Just as we ignore the
clippings from our beards and hair, so the divine soul on leaving a
man thinks it no more relevant to itself where its container ends up
– whether destroyed by fire or covered by earth or mangled by wild
animals – than the after–birth matters to a new–born baby.
Whether it is cast out to be torn by birds of prey, or consumed
              'Thrown to the dogfish as their spoil',

35. what does it matter to that which has gone?   But even while it is
part of mortality the soul fears no threats after death from things
which up to the point of death are not worth fearing. 'I fear', it
will say, 'neither the executioner's hook nor the shameful mangling of
a corpse displayed as a dreadful sight to beholders. I ask no one to
do me the final honours; I bequeath my remains to no one. Nature
has taken care that no man remains unburied: if anyone is left
exposed by brutality, time will lay him to rest.' Maecenas puts it
eloquently:
      'I care for no tomb: the abandoned are buried by nature'.
You would think this was said by a man girded for action, and indeed
he had a noble and manly spirit had it not been enervated by
prosperity.

LETTER 104

1.   I have escaped to my place at Nomentum – escaped from
what, do you think? The city? No, a fever, and one that was
insidiously attacking me: it had already laid hold of me. My doctor
said it was beginning when my pulse was increased and unnaturally

Protinus itaque parari vehiculum iussi; Paulina mea retinente exire perseveravi. Illud mihi in ore erat domini mei Gallionis, qui cum in Achaia febrem habere coepisset, protinus navem escendit clamitans non

2. corporis esse sed loci morbum. Hoc ego Paulinae meae dixi, quae mihi valetudinem meam commendat. Nam cum sciam spiritum illius in meo verti, incipio, ut illi consulam, mihi consulere. Et cum me fortiorem senectus ad multa reddiderit, hoc beneficium aetatis amitto; venit enim mihi in mentem in hoc sene et adulescentem esse cui parcitur. Itaque quoniam ego ab illa non inpetro ut me fortius amet,

3. <a me> inpetrat illa ut me diligentius amem. Indulgendum est enim honestis adfectibus; et interdum, etiam si premunt causae, spiritus in honorem suorum vel cum tormento revocandus et in ipso ore retinendus est, cum bono viro vivendum sit non quamdiu iuvat sed quamdiu oportet: ille qui non uxorem, non amicum tanti putat ut diutius in vita commoretur, qui perseverabit mori, delicatus est. Hoc quoque imperet sibi animus, ubi utilitas suorum exigit, nec tantum si

4. vult mori, sed si coepit, intermittat et <se> suis commodet. Ingentis animi est aliena causa ad vitam reverti, quod magni viri saepe fecerunt; sed hoc quoque summae humanitatis existimo, senectutem suam, cuius maximus fructus est securior sui tutela et vitae usus animosior, attentius <curare>, si scias alicui id tuorum esse dulce,

5. utile, optabile. Habet praeterea in se non mediocre ista res gaudium et mercedem; quid enim iucundius quam uxori tam carum esse ut propter hoc tibi carior fias? Potest itaque Paulina mea non tantum suum mihi timorem inputare sed etiam meum.

6. Quaeris ergo quomodo mihi consilium profectionis cesserit? Ut primum gravitatem urbis excessi et illum odorem culinarum fumantium quae motae quidquid pestiferi vaporis sorbuerunt cum pulvere effundunt, protinus mutatam valetudinem sensi. Quantum deinde adiectum putas viribus postquam vineas attigi? in pascuum emissus cibum meum invasi. Repetivi ergo iam me; non permansit marcor ille corporis dubii et male cogitantis. Incipio toto animo studere.

irregular. So I straightway ordered my carriage to be prepared, and though my dear Paulina was trying to restrain me I persisted in leaving. I kept repeating the remark of my mentor Gallio, who, when he felt a fever coming on in Achaea, at once boarded ship, exclaiming that the illness arose from the place and not from his

2. body. I told my Paulina this as she makes my health a cause of concern to me. For since I realize that her existence depends on mine, I am beginning to look after myself in order to look after her. And although old age has made me tougher to face many things, I am losing this advantage of my years; for I now have the idea that inside this old man there also exists a young man to whom indulgence is due. So since I can't get her to show more fortitude in her love for me, she gets me to show more care in my love for myself.

3. For we must respect genuine feelings, and sometimes even against physical pressures our last breath has to be summoned back and kept from passing our lips for the sake of our dear ones, and even at the cost of great pain, since it is the good man's duty to live not as long as he wants but as long as he should. The man who does not value his wife or his friend enough to stay alive a little longer, and insists on dying, is self—indulgent. This is also a command the soul should give itself when the needs of our dear ones require it; and not merely if it desires death, but if it has already

4. begun to die, it must pause and consult their interests. It is the mark of a noble spirit to return to life for the sake of someone else, as great men have often done. But in my view it is also a sign of the highest human feeling to take greater care of your old age, if you know this would be pleasing, helpful or desirable to any of your dear ones, even though the biggest advantage of old age is that you can be more free and easy in looking after yourself and enjoy a more

5. spirited life—style. Besides this attitude itself brings no small joy and reward; for what could be pleasanter than to be so dear to your wife that you thereby become more dear to yourself? And so Paulina is able to make me responsible both for her anxiety on my behalf and for my own.

6. So, you're wondering how my plan to go away turned out? As soon as I had escaped the oppressive atmosphere of the city and the smell of reeking kitchens, which as soon as they start operating pour out a mixture of ash and all the foul fumes they have generated, I felt an immediate physical change for the better. You can imagine how much stronger I went on to feel when I arrived at my vineyards — I simply attacked my food, like a creature turned out to pasture! The result is I am my old self again: gone is that apathy due to a listless body and an inability to think straight. I'm starting to work with all my old enthusiasm.

7.   Non multum ad hoc locus confert nisi se sibi praestat animus, qui
     secretum in occupationibus mediis si volet habebit: at ille qui regiones
     eligit et otium captat ubique quo distringatur inveniet.   Nam Socraten
     querenti cuidam quod nihil sibi peregrinationes profuissent respondisse
8.   ferunt, 'non inmerito hoc tibi evenit; tecum enim peregrinabaris'.   O
     quam bene cum quibusdam ageretur, si a se aberrarent!   Nunc
     premunt se ipsi, sollicitant, corrumpunt, territant.   Quid prodest mare
     traicere et urbes mutare? si vis ista quibus urgueris effugere, non
     aliubi sis oportet sed alius.   Puta venisse te Athenas, puta Rhodon;
     elige arbitrio tuo civitatem: quid ad rem pertinet quos illa mores
9.   habeat? tuos adferes.   Divitias iudicabis bonum: torquebit te paupertas,
     quod est miserrimum, falsa.   Quamvis enim multum possideas, tamen,
     quia aliquis plus habet, tanto tibi videris defici quanto vinceris.
     Honores iudicabis bonum: male te habebit ille consul factus, ille etiam
     refectus; invidebis quotiens aliquem in fastis saepius legeris.   Tantus
     erit ambitionis furor ut nemo tibi post te videatur si aliquis ante te
10. fuerit.   Maximum malum iudicabis mortem, cum <in> illa nihil sit
     mali nisi quod ante ipsam est, timeri.   Exterrebunt te non tantum
     pericula sed suspiciones; vanis semper agitaberis.   Quid enim proderit
                     evasisse tot urbes
               Argolicas mediosque fugam tenuisse per hostis?
     Ipsa pax timores sumministrabit; ne tutis quidem habebitur fides
     consternata semel mente, quae ubi consuetudinem pavoris inprovidi
     fecit, etiam ad tutelam salutis suae inhabilis est.   Non enim vitat sed
11. fugit; magis autem periculis patemus aversi.   Gravissimum iudicabis
     malum aliquem ex his quos amabis amittere, cum interim hoc tam
     ineptum erit quam flere quod arboribus amoenis et domum tuam
     ornantibus decidant folia.   Quidquid te delectat aeque vide †ut
     videres†: dum virent, utere.   Alium alio die casus excutiet, sed
     quemadmodum frondium iactura facilis est quia renascuntur, sic istorum

7.   Mere surroundings cannot do much to produce this effect unless the soul is wholly in command of itself and can create its own privacy, if it wishes, even in the midst of distractions. On the contrary, the man who flits from place to place looking for peace and quiet, will find everywhere something to make him fretful. There is a story that somebody once complained to Socrates that his foreign travels had done him no good, and was told in reply: 'That's not
8.   surprising, since you took yourself abroad with you'.   What a good thing it would be for some people if they could escape from. themselves.   As it is, they are a burden and an anxiety to themselves, they cause their own demoralization and their own terrors. What is the use of crossing the sea and moving from city to city? If you want to avoid the things that afflict you, you have to be a different person, not just in a different place.   Suppose it's Athens you've come to, suppose it's Rhodes; take any state you fancy: what does the character of that place matter when you'll be taking your
9.   own there? You will still be judging wealth to be a good thing; you will be tormented by poverty − imaginary poverty, which is the most pitiable state to be in.   For however much you have, because someone else has more you imagine yourself lacking just those things in which he outstrips you.   You will judge public honours to be a good thing and you will resent it when so−and−so is elected consul, and so−and−so re−elected; you will feel envy whenever you see someone's name appearing too often in the consular lists.   Such will be your frenzied ambition that no one will seem to be behind you in
10. the race so long as someone is ahead.   You will judge death the greatest of evils, though there is nothing evil in death except what precedes it − our fears of it.   Not just dangers but presentiments of them will throw you into a panic; you will always suffer from imaginary distresses.   What will you gain by having

'passed by so many Argive towns
And gained your flight right through the foemen's ranks'?

Peace itself will offer you terrors.   Once it is in a state of shock the mind will have no trust even in conditions of security, for when it has become habituated to blind panic it is incapable even of looking after its own well−being.   Instead of steering clear of trouble it flees wildly, but we are more exposed to dangers when we turn our backs
11. on them.   You will judge it the worst of afflictions to lose one of your loved ones, though this will be as silly as weeping because the leaves are falling from the lovely trees that adorn your home.   Be reasonable in your view of everything that delights you, and enjoy them while they last.   Chance will cast away one of them on one day and another on another day; but just as the falling of the leaves does not bother us because they grow again, so you should bear the

quos amas quosque oblectamenta vitae putas esse damnum, quia
12. reparantur etiam si non renascuntur. 'Sed non erunt idem.' Ne tu
quidem idem eris. Omnis dies, omnis hora te mutat; sed in aliis
rapina facilius apparet, hic latet, quia non ex aperto fit. Alii
auferuntur, at ipsi nobis furto subducimur. Horum nihil cogitabis nec
remedia vulneribus oppones, sed ipse tibi seres sollicitudinum causas
alia sperando, alia desperando? Si sapis, alterum alteri misce: nec
speraveris sine desperatione nec desperaveris sine spe.

13.   Quid per se peregrinatio prodesse cuiquam potuit? Non
voluptates illa temperavit, non cupiditates refrenavit, non iras repressit,
non indomitos amoris impetus fregit, nulla denique animo mala eduxit.
Non iudicium dedit, non discussit errorem, sed ut puerum ignota
14. mirantem ad breve tempus rerum aliqua novitate detinuit. Ceterum
inconstantiam mentis, quae maxime aegra est, lacessit, mobiliorem
levioremque reddit ipsa iactatio. Itaque quae petierant cupidissime
loca cupidius deserunt et avium modo transvolant citiusque quam
15. venerant abeunt. Peregrinatio notitiam dabit gentium, novas tibi
montium formas ostendet, invisitata spatia camporum et inriguas
perennibus aquis valles; alicuius fluminis < singularem ponet> sub
observatione naturam, sive ut Nilus aestivo incremento tumet, sive ut
Tigris eripitur ex oculis et acto per occulta cursu integrae magnitudinis
redditur, sive ut Maeander, poetarum omnium exercitatio et ludus,
implicatur crebris anfractibus et saepe in vicinum alveo suo admotus,
antequam sibi influat, flectitur: ceterum neque meliorem faciet neque
16. saniorem. Inter studia versandum est et inter auctores sapientiae ut
quaesita discamus, nondum inventa quaeramus; sic eximendus animus
ex miserrima servitute in libertatem adseritur. Quamdiu quidem
nescieris quid fugiendum, quid petendum, quid necessarium, quid
supervacuum, quid iustum, quid iniustum, quid honestum, quid
17. inhonestum sit, non erit hoc peregrinari sed errare. Nullam tibi opem
feret iste discursus; peregrinaris enim cum adfectibus tuis et mala te
tua sequuntur. Utinam quidem sequerentur! Longius abessent: nunc

loss of your loved ones, whom you regard as gladdening your life,
12.   because though they do not grow again they are replaced.   'But they
won't be the same ones.'   Well, you won't be the same either.
Every day, every hour alters you; but the ravages are easier to see in
others, whereas in ourselves they are unnoticed because they aren't
obvious to us.   Other people are being taken away from us, while we
are furtively being snatched from ourselves.   Will you never give a
thought to these things and apply remedies to your wounds, rather
than sowing seeds of anxiety for yourself by hoping to have some
things and despairing of having others?   Be wise and unite the two
feelings: don't hope without a mixture of despair, nor despair
without a mixture of hope.

13.   What good has travel in itself been able to do anyone?   It has
not tempered pleasures, nor restrained desires, nor checked anger, nor
quelled the impetuous outbursts of love: in a word, it has rid the
soul of no faults whatever.   It has not instilled judgment into us, nor
cast off our mistakes, but simply distracted us for a short time by
some novel experience, like a child staring open–mouthed at a
14.   strange sight.   What is more, it aggravates any acute mental
instability, as the effect of movement itself is to increase its fitfulness
and irritability.   That is why people are even more eager to leave the
places they were desperately eager to see, and like birds they migrate
onwards, departing more quickly than they came.

15.   Travel will give you knowledge of other nations, and show you
the outlines of unfamiliar mountains, wide unknown plains, valleys
watered by ever–flowing rivers.   It will give you the chance to
observe the unusual nature of some or other river – how the Nile
floods in the summer; or how the Tigris disappears from sight, and
after a hidden course underground emerges again with undiminished
force; or how the Maeander, that theme on which every poet has
enjoyed practising his craft, winds around in innumerable loops and,
often approaching close to its own stream, turns away just before it
flows back into itself.   But travel will not make you a better or a
16.   more sensible man.   Rather we should spend our time studying,
surrounded by wise writers, so that we may learn what has already
been discovered, and pursue the search for what is yet unknown: in
this way is a soul liberated which needs to be delivered from a
wretched state of slavery.   Indeed, as long as you don't know what is
to be avoided and what sought, what is essential and what
superfluous, what is just and what unjust, what is honourable and
17.   what dishonourable, you will not be travelling but wandering.   That
bustling about will not help you, for you are taking your passion on
your travels, and your troubles are following you.   Would that they
were only following you!   They would be further away; as it is you

fers illa, non ducis. Itaque ubique te premunt et paribus incommodis
18. urunt. Medicina aegro, non regio quaerenda est. Fregit aliquis crus
aut extorsit articulum: non vehiculum navemque conscendit, sed
advocat medicum ut fracta pars iungatur, ut luxata in locum
reponatur. Quid ergo? animum tot locis fractum et extortum credis
locorum mutatione posse sanari? Maius est istud malum quam ut
19. gestationę curetur. Peregrinatio non facit medicum, non oratorem;
nulla ars loco discitur: quid ergo? sapientia, ars omnium maxima, in
itinere colligitur? Nullum est, mihi crede, iter quod te extra
cupiditates, extra iras, extra metus sistat; aut si quod esset, agmine
facto gens illuc humana pergeret. Tamdiu ista urguebunt mala
macerabuntque per terras ac maria vagum quamdiu malorum gestaveris
20. causas. Fugam tibi non prodesse miraris? tecum sunt quae fugis. Te
igitur emenda, onera tibi detrahe et [emenda] desideria intra salutarem
modum contine; omnem ex animo erade nequitiam. Si vis peregrin—
ationes habere iucundas, comitem tuum sana. Haerebit tibi avaritia
quamdiu avaro sordidoque convixeris; haerebit tumor quamdiu superbo
conversaberis; numquam saevitiam in tortoris contubernio pones;
21. incendent libidines tuas adulterorum sodalicia. Si velis vitiis exui,
longe a vitiorum exemplis recedendum est. Avarus, corruptor, saevus,
fraudulentus, multum nocituri si prope a te fuissent, intra te sunt.
Ad meliores transi: cum Catonibus vive, cum Laelio, cum Tuberone.
Quod si convivere etiam Graecis iuvat, cum Socrate, cum Zenone
versare: alter te docebit mori si necesse erit, alter antequam necesse
22. erit. Vive cum Chrysippo, cum Posidonio: hi tibi tradent humanorum
divinorumque notitiam, hi iubebunt in opere esse nec tantum scite
loqui et in oblectationem audientium verba iactare, sed animum
indurare et adversus minas erigere. Unus est enim huius vitae
fluctuantis et turbidae portus eventura contemnere, stare fidenter ac
paratum tela fortunae adverso pectore excipere, non latitantem nec
23. tergiversantem. Magnanimos nos natura produxit, et ut quibusdam
animalibus ferum dedit, quibusdam subdolum, quibusdam pavidum, ita
nobis gloriosum et excelsum spiritum quaerentem ubi honestissime, non

are carrying them on you, not going ahead of them. That's why they oppress you wherever you are with the same stinging discomfort.

18. When you are ill it is medicine you need, not a particular place. Someone has broken a leg or dislocated a joint: he doesn't take a carriage or board a ship, but sends for a doctor to set the fracture or reduce the dislocation. Well, then: if your soul has been broken and dislocated in so many places do you think it can be healed by a change of scene? This is too great an affliction to be cured by going on a journey.

19. Travel does not make one a doctor or an orator; no art is learnt just from the place you are in. So could you say that wisdom, the greatest of all arts, is acquired by taking a journey? Believe me, there is no journey which can free you of your greedy desires, your fits of anger, your fears — or if there were, the human race would all troop there together. Those troubles of yours will go on oppressing and tormenting you wherever you wander on land and sea,

20. so long as you carry with you the sources of the troubles. Are you surprised that running away does you no good? The things you are running away from are still with you. You must, then, reform yourself, cast off this burden, and contain your desires within healthy limits: root out all wickedness from your soul. If you want your journeys to be pleasant, you must heal your companion. Avarice will stick to you as long as you keep company with a mean and avaricious man. Conceit will stick to you as long as you associate with an arrogant man. You'll never get rid of cruelty while you share

21. lodgings with a torturer. You will inflame your lusts if you fraternize with adulterers. If you wish to be rid of your vices you must steer well clear of examples set by the vicious. The miser, the seducer, the cruel man, the cheat, who would be highly damaging to you just by being close by, are right inside you. Turn to better men: live with the Catos, with Laelius, with Tubero. If you enjoy Greek company too, cultivate Socrates and Zeno: the one will teach you how to die if you have to, the other how to die before you have

22. to. Live with Chrysippus, with Posidonius: these will give you a knowledge of things human and divine; these will instruct you in practical activity, not just in clever talking and pretentious speechifying aimed at entertaining an audience, but in toughening your soul and rousing it to face anything that threatens. The only harbour in the stormy tossing sea of life is to be untroubled about the future, to brace yourself and stand prepared to face fortune's missiles, without skulking away or turning your back.

23. Nature made us high—souled creatures, and as she gave certain animals the quality of ferocity, and certain ones cunning, and certain ones timidity, so she gave us a noble and exalted spirit which seeks

ubi tutissime vivat, simillimum mundo, quem quantum mortalium passibus licet sequitur aemulaturque; profert se, laudari et aspici credit.

24. <Dominus> omnium est, supra omnia est; itaque nulli se rei summittat, nihil illi videatur grave, nihil quod virum incurvet.

Terribiles visu formae, Letumque Labosque:

minime quidem, si quis rectis oculis intueri illa possit et tenebras perrumpere; multa per noctem habita terrori dies vertit ad risum.

Terribiles visu formae, Letumque Labosque:

25. egregie Vergilius noster non re dixit terribiles esse sed visu, id est videri, non esse. Quid, inquam, in istis est tam formidabile quam fama vulgavit? quid est, obsecro te, Lucili, cur timeat laborem vir, mortem homo? Totiens mihi occurrunt isti qui non putant fieri posse

26. quidquid facere non possunt, et aiunt nos loqui maiora quam quae humana natura sustineat. At quanto ego de illis melius existimo! ipsi quoque haec possunt facere, sed nolunt. Denique quem umquam ista destituere temptantem? cui non faciliora apparuere in actu? Non quia

27. difficilia sunt non audemus, sed quia non audemus difficilia sunt.

Si tamen exemplum desideratis, accipite Socraten, perpessicium senem, per omnia aspera iactatum, invictum tamen et paupertate, quam graviorem illi domestica onera faciebant, et laboribus, quos militares quoque pertulit. Quibus ille domi exercitus, sive uxorem eius moribus feram, lingua petulantem, sive liberos indociles et matri quam patri similiores †sivere† aut in bello fuit aut in tyrannide aut in

28. libertate bellis ac tyrannis saeviore. Viginti et septem annis pugnatum est; post finita arma triginta tyrannis noxae dedita est civitas, ex quibus plerique inimici erant. Novissime damnatio est sub gravissimis nominibus impleta: obiecta est et religionum violatio et iuventutis corruptela, quam inmittere in deos, in patres, in rem publicam dictus est. Post haec carcer et venenum. Haec usque eo animum Socratis non moverant ut ne vultum quidem moverint. <O> illam mirabilem laudem et singularem! usque ad extremum nec hilariorem quisquam nec tristiorem Socraten vidit; aequalis fuit in tanta inaequalitate fortunae.

29. Vis alterum exemplum? accipe hunc M. Catonem recentiorem,

the most honourable life, not the safest one; a spirit most like the cosmos, which, so far as mortal steps can, it follows and emulates.

24. It asserts itself and is confident of glory and respect. It is lord of all things, it is above all things: let it therefore humble itself before nothing, let nothing seem too heavy for it, so as to make a man bow down under the weight.

'Shapes terrible to see, Hardship and Death'

— not in the least, if you can pierce the darkness and look them straight in the eye. Many things which inspire terror at night daylight makes us laugh at.

'Shapes terrible to see, Hardship and Death':

25. our Virgil admirably says they are not terrible in reality, but only to look at, that is, they seem so but are not. What, I ask, is there so fearful in them as legend has spread abroad? Do tell me, Lucilius, why a real man should fear hardship, and any man should fear death? So often do I come across people who think that whatever they can't do cannot be done, and who say that we Stoics are

26. suggesting greater burdens than human nature could bear. How much more highly do I think of these people than they do! Of course they too can do these things, but they don't want to. Anyway, what man ever had to give them up after trying? Who has not found them easier when actually doing them? It is not because they are difficult that our courage fails us, but because our courage fails us they are difficult.

27. But if you want a precedent, consider Socrates, an old man who endured so much, knocked about in every kind of hardship, yet unconquered either by poverty, which his domestic burdens made still more grievous for him, or by his sufferings, including those he endured as a soldier. Besides his afflictions at home — his wife with her bullying behaviour and nagging tongue, his undisciplined children, more like their mother than their father — his life was passed either in wartime or under tyranny or in a political freedom which was

28. actually more savage than wars and tyrants. The war lasted twenty—seven years; at the end of it the state was handed over to the excesses of the Thirty Tyrants, a great many of whom were his enemies. Finally came his condemnation on the most serious charges: he was accused of blasphemy and of corrupting young people, whom he was said to be stirring up against the gods, their parents and the state. Then came prison and the poison. All this, so far from affecting Socrates' spirit, did not even affect his countenance. What a rare and glorious example to marvel at! Right to the end nobody saw Socrates specially cheerful or depressed: he stayed constant through all the inconstancy of his fortunes.

29. Do you want another precedent? Consider Marcus Cato, nearer

cum quo et infestius fortuna egit et pertinacius. Cui cum omnibus locis obstitisset, novissime et in morte, ostendit tamen virum fortem posse invita fortuna vivere, invita mori. Tota illi aetas aut in armis est exacta civilibus aut †intacta† concipiente iam civile bellum; et hunc licet dicas non minus quam Socraten †inseruisse dixisse† nisi forte Cn. Pompeium et Caesarem et Crassum putas libertatis socios

30. fuisse. Nemo mutatum Catonem totiens mutata re publica vidit; eundem se in omni statu praestitit, in praetura, in repulsa, in accusatione, in provincia, in contione, in exercitu, in morte. Denique in illa rei publicae trepidatione, cum illinc Caesar esset decem legionibus pugnacissimis subnixus, totis exterarum gentium praesidiis, hinc Cn. Pompeius, satis unus adversus omnia, cum alii ad Caesarem inclinarent, alii ad Pompeium, solus Cato fecit aliquas et rei publicae

31. partes. Si animo conplecti volueris illius imaginem temporis, videbis illinc plebem et omnem erectum ad res novas vulgum, hinc optumates et equestrem ordinem, quidquid erat in civitate sancti et electi, duos in medio relictos, rem publicam et Catonem. Miraberis, inquam, cum animadverteris

> Atriden Priamumque et saevom ambobus Achillen;

32. utrumque enim inporbat, utrumque exarmat. Hanc fert de utroque sententiam: ait se, si Caesar vicerit, moriturum, si Pompeius, exulaturum. Quid habebat quod timeret qui ipse sibi et victo et victori constituerat quae constituta esse ab hostibus iratissimis poterant?

33. Perit itaque ex decreto suo. Vides posse homines laborem pati: per medias Africae solitudines pedes duxit exercitum. Vides posse tolerari sitim: in collibus arentibus sine ullis inpedimentis victi exercitus reliquias trahens inopiam umoris loricatus tulit et, quotiens aquae fuerat occasio, novissimus bibit. Vides honorem et notam posse contemni: eodem quo repulsus est die in comitio pila lusit. Vides posse non timeri potentiam superiorum: et Pompeium et Caesarem, quorum nemo alterum offendere audebat nisi ut alterum demereretur, simul provocavit. Vides tam mortem posse contemni quam exilium: et

34. exilium sibi indixit et mortem et interim bellum. Possumus itaque adversus ista tantum habere animi, libeat modo subducere iugo collum.

to our own times, whom fortune treated with even more unremitting cruelty. Though she blocked him at every point — at the end even in his death — yet he showed how a brave man can live against fortune's will, and die against fortune's will. He spent his whole life either in civil war or with civil war about to break out, and you could say of him no less than of Socrates that he avoided slavery — unless you happen to think that Pompey and Caesar and Crassus were
30. friends of freedom. With the state so often changing, no man ever saw Cato change: under all conditions he showed himself the same, whether acting as praetor, or suffering political defeat, or making an accusation in court, or governing his province, or at a public assembly, or on a military campaign, or at his death. Indeed, at that time of confusion and alarm for the state, with Caesar lined up on one side, backed by ten crack legions and the full military support of foreign nations, and Pompey on the other, prepared to face the world alone, and when different groups were rallying to the support of each of them, Cato alone formed a kind of party — the party of the
31. Republic. If you want to form a mental picture of that time, you will see on the one side the populace, the whole rabble intent on revolution, on the other side Rome's choice and revered classes, the nobility and the knights, and two figures in the middle, the Republic and Cato. You will be impressed, I tell you, as you observe

'Atreus' son and Priam, and Achilles wroth with each';
32. for Cato is condemning each and trying to disarm each. This is his resolution about them both, that if Caesar won he would kill himself, if Pompey won he would go into exile. What did he have to fear who had decreed for himself in defeat or victory what could have been decreed for him by his most implacable enemies? And so he died by his own sentence.
33. You see how men can suffer hardship: on foot he led his army right across the deserts of Africa. You see how thirst can be endured: wearing full armour he suffered from the drought as he trailed the remnants of a defeated army without supplies among parched hills, and whenever they came across any water he was the last to drink. You see how both honours and humiliations can be treated with scorn: on the very day of his election defeat he played ball at the place of polling. You see how the power of our superiors can be defied: he challenged simultaneously both Pompey and Caesar, though no one ever dared to offend either of them except to win the favour of the other. You see how death can be treated with as much scorn as exile: he condemned himself to both exile and death, and meanwhile to war.
34. So we can show just as much courage in the face of these things provided we choose to rid our necks of the yoke. But first we

In primis autem respuendae voluptates: enervant et effeminant et multum petunt, multum autem fortuna petendum est. Deinde spernendae opes: auctoramenta sunt servitutum. Aurum et argentum et quidquid aliud felices domos onerat relinquatur: non potest gratis constare libertas. Hanc si magno aestimas, omnia parvo aestimanda sunt. Vale.

LETTER 110

1.   Ex Nomentano meo te saluto et iubeo habere mentem bonam, hoc est propitios deos omnis, quos habet placatos et faventes quisquis sibi se propitiavit. Sepone in praesentia quae quibusdam placent, unicuique nostrum paedagogum dari deum, non quidem ordinarium, sed hunc inferioris notae ex eorum numero quos Ovidius ait 'de plebe deos'. Ita tamen hoc seponas volo ut memineris maiores nostros qui crediderunt Stoicos fuisse; singulis enim et Genium et Iunonem

2. dederunt. Postea videbimus an tantum dis vacet ut privatorum negotia procurent: interim illud scito, sive adsignati sumus sive neglecti et fortunae dati, nulli te posse inprecari quicquam gravius quam si inprecatus fueris ut se habeat iratum. Sed non est quare cuiquam quem poena putaveris dignum optes ut infestos deos habeat: habet,

3. inquam, etiam si videtur eorum favore produci. Adhibe diligentiam tuam et intuere quid sint res nostrae, non quid vocentur, et scies plura mala contingere nobis quam accidere. Quotiens enim felicitatis et causa et initium fuit quod calamitas vocabatur! quotiens magna gratulatione excepta res gradum sibi struxit in praeceps et aliquem iam eminentem adlevavit etiamnunc, tamquam adhuc ibi staret unde tuto

4. cadunt! Sed ipsum illud cadere non habet in se mali quicquam si exitum spectes, ultra quem natura neminem deiecit. Prope est rerum omnium terminus, prope est, inquam, et illud unde felix eicitur et illud unde infelix emittitur: nos utraque extendimus et longa spe ac metu facimus. Sed, si sapis, omnia humana condicione metire; simul et quod gaudes et quod times contrahe. Est autem tanti nihil diu gaudere ne quid diu timeas.

must reject pleasures: they weaken and unman us, and make many demands, which forces us in turn to make many demands on fortune. Then wealth must be despised: it is the wages of slavery. Gold and silver and all else that encumbers our prosperous homes must be discarded: freedom cannot cost us nothing. If you value this highly everything else must be valued at little.

LETTER 110

1.   I greet you from my place at Nomentum and wish you health of mind, that is, the favour of all the gods — and anyone who has won his own favour has the gods at peace and well—disposed towards him. Put aside for the time being the belief of certain people that each of us has a god appointed to him as a guardian — not indeed a god from the regular ranks, but one of lesser quality belonging to the group which Ovid calls 'lower—class gods'. However, while you are putting aside this belief I want you to remember that our ancestors who entertained it were essentially Stoics; for they attributed to every

2. single man or woman a Genius or a Juno. We shall see presently whether the gods have enough time to look after the affairs of individuals; in the meantime you must realize that whether we have been allotted to a god's protection, or abandoned to the whim of fortune, you cannot invoke a worse curse on anyone than to wish him to be on bad terms with himself. But there is no reason for you to pray for the hostility of the gods towards anybody you think deserves punishment: he has their hostility, I tell you, even if he appears to be getting on well through their favour.

3.   Use your wits and look hard at human affairs as they are, not as they are described, and you will realize that our troubles more often turn out well than badly for us. See how often what was described as a disaster proved to be the initial cause of a blessing! How often an occurrence welcomed with loud rejoicing has in fact created steps to the edge of a precipice, and has raised even higher someone already highly placed, as if till then he was standing where

4. one might safely fall! Still, this fall is not in itself an evil if you consider the final point beyond which nature has cast no one down. At hand is the end of all things, at hand, I tell you, is that point where the happy man is thrown out and the unhappy man is let out. With our hopes and fears we prolong and extend both our happiness and our unhappiness. But if you're wise you should measure all things in human terms, and contract the limits of your joys and your fears. Moreover, it is worth while enjoying nothing for long so that you don't fear anything for long.

5.   Sed quare istuc malum adstringo?   Non est quod quicquam
timendum putes: vana sunt ista quae nos movent, quae attonitos
habent.   Nemo nostrum quid veri esset excussit, sed metum alter
alteri tradidit; nemo ausus est ad id quo perturbabatur accedere et
naturam ac bonum timoris sui nosse.   Itaque res falsa et inanis habet
6.   adhuc fidem quia non coarguitur.   Tanti putemus oculos intendere:
iam apparebit quam brevia, quam incerta, quam tuta timeantur.   Talis
est animorum nostrorum confusio qualis Lucretio visa est:
         nam veluti pueri trepidant atque omnia caecis
         in tenebris metuunt, ita nos in luce timemus.
Quid ergo? non omni puero stultiores sumus qui in luce timemus?
7.   Sed falsum est, Lucreti, non timemus in luce: omnia nobis fecimus
tenebras.   Nihil videmus, nec quid noceat nec quid expediat; tota vita
incursitamus nec ob hoc resistimus aut circumspectius pedem ponimus.
Vides autem quam sit furiosa res in tenebris impetus.   At mehercules
id agimus ut longius revocandi simus, et cum ignoremus quo feramur,
velociter tamen illo quo intendimus perseveramus.   Sed lucescere, si
8   velimus, potest.   Uno autem modo potest, si quis hanc humanorum
divinorumque notitiam [scientia] acceperit, si illa se non perfuderit sed
infecerit, si eadem, quamvis sciat, retractaverit et ad se saepe
rettulerit, si quaesierit quae sint bona, quae mala, quibus hoc falso sit
nomen adscriptum, si quaesierit de honestis et turpibus, de providentia.
9.   Nec intra haec humani ingenii sagacitas sistitur: prospicere et ultra
mundum libet, quo feratur, unde surrexerit, in quem exitum tanta
rerum velocitas properet.   Ab hac divina contemplatione abductum
animum in sordida et humilia pertraximus, ut avaritiae serviret, ut
relicto mundo terminisque eius et dominis cuncta versantibus terram
rimaretur et quaereret quid ex illa mali effoderet, non contentus
10.   oblatis.   Quidquid nobis bono futurum erat deus et parens noster in
proximo posuit; non expectavit inquisitionem nostram et ultro dedit:
nocitura altissime pressit.   Nihil nisi de nobis queri possumus: ea
quibus periremus nolente rerum natura et abscondente protulimus.
Addiximus animum voluptati, cui indulgere initium omnium malorum

5.   But why am I trying to restrict this evil of fear? You have no reason to regard anything as fearful: the things which disturb us and keep us petrified are quite illusory. None of us has tested their reality, but one man's fear rubs off on another. No one has dared to approach the source of his anxiety and to learn the nature of the fear and any good there might be in it. Consequently, a false and empty circumstance still looks genuine because it has not been refuted.

6. We must think it worthwhile to look hard at our fears, and it will soon be obvious how short—lived, uncertain and reassuring they are. This is the sort of confusion in our minds which struck Lucretius:

    'As at night children tremble, dreading all in the dark,
    So even in daylight our fears do afflict us'.

7. Well, then: with our daylight fears are we not more silly than any child? But you are wrong, Lucretius: it is not that we have fears in the daylight, but that we have entirely created darkness for ourselves. We see nothing either to harm us or to do us good. All our lives we rush around bumping into things, without pausing on this account or treading more carefully. You see how lunatic it is to run at something in the dark; yet, goodness me, that's what we are doing, so that we have to be summoned back from further away, and though we don't know whither we are rushing we still keep on full tilt in

8. our course. Yet daylight can come if we want it to, but only if a man has acquired this knowledge of things human and divine; if he has not just let it wash over him but has become deep—dyed in it; if he has considered over and over again the same notions, even though he may have grasped them, and has applied them frequently to himself; if he has asked himself what things are good and what are bad and what bear one of these names falsely; if he has asked himself about things honourable and disgraceful, and about providence.

9. Nor is the keenness of the human intellect restricted within these limits. It can also gaze beyond the universe, pondering whither this is being borne, when it arose, to what final end all that rushing mass of matter is hurtling. From this divine spectacle we have withdrawn our minds and dragged them to sordid and lowly areas, to be slaves to greed, to abandon the universe and its limits and its all—powerful masters, and to explore the earth and see what evils they can dig out

10. of it, not satisfied with what is freely offered. Whatever was to be of benefit to us god, our parent, put within our reach: he anticipated our searching for it and gave it unasked. The things that would harm us he buried deep down. We have nothing to complain of but ourselves. It is we who have brought to light the instruments of our destruction against nature's wishes and when she was hiding them from view. We have enslaved our souls to pleasure, indulgence in which is the beginning of all evils; we have betrayed them to

est, tradidimus ambitioni et famae, ceteris aeque vanis et inanibus.

11.　　　　Quid ergo nunc te hortor ut facias? nihil novi — nec enim novis malis remedia quaeruntur — sed hoc primum, ut tecum ipse dispicias quid sit necessarium, quid supervacuum.　Necessaria tibi ubique occurrent: supervacua et semper et toto animo quaerenda sunt.

12.　Non est autem quod te nimis laudes si contempseris aureos lectos et gemmeam supellectilem; quae est enim virtus supervacua contemnere? Tunc te admirare cum contempseris necessaria.　Non magnam rem facis quod vivere sine regio apparatu potes, quod non desideras milliarios apros nec linguas phoenicopterorum et alia portenta luxuriae iam tota animalia fastidientis et certa membra ex singulis eligentis: tunc te admirabor si contempseris etiam sordidum panem, si tibi persuaseris herbam, ubi necesse est, non pecori tantum sed homini nasci, si scieris cacumina arborum explementum esse ventris in quem sic pretiosa congerimus tamquam recepta servantem.　Sine fastidio implendus est; quid enim ad rem pertinet quid accipiat, perditurus

13.　quidquid acceperit?　Delectant te disposita quae terra marique capiuntur, alia eo gratiora si recentia perferuntur ad mensam, alia si diu pasta et coacta pinguescere fluunt ac vix saginam continent suam; delectat te nitor horum arte quaesitus.　At mehercules ista sollicite scrutata varieque condita, cum subierint ventrem, una atque eadem foeditas occupabit.　Vis ciborum voluptatem contemnere? exitum specta.

14.　　　　Attalum memini cum magna admiratione omnium haec dicere: 'diu' inquit 'mihi inposuere divitiae.　Stupebam ubi aliquid ex illis alio atque alio loco fulserat; existimabam similia esse quae laterent his quae ostenderentur.　Sed in quodam apparatu vidi totas opes urbis, caelata et auro et argento et iis quae pretium auri argentique vicerunt, exquisitos colores et vestes ultra non tantum nostrum sed ultra finem hostium advectas; hinc puerorum perspicuos cultu atque forma greges, hinc feminarum, et alia quae res suas recognoscens summi imperii

15.　fortuna protulerat.　"Quid hoc est" inquam "aliud inritare cupiditates hominum per se incitatas? quid sibi vult ista pecuniae pompa? ad discendam avaritiam convenimus?"　At mehercules minus cupiditatis istinc effero quam adtuleram. Contempsi divitias, non quia supervacuae

ambition and public opinion, and everything else which is equally empty and vain.

11.   So, what am I urging you to do? Nothing new — it isn't for new maladies that we are seeking cures, — but this first and foremost, that you distinguish clearly for yourself the essential and the superfluous. Essentials you will find everywhere; superfluous things

12. have to be sought by a constant effort of the whole soul. But there is no reason to overpraise yourself if you have come to despise golden couches and bejewelled furniture: for what virtue lies in despising superfluities? You can admire yourself when you have come to despise essentials. It's no great achievement if you can live without regal trappings, and do without boars weighing a thousand pounds and flamingoes' tongues, and the other extravagances of a luxury which is now disgusted with whole animals and only chooses certain parts from individual ones. I shall admire you if you come to despise coarse bread, if you can persuade yourself that when necessary grass grows for man as well as beast, if you have realized that shoots from trees can serve to fill the belly, which we stuff full of expensive food as though it could retain what it receives. No, it must be filled without squeamishness; for how can it matter what it accepts, since it is

13. bound to get rid of all it has accepted? You love to see the game taken on land and sea laid out in front of you, some all the more desirable if brought fresh to your table, some if force—fed and stuffed for so long it scarcely holds the fat it's overflowing with — what you love is the sheen that is thus skilfully imparted to it. Yet, goodness me, when those dishes, so anxiously sought for and diversely seasoned, have entered the stomach they become one uniform horrid mess. Do you want to despise the pleasure of food? Look at what happens to it.

14.   I remember Attalus winning great admiration from all who heard him with these words: 'For a long time I was impressed by riches. I was fascinated in whatever place their brilliance shone forth, and I presumed that what lay concealed was similar to what was displayed. But I happened to witness a ceremonial display of all the city's wealth: objects carved in gold and silver and in materials surpassing the value of gold and silver; choice dyes and fabrics imported from beyond not only our boundaries but those of our enemies; matching groups of boys and girls conspicuous for their adornment and their beauty; and everything else that a successful

15. imperial power puts on parade when reviewing its resources. "What else", I said to myself, "does all this do but kindle men's greedy passions already naturally aroused? What is the point of that parade of wealth? Have we assembled here to be taught avarice?" Yet, I do assure you I left that sight with less capacity for greed than I took

16. sed quia pusillae sunt. Vidistine quam intra paucas horas ille ordo quamvis lentus dispositusque transierit? Hoc totam vitam nostram occupabit quod totum diem occupare non potuit? Accessit illud quoque: tam supervacuae mihi visae sunt habentibus quam fuerunt

17. spectantibus. Hoc itaque ipse mihi dico quotiens tale aliquid praestrinxerit oculos meos, quotiens occurrit domus splendida, cohors culta servorum, lectica formonsis inposita calonibus: "quid miraris? quid stupes? pompa est. Ostenduntur istae res, non possidentur, et dum

18. placent transeunt". Ad veras potius te converte divitias; disce parvo esse contentus et illam vocem magnus atque animosus exclama: habemus aquam, habemus polentam; Iovi ipsi controversiam de felicitate faciamus. Faciamus, oro te, etiam si ista defuerint; turpe est

19. beatam vitam in auro et argento reponere, aeque turpe in aqua et polenta. "Quid ergo faciam si ista non fuerint?" Quaeris quod sit remedium inopiae? Famem fames finit: alioquin quid interest magna sint an exigua quae servire te cogant? quid refert quantulum sit quod

20. tibi possit negare fortuna? Haec ipsa aqua et polenta in alienum arbitrium cadit; liber est autem non in quem parum licet fortunae, sed in quem nihil. Ita est: nihil desideres oportet si vis Iovem provocare nihil desiderantem.'

Haec nobis Attalus dixit, natura omnibus dixit; quae si voles frequenter cogitare, id ages ut sis felix, non ut videaris, et ut tibi videaris, non aliis. Vale.

LETTER 114

1.   Quare quibusdam temporibus provenerit corrupti generis oratio quaeris et quomodo in quaedam vitia inclinatio ingeniorum facta sit, ut aliquando inflata explicatio vigeret, aliquando infracta et in morem cantici ducta; quare alias sensus audaces et fidem egressi placuerint, alias abruptae sententiae et suspiciosae, in quibus plus intellegendum esset quam audiendum; quare aliqua aetas fuerit quae translationis iure uteretur inverecunde. Hoc quod audire vulgo soles, quod apud Graecos in proverbium cessit: talis hominibus fuit oratio qualis vita.

2. Quemadmodum autem uniuscuiusque actio †dicendi† similis est, sic genus dicendi aliquando imitatur publicos mores, si disciplina civitatis laboravit et se in delicias dedit. Argumentum est luxuriae publicae

to it. I despised riches, not because they are superfluous but because
16. they are insignificant. You saw in how few hours that procession
passed by, though organized in slow stages? Is that going to fill our
whole lives which could not fill a whole day? This point too
occurred to me, that these riches are as superfluous to the possessors
17. as to the spectators. So, whenever some such sight dazzles my eyes
— a luxurious house, an elegant troop of slaves, a litter carried by
handsome servants — I tell myself: "What are you admiring? What
are you gaping at? It's only a procession. Those things are for
show, not for possession, and even as they please us they pass away."
18. Turn instead to real wealth; learn to be content with little and call
out loudly and boldly: We have water, we have barley: we may vie
with Jupiter himself in happiness. We may, I assure you, even if
those were lacking. It is disgraceful to base one's life on gold and
silver, and equally disgraceful to base it on water and barley. "Then
19. what am I to do if I don't have them?" You are asking for the
remedy for destitution? Hunger ends hunger. In any case, what
difference does it make if the things are great or scanty which enslave
you? What's it matter how trifling is the amount that fortune can
20. deny you? This very water and barley is under someone else's
control; but the free man is not the one over whom fortune has just
a small hold, but the one over whom fortune has no hold at all. So
there you are: you must want nothing, if you wish to challenge
Jupiter who himself wants nothing.'

Attalus has told us this; nature has told all men this. If you
are willing to meditate it constantly you will be on the way to being
happy, not just seeming happy, and seeming so not to others, but to
yourself.

LETTER 114

1.   You ask why at certain periods a corrupt style of speech has
appeared and how it is that writers have tended to adopt certain
faults, so that sometimes a bombastic style of utterance has been
fashionable, sometimes an effeminate sing—song effect; why at times
daring and extravagant thoughts have been popular, and at other times
brief, allusive sayings in which you had to understand more than you
heard; why at one time there was a shameless over—indulgence in
metaphor. The answer lies in the commonly quoted Greek proverb:
2. 'Men's style of speech reflects their lives'. Now as each man's
behaviour is like his style of speaking, so style in speaking sometimes
imitates public standards of behaviour, if these have become corrupted
by loose living. A dissolute style of oratory is a proof of luxury in

orationis lascivia, si modo non in uno aut in altero fuit, sed adprobata
3. est et recepta. Non potest alius esse ingenio, alius animo color. Si
ille sanus est, si compositus, gravis, temperans, ingenium quoque
siccum ac sobrium est: illo vitiato hoc quoque adflatur. Non vides, si
animus elanguit, trahi membra et pigre moveri pedes? si ille
effeminatus est, in ipso incessu apparere mollitiam? si ille acer est et
ferox, concitari gradum? si furit aut, quod furori simile est, irascitur,
turbatum esse corporis motum nec ire sed ferri? Quanto hoc magis
accidere ingenio putas, quod totum animo permixtum est, ab illo
fingitur, illi paret, inde legem petit?
4.   Quomodo Maecenas vixerit notius est quam ut narrari nunc
debeat quomodo ambulaverit, quam delicatus fuerit, quam cupierit
videri, quam vitia sua latere noluerit. Quid ergo? non oratio eius
aeque soluta est quam ipse discinctus? non tam insignita illius verba
sunt quam cultus, quam comitatus, quam domus, quam uxor? Magni
vir ingenii fuerat si illud egisset via rectiore, si non vitasset intellegi,
si non etiam in oratione difflueret. Videbis itaque eloquentiam ebrii
hominis involutam et errantem et licentiae plenam. [Maecenas de
5. cultu suo.] Quid turpius 'amne silvisque ripa comantibus'? Vide ut
'alveum lyntribus arent versoque vado remittant hortos'. Quid? si quis
'feminae cinno crispat et labris columbatur incipitque suspirans, ut
cervice lassa fanantur nemoris tyranni'. 'Inremediabilis factio rimantur
epulis lagonaque temptant domos et spe mortem exigunt.' 'Genium
festo vix suo testem.' 'Tenuisve cerei fila et crepacem molam.'
6. 'Focum mater aut uxor investiunt.' Non statim cum haec legeris hoc
tibi occurret, hunc esse qui solutis tunicis in urbe semper incesserit
(nam etiam cum absentis Caesaris partibus fungeretur, signum a
discincto petebatur); hunc esse qui < in> tribunali, in rostris, in omni
publico coetu sic apparuerit ut pallio velaretur caput exclusis utrimque
auribus, non aliter quam in mimo fugitivi divitis solent; hunc esse cui
tunc maxime civilibus bellis strepentibus et sollicita urbe et armata
comitatus hic fuerit in publico, spadones duo, magis tamen viri quam
7. ipse; hunc esse qui uxorem milliens duxit, cum unam habuerit? Haec
verba tam inprobe structa, tam neglegenter abiecta, tam contra

3.   public life, provided that it is not restricted to one or two cases but is popular and generally accepted. A man's mind and his moral character have the same complexion: if his character is healthy, if it is sober, orderly and prudent, his mind too is serious and temperate. But if his character becomes depraved his mind too is infected. Don't you see that if the character is depressed the limbs droop and the feet move sluggishly? If it is effeminate the softness actually shows in the gait? If it is lively and fierce the pace is brisk? If it is mad or — what is much the same thing — angry, the movement of the body is agitated and it is swept along without volition? Is this not even more true of the mind, which is totally mingled with the character — formed by it, obedient to it, and seeking guidance from it?

4.   The life—style of Maecenas is too well known for me to have to describe how he walked, how self—indulgent he was, how he wished to be seen, how he did not wish to conceal his faults. Well, then, is not his literary style as loose as his own appearance was careless? Isn't his vocabulary as conspicuous as his dress, his attendants, his house, his wife? He would have shown high talent if he had pursued a more direct path, if he had not avoided being understood through flabbiness even in his style. Thus you will find his eloquence is that of a drunkard, complex, rambling and wanton.

5.   What could be worse than the phrase 'the river bank with tresses of water and woods'? Look at 'they plough the channel with boats and by stirring up the shallows send back the gardens.' Imagine somebody who 'puckers up his face with a grimace at a lady and bills with his lips and begins sighing, as the lords of the forest rut with drooping necks'. Or 'the unregenerate conspirators probe with feasts, assail houses with the wine—bottle and demand death for hope'. Or 'guardian spirit scarcely to be called to witness on his own festive day'. Or 'threads of slender candle and crackling grain'. Or

6.   'mother or wife accoutre the hearth'. When you read this sort of thing doesn't it strike you at once that this is the man who always went about the city sloppily dressed (for even when he was acting for Augustus during his absence he gave out the daily password unbelted)? The man who at the tribunal, at the speakers' platform, at every public assembly appeared with his head covered in a cloak, with only his ears showing, exactly like a rich man's runaway slaves in a mime? The man who, when the civil wars were at their height and Rome was in an armed state of panic, had for his entourage two eunuchs (though they were more men than he)? The man who had one wife but married her a thousand times?

7.   The words I have quoted, so audaciously arranged, so carelessly flung down, employed with such disregard for normal usage, reveal a

consuetudinem omnium posita ostendunt mores quoque non minus novos et pravos et singulares fuisse. Maxima laus illi tribuitur mansuetudinis: pepercit gladio, sanguine abstinuit, nec ulla alia re quid posset quam licentia ostendit. Hanc ipsam laudem suam corrupit istis orationis portentosissimae delicis; apparet enim mollem fuisse, non

8.   mitem. Hoc istae ambages compositionis, hoc verba transversa, hoc sensus miri, magni quidem saepe sed enervati dum exeunt, cuivis manifestum facient: motum illi felicitate nimia caput. Quod vitium

9.   hominis esse interdum, interdum temporis solet. Ubi luxuriam late felicitas fudit, cultus primum corporum esse diligentior incipit; deinde supellectili laboratur; deinde in ipsas domos inpenditur cura ut in laxitatem ruris excurrant, ut parietes advectis trans maria marmoribus fulgeant, ut tecta varientur auro, ut lacunaribus pavimentorum respondeat nitor; deinde ad cenas lautitia transfertur et illic commendatio ex novitate et soliti ordinis commutatione captatur, ut ea quae includere solent cenam prima ponantur, ut quae advenientibus

10. dabantur exeuntibus dentur. Cum adsuevit animus fastidire quae ex more sunt et illi pro sordidis solita sunt, etiam in oratione quod novum est quaerit et modo antiqua verba atque exoleta revocat ac profert, modo fingit †et ignota ac† deflectit, modo, id quod nuper

11. increbruit, pro cultu habetur audax translatio ac frequens. Sunt qui sensus praecidant et hoc gratiam sperent, si sententia pependerit et audienti suspicionem sui fecerit; sunt qui illos detineant et porrigant; sunt qui non usque ad vitium accedant (necesse est enim hoc facere aliquid grande temptanti) sed qui ipsum vitium ament.

Itaque ubicumque videris orationem corruptam placere, ibi mores quoque a recto descivisse non erit dubium. Quomodo conviviorum luxuria, quomodo vestium aegrae civitatis indicia sunt, sic orationis licentia, si modo frequens est, ostendit animos quoque a quibus verba

12. exeunt procidisse. Mirari quidem non debes corrupta excipi non tantum a corona sordidiore sed ab hac quoque turba cultiore; togis enim inter se isti, non iudicis distant. Hoc magis mirari potes, quod non tantum vitiosa sed vitia laudentur. Nam illud semper factum est: nullum sine venia placuit ingenium. Da mihi quemcumque vis magni nominis virum: dicam quid illi aetas sua ignoverit, quid in illo sciens dissimulaverit. Multos tibi dabo quibus vitia non nocuerint, quosdam quibus profuerint. Dabo, inquam, maximae famae et inter admiranda

character no less strange, distorted and unusual. The highest compliment we can pay him is that he was merciful: he spared the sword and refrained from bloodshed, showing his power only in his unconventional behaviour. But he spoiled even this compliment by those outlandish freaks of style which show that he was not mild but
8. soft. That obscure word—order, the words that trip you up, the extraordinary ideas, often indeed noble, but emasculated in the utterance — all these make it clear that too much prosperity had turned his head.

9. This is a fault sometimes of a man, sometimes of an age. When prosperity has produced widespread luxury, first people begin to take pains with their personal appearance; then furniture becomes elaborate; then care is devoted to the houses themselves, so that they emulate country estates in their extent, with walls gleaming with imported marble, and gilded ceilings whose panels are matched by the gleaming paved floors. Then extravagance is applied to food and praise is sought from novelty and unusual order in presenting dishes, so that what usually concludes the meal becomes the first course and departing guests receive what used to be given them on arrival.

10. When the mind has grown accustomed to disdain the conventional and to regard what is normal as vulgar, it seeks novelty in speech too, sometimes reviving and exhibiting old, obsolete words, sometimes coining new words or varying the forms of existing ones, sometimes — a popular habit recently — considering a bold and frequent use of
11. metaphor as sophisticated. Some speakers cut short their sentences and expect to win favour by letting a thought hang fire and making their audience guess its import. Others cling to their sentences and stretch them out. Others again don't just fall into a stylistic fault (that is inevitable if one is aiming high), but love the fault for its own sake.

So wherever you see a corrupt style is popular there you can be sure that morality had gone astray. Just as luxurious banquets and clothes are signs of a sick society, so too licentious style, if it is widespread, reveals the degeneracy of the minds from which the words
12. proceed. Indeed you shouldn't be surprised that corrupt work is accepted not only by the man in the street but by the intelligentsia too: they differ in their clothes, not in their taste. You could be more surprised at the fact that they admire not just faulty works but the faults themselves. It has of course always been true that no great talent has been admired without some allowance for shortcomings. Name anyone of high reputation and I'll tell you what his contemporaries forgave in him or willingly overlooked. I'll show you many whose faults did them no harm, and some whose faults actually helped them. I'll show you men of the greatest renown, held up to

propositos, quos si quis corrigit, delet; sic enim vitia virtutibus inmixta sunt ut illas secum tractura sint.

13.   Adice nunc quod oratio certam regulam non habet: consuetudo illam civitatis, quae numquam in eodem diu stetit, versat. Multi ex alieno saeculo petunt verba, duodecim tabulas loquuntur; Gracchus illis et Crassus et Curio nimis culti et recentes sunt, ad Appium usque et Coruncanium redeunt. Quidam contra, dum nihil nisi tritum et

14. usitatum volunt, in sordes incidunt. Utrumque diverso genere corruptum est, tam mehercules quam nolle nisi splendidis uti ac sonantibus et poeticis, necessaria atque in usu posita vitare. Tam hunc dicam peccare quam illum: alter se plus iusto colit, alter plus iusto neglegit; ille et crura, hic ne alas quidem vellit.

15.   Ad compositionem transeamus. Quot genera tibi in hac dabo quibus peccetur? Quidam praefractam et asperam probant; disturbant de industria si quid placidius effluxit; nolunt sine salebra esse iuncturam; virilem putant et fortem quae aurem inaequalitate percutiat. Quorundam non est compositio, modulatio est; adeo blanditur et

16. molliter labitur. Quid de illa loquar in qua verba differuntur et diu expectata vix ad clausulas redeunt? Quid illa in exitu lenta, qualis Ciceronis est, devexa et molliter detinens nec aliter quam solet ad morem suum pedemque respondens?

Non tantum *** in genere sententiarum vitium est, si aut pusillae sunt et pueriles aut inprobae et plus ausae quam pudore salvo licet, si floridae sunt et nimis dulces, si in vanum exeunt et sine effectu nihil amplius quam sonant.

17.   Haec vitia unus aliquis inducit, sub quo tunc eloquentia est, ceteri imitantur et alter alteri tradunt. Sic Sallustio vigente anputatae sententiae et verba ante expectatum cadentia et obscura brevitas fuere pro cultu. L. Arruntius, vir rarae frugalitatis, qui historias belli Punici scripsit, fuit Sallustianus et in illud genus nitens. Est apud Sallustium 'exercitum argento fecit', id est, pecunia paravit. Hoc Arruntius amare coepit; posuit illud omnibus paginis. Dicit quodam loco 'fugam nostris fecere', alio loco 'Hiero rex Syracusanorum bellum fecit', et

18. alio loco 'quae audita Panhormitanos dedere Romanis fecere'. Gustum tibi dare volui: totus his contexitur liber. Quae apud Sallustium rara fuerunt apud hunc crebra sunt et paene continua, nec

us as objects of admiration, who would be destroyed if their faults were corrected: their vices and virtues are so closely linked that they stand or fall together.

13.   Consider too that style has no fixed rules: it is governed by the ordinary usage of a society, and that frequently changes. Many seek their vocabulary from a different age and talk the language of the Twelve Tables. Gracchus and Crassus and Curio are too elegant and modern for them, so they go right back to Appius and Coruncanius. On the other hand, some aiming solely at what is trite

14. and well−worn fall into banality. Both types are corrupt in their different ways − just as much, to be sure, as the wish to use nothing but florid, resounding and poetic expressions and to avoid obvious everyday ones. The one man is as much at fault as the other: one is too elegant, the other too careless; one shaves even his legs, the other not even his armpits.

15.   Let us turn to word−order. How many kinds of fault shall I show you here? Some like a rough and broken rhythm, and wilfully disturb the flow if it is too smooth; they must have a jolting sequence of words; they think a rhythm is virile and forceful if it strikes the ear with its irregularity. Some aim at singing not rhythm, so alluring

16. and smooth is the flow of their words. And what of the fashion of delaying words so that we keep waiting for them and they only just turn up at the close of the period? Or that lingering cadence, like Cicero's, gently slowing the reader with its diminuendo and never altering its customary metrical rhythm?

17.   There is also a fault in the field of epigrams, if they are trivial and childish, or offensive and indecently bold; if they are flowery and over−elegant; if they are ultimately pointless and have no effect beyond the sound of the words.

These faults are introduced by some one individual who dominates rhetoric at the time, and they are copied by others who pass them on one to another. Thus in Sallust's heyday there was a fashion for clipped sentences, phrases ending unexpectedly, and brevity carried to the point of obscurity. Lucius Arruntius, a man of unusual austerity, who wrote a history of the Punic War, was a disciple of Sallust and tried hard to adopt his style. You'll find in Sallust 'He created an army with silver' (that is, he levied it by paying money). Arruntius adopted the phrase devotedly and put it on every page. In one place he has 'They created flight for our men'; elsewhere 'Hiero, king of Syracuse, created war'; and again 'This report created the

18. Panhormitan surrender to the Romans'. I wanted to give you just a taste of this, but the whole book is a texture of these expressions. What was rare in Sallust is frequent and almost continuous in Arruntius, for the obvious reason that Sallust hit upon these phrases

19. sine causa; ille enim in haec incidebat, at hic illa quaerebat.   Vides autem quid sequatur ubi alicui vitium pro exemplo est.   Dixit Sallustius 'aquis hiemantibus'.   Arruntius in primo libro belli Punici ait 'repente hiemavit tempestas', et alio loco cum dicere vellet frigidum annum fuisse ait 'totus hiemavit annus', et alio loco 'inde sexaginta onerarias leves praeter militem et necessarios nautarum hiemante aquilone misit'.   Non desinit omnibus locis hoc verbum infulcire. Quodam loco dicit Sallustius 'dum inter arma civilia aequi bonique famas petit'.   Arruntius non temperavit quominus primo statim libro

20. poneret ingentes esse 'famas' de Regulo.   Haec ergo et eiusmodi vitia, quae aliciui inpressit imitatio, non sunt indicia luxuriae nec animi corrupti; propria enim esse debent et ex ipso nata ex quibus tu aestimes alicius adfectus: iracundi hominis iracunda oratio est,

21. commoti nimis incitata, delicati tenera et fluxa.   Quod vides istos sequi qui aut vellunt barbam aut intervellunt, qui labra pressius tondent et adradunt servata et summissa cetera parte, qui lacernas coloris inprobi sumunt, qui perlucentem togam, qui nolunt facere quicquam quod hominum oculis transire liceat: inritant illos et in se avertunt, volunt vel reprehendi dum conspici.   Talis est oratio Maecenatis omniumque aliorum qui non casu errant sed scientes

22. volentesque.   Hoc a magno animi malo oritur: quomodo in vino non ante lingua titubat quam mens cessit oneri et inclinata vel prodita est, ita ista orationis quid aliud quam ebrietas nulli molesta est nisi animus labat.   Ideo ille curetur: ab illo sensus, ab illo verba exeunt, ab illo nobis est habitus, vultus, incessus.   Illo sano ac valente oratio quoque robusta, fortis, virilis est: si ille procubuit, et cetera ruinam sequuntur.

23.   Rege incolumi mens omnibus una est:
                 amisso rupere fidem
Rex noster est animus; hoc incolumi cetera manent in officio, parent, obtemperant: cum ille paulum vacillavit, simul dubitant.   Cum vero cessit voluptati, artes quoque eius actusque marcent et omnis ex languido fluidoque conatus est.

24.   Quoniam hac similitudine usus sum, perseverabo.   Animus noster modo rex est, modo tyrannus: rex cum honesta intuetur, salutem commissi sibi corporis curat et illi nihil imperat turpe, nihil sordidum; ubi vero inpotens, cupidus, delicatus est, transit in nomen detestabile

by chance whereas Arruntius deliberately sought them out. You see what follows when a fault is used as a model. Sallust said 'When

19. the waters wintered'. Arruntius in the first book of his *Punic War* has 'The storm suddenly wintered', and elsewhere when he wished to say it was a cold year says 'The whole year wintered', and elsewhere 'Then he despatched sixty transport vessels lightly laden except for soldiers and essential crew, while the north wind wintered'. He insists on stuffing this word in everywhere. In one place Sallust says 'While amid civil war he seeks fames for integrity and goodness'. Arruntius could not resist putting in his very first book that there were tremendous 'fames' about Regulus.

20. Now these and similar faults, which imitation has instilled into a writer, are not signs of self—indulgence or immorality. You have to assess a man's nature from characteristics which are individual to him and inborn: an angry person's speech is angry, an agitated person's

21. is over—excited, a fastidious person's is soft and mincing. This is the aim of those people who pluck or partially pluck their beards, who shave their lips close and smooth, leaving the rest to grow long, who wear cloaks of outlandish colours or transparent togas, who refuse to do anything which might pass unnoticed: they are chivying others into paying them attention, willing even to be criticised so long as they are conspicuous. Such is the style of Maecenas and of all others whose errors arise not from chance but consciously and willingly.

22. This is due to a serious defect of character. When someone has had too much to drink his mind succumbs to the pressure, yielding and betrayed, before his tongue starts stuttering: in the same way nobody suffers from what can only be called a drunken style unless his mind is losing its grip. So let the treatment start there: from there our thoughts and our words proceed, from there we derive our dress, our demeanour, our gait. When the mind is sound and healthy, style of speech too is forceful, firm and virile. If the mind has given way the rest follows its collapse.

23. 'The king being safe all have a single aim;
He's lost, and anarchy prevails'.
The mind is our king: as long as it is unharmed all else remains at its post of duty, compliant and obedient. If it wavers slightly they share its uncertainty. But when it has yielded to pleasure its functions and actions also decay, and all its impulses become feeble and infirm.

24. Since I have used this analogy I shall pursue it. Our mind is sometimes a king, sometimes a tyrant. It is a king when it contemplates honourable courses, and cares for the welfare of the body in its charge and gives it no mean or disgraceful orders. But when it lacks self—control and gives way to desires and

ac dirum et fit tyrannus.   Tunc illum excipiunt adfectus inpotentes et instant; qui initio quidem gaudet, ut solet populus largitione nocitura
25. frustra plenus et quae non potest haurire contrectans; cum vero magis ac magis vires morbus exedit et in medullas nervosque descendere deliciae, conspectu eorum quibus se nimia aviditate inutilem reddidit laetus,   pro   suis   voluptatibus   habet   alienarum   spectaculum, sumministrator libidinum testisque, quarum usum sibi ingerendo abstulit. Nec illi tam gratum est abundare iucundis quam acerbum quod non omnem illum apparatum per gulam ventremque transmittit, quod non cum omni exoletorum feminarumque turba convolutatur, maeretque quod magna pars suae felicitatis exclusa corporis angustiis cessat.
26. Numquid enim, mi Lucili, <non> in hoc furor est, quod nemo nostrum mortalem se cogitat, quod nemo inbecillum? immo quod nemo nostrum unum esse se cogitat?   Aspice culinas nostras et concursantis inter tot ignes cocos: unum videri putas ventrem cui tanto tumultu comparatur   cibus?   Aspice   veteraria   nostra   et   plena   multorum saeculorum vindemiis horrea: unum putas videri ventrem cui tot consulum regionumque vina cluduntur?   Aspice   quot   locis   terra vertatur, quot millia colonorum arent, fodiant: unum videri putas
27. ventrem cui et in Sicilia et in Africa seritur?   Sani erimus et modica concupiscemus si unusquisque se numeret, metiatur simul corpus, sciat quam nec multum capere nec diu possit.   Nihil tamen aeque tibi profuerit ad temperantiam omnium rerum quam frequens cogitatio brevis aevi et huius incerti: quidquid facies, respice ad mortem.   Vale.

LETTER 122

1.   Detrimentum iam dies sensit; resiluit aliquantum, ita tamen ut liberale adhuc spatium sit si quis cum ipso, ut ita dicam, die surgat. Officiosior meliorque si quis illum expectat et lucem primam excipit: turpis qui alto sole semisomnus iacet, cuius vigilia medio die incipit;
2. et adhuc multis hoc antelucanum est.   Sunt qui officia lucis noctisque perverterint nec ante diducant oculos hesterna graves crapula quam adpetere nox coepit.   Qualis illorum condicio dicitur quos natura, ut

self—indulgence, it gains instead that dreaded and accursed name of tyrant. Then wanton passions grip and plague it, in which at first it takes delight — as happens to a populace vainly sated with largesse which will only harm it, and which it can handle but not fully enjoy.

25. But when the disease has increasingly sapped the man's strength and self—indulgence has probed his physical vitals, then he can only delight in the sight of those things of which his excessive desires have now made him incapable; the sight of others' pleasures replaces the enjoyment of his own; and he becomes the purveyor and witness of wanton delights of which he has deprived himself by over—indulgence. His is not the pleasure of having a rich abundance so much as the bitterness of not being able to force all that sumptious store down his own gullet, or to cavort with the whole crowd of his male and female lovers: he grieves because his physical limitations cut him off from a large part of his bliss.

26. My dear Lucilius, is it not madness that none of us thinks of himself as mortal, or as frail, or even as a single individual? Look at our kitchens and our cooks milling around so many fires: can you believe that all that bustle is to prepare food for just one stomach? Look at our wine—cellars and our barns full of the grape—harvests of many generations: can you believe that wines of so many vintages and regions are stored for just one stomach? Look at all the estates where the land is being tilled, the thousands of farmers who are ploughing and digging: can you believe that both Sicily and Africa

27. are being cultivated for just one stomach? We shall recover our senses and moderate our desires if each man assesses himself and measures his body, realizing that he cannot hold much or hold it for long. But nothing will be so conducive to self—control in all things as frequent reflection on the brevity and uncertainty of life: whatever you do you must turn your thoughts to death.

LETTER 122

1. The days are closing in now, and have shrunk somewhat, though still leaving a plentiful amount of light for anyone prepared to rise, as it were, with the day itself. Even more industrious and praiseworthy is the man who is waiting for the day and welcomes the first light. Shame on the man who is still lying half—asleep when the sun is high in the heavens, and whose conscious day begins at

2. noon — and for many people even then the day has not yet dawned. Some people reverse the functions of day and night, and don't open their eyes, heavy with yesterday's drunken orgy, before night comes on. The life—style of these people, if not their geographical position,

  ait Vergilius, pedibus nostris subditos e contrario posuit,

     nosque ubi primus equis Oriens adflavit anhelis,

     illis sera rubens accendit lumina Vesper,

3. talis horum contraria omnibus non regio sed vita est. Sunt quidam in
eadem urbe antipodes qui, ut M. Cato ait, nec orientem umquam
solem viderunt nec occidentem. Hos tu existimas scire quemadmodum
vivendum sit, qui nesciunt quando? Et hi mortem timent, in quam se
vivi condiderunt? tam infausti ominis quam nocturnae aves sunt. Licet
in vino unguentoque tenebras suas exigant, licet epulis et quidem in
multa fericula discoctis totum perversae vigiliae tempus educant, non
convivantur sed iusta sibi faciunt. Mortuis certe interdiu parentatur.
At mehercules nullus agenti dies longus est. Extendamus vitam: huius
et officium et argumentum actus est. Circumscribatur nox et aliquid

4. ex illa in diem transferatur. Aves quae conviviis comparantur, ut
inmotae facile pinguescant, in obscuro continentur; ita sine ulla
exercitatione iacentibus tumor pigrum corpus invadit et †superba
umbra† iners sagina subcrescit. At istorum corpora qui se tenebris
dicaverunt foeda visuntur, quippe suspectior illis quam morbo
pallentibus color est: languidi et evanidi albent, et in vivis caro
morticina est. Hoc tamen minimum in illis malorum dixerim: quanto
plus tenebrarum in animo est! ille in se stupet, ille caligat, invidet
caecis. Quis umquam oculos tenebrarum causa habuit?

5. Interrogas quomodo haec animo pravitas fiat aversandi diem et
totam vitam in noctem transferendi? Omnia vitia contra naturam
pugnant, omnia debitum ordinem deserunt; hoc est luxuriae
propositum, gaudere perversis nec tantum discedere a recto sed quam

6. longissime abire, deinde etiam e contrario stare. Non videntur tibi
contra naturam vivere <qui> ieiuni bibunt, qui vinum recipiunt
inanibus venis et ad cibum ebrii transeunt? Atqui frequens hoc
adulescentium vitium est, qui vires excolunt <ut> in ipso paene
balinei limine inter nudos bibant, immo potent et sudorem quem
moverunt potionibus crebris ac ferventibus subinde destringant. Post
prandium aut cenam bibere vulgare est; hoc patres familiae rustici
faciunt et verae voluptatis ignari: merum illud delectat quod non

is opposite to everybody else, resembling the condition of those whom nature, as Virgil says, has placed diametrically beneath our feet:

'When Dawn first on us breathes with panting steeds,
For them does Evening light her tardy lamps'.

3. There are certain antipodeans living in this very city who, to quote Marcus Cato, have never seen the sun either rising or setting. Do you think these people know how one should live if they don't know when? And can they be afraid of death if that is what they have plunged themselves into while still alive? They are as ill—omened as nocturnal birds. They may be occupying their hours of darkness in wine and perfumes; they may be spending the whole of their unnaturally wakeful time in eating feasts which are, indeed, cooked and served individually throughout many courses; nevertheless they are not banqueting, but conducting their own obsequies. At least the dead have their rites celebrated during daylight. But, good heavens, no day is long to an active man. Let us extend our life: action is its duty and its theme. Let night be curtailed and some of it

4. transferred to day. Birds which are reared for the table are kept in the dark, so that they won't move about and will fatten easily: so they lie around, taking no exercise, as their bodies get torpid and swollen and the sluggish fat gradually covers them in their dark surroundings. Look now at the foul physical appearance of those who have devoted themselves to darkness: their complexion is more worrying than the pallor of invalids; they turn white, sickly and drooping; and you can read death on the flesh of their living bodies. Yet I would say this is the least of their ills: how much darker is the state of their souls — stupefied, dazed and envious of the blind! Who ever had eyes for the sake of the dark?

5. You ask how comes the soul to have this perverse dislike of daylight and transference of all its life to the night? All vices fight against nature, all desert the established order of things. This is luxury's aim, to delight in abnormality, and not only to depart from the right course, but to move away as far as possible and eventually

6. to take up a position diametrically opposed to it. Don't you think people are living in opposition to nature when they drink on an empty stomach, taking wine into a void alimentary system, and eating when they are already drunk? Yet this is a common vice of young people, who cultivate their physical resources so that almost at the moment of entering the bath—house they are drinking — soaking, I should say — in naked groups, and from time to time wiping off the sweat brought on by their continual hot potations. To drink after lunch or dinner is a vulgar habit, indulged in by rustic householders who don't know how to find real pleasure. The pure wine that gives delight is that which does not float on food, but makes its way freely

7. innatat cibo, quod libere penetrat ad nervos; illa ebrietas iuvat quae in vacuum venit. Non videntur tibi contra naturam vivere qui commutant cum feminis vestem? Non vivunt contra naturam qui spectant ut pueritia splendeat tempore alieno? Quid fieri crudelius vel miserius potest? numquam vir erit, ut diu virum pati possit? et cum illum contumeliae sexus eripuisse debuerat, non ne aetas quidem

8. eripiet? Non vivunt contra naturam qui hieme concupiscunt rosam fomentoque aquarum calentium et locorum apta mutatione bruma lilium [florem vernum] exprimunt? Non vivunt contra naturam qui pomaria in summis turribus serunt? quorum silvae in tectis domuum ac fastigiis nutant, inde ortis radicibus quo inprobe cacumina egissent? Non vivunt contra naturam qui fundamenta thermarum in mari iaciunt et delicate natare ipsi sibi non videntur nisi calentia stagna fluctu ac

9. tempestate feriantur? Cum instituerunt omnia contra naturae consuetudinem velle, novissime in totum ab illa desciscunt. 'Lucet: somni tempus est. Quies est: nunc exerceamur, nunc gestemur, nunc prandeamus. Iam lux propius accedit: tempus est cenae. Non oportet id facere quod populus; res sordida est trita ac vulgari via vivere. Dies publicus relinquatur: proprium nobis ac peculiare mane

10. fiat.' Isti vero mihi defunctorum loco sunt; quantulum enim a funere absunt et quidem acerbo qui ad faces et cereos vivunt?

Hanc vitam agere eodem tempore multos meminimus, inter quos et Acilium Butam praetorium, cui post patrimonium ingens consumptum Tiberius paupertatem confitenti 'sero' inquit 'experrectus

11. es'. Recitabat Montanus Iulius carmen, tolerabilis poeta et amicitia Tiberi notus et frigore. Ortus et occasus libentissime inserebat; itaque cum indignaretur quidam illum toto die recitasse et negaret accedendum ad recitationes eius, Natta Pinarius ait: 'numquid possum liberalius agere? paratus sum illum audire ab ortu ad occasum'. Cum

12. hos versus recitasset

incipit ardentes Phoebus producere flammas,
spargere < se> rubicunda dies; iam tristis hirundo
argutis reditura cibos inmittere nidis
incipit et molli partitos ore ministrat,

Varus eques Romanus, M. Vinicii comes, cenarum bonarum adsectator,

to our vitals: it's the drunkenness which comes on an empty stomach which they enjoy.

7.   Don't you think people are living in opposition to nature when they exchange clothes with women? Aren't they living against nature who aim at preserving the glow of youth when that age is past? What could be more cruel or pathetic than for a boy never to become a man so that he can long continue to gratify a man? Will not even his age rescue him from the affronts from which his sex

8.   ought to have rescued him? Aren't they living against nature who long for roses during winter, and by nurturing them with warm water and suitable change of environment manage to force lilies in midwinter? Aren't they living against nature who plant orchards on the tops of towers? Who have woodland trees waving their branches on the roofs and gables of houses, with their roots springing from a height which it would have been presumptuous for their tops to reach? Aren't they living against nature who lay foundations for hot baths in the sea, and don't reckon they are swimming luxuriously enough unless their heated pools are exposed to violent waves and

9.   storms? Having once begun to long for everything contrary to the normal practice of nature, they end by totally rejecting her. 'It's daylight: time to sleep. All is quiet: now for our exercise, now for a drive, now for a meal. Dawn is approaching: time for dinner. We mustn't do what the world does: it's vulgar to follow the well−worn everyday track in life. Let us abandon the day to the mass of people and have the dawn hours to be especially our own.'

10.   Really, I regard these people as virtually dead. For can they be at all far from the grave − and indeed an untimely one − if they live by the light of torches and candles? I remember many who led this sort of life at the same time, including the ex−praetor Acilius Buta. After he had squandered a huge fortune and was admitting his poverty to Tiberius, the latter replied 'You have woken

11.   up a bit late.' Montanus Julius, a reasonably good poet and well known for his friendship with Tiberius and his subsequent disgrace, used to give recitations of his works. He was particularly fond of including descriptions of sunrises and sunsets; so when somebody once complained that he had been reciting for a whole day and that his recitations were not worth attending, Natta Pinarius remarked 'Here's a generous offer: I'm ready to listen to him from sunrise to sunset.'

12. When Montanus had recited these verses:

"Phoebus begins to show his fiery flames,
  The rosy day to spread; the plaintive swallow
  Begins her journeys to and fro, with gentle beak
  To feed shrill nestlings, giving each its share,"

Varus, a Roman knight and a pal of Marcus Vinicius, a frequenter c

quas inprobitate linguae merebatur, exclamavit 'incipit Buta dormire'.
13. Deinde cum subinde recitasset

      iam sua pastores stabulis armenta locarunt,
      iam dare sopitis nox pigra silentia terris
      incipit,

idem Varus inquit 'quid dicis? iam nox est? ibo et Butam salutabo'.
    Nihil erat notius hac eius vita in contrarium circumacta; quam,
14. ut dixi, multi eodem tempore egerunt. Causa autem est ita vivendi
quibusdam, non quia aliquid existiment noctem ipsam habere iucundius,
sed quia nihil iuvat solitum, et gravis malae conscientiae lux est, et
omnia concupiscenti aut contemnenti prout magno aut parvo empta
sunt fastidio est lumen gratuitum. Praeterea luxuriosi vitam suam esse
in sermonibus dum vivunt volunt; nam si tacetur, perdere se putant
operam. Itaque aliquotiens faciunt quod excitet famam. Multi bona
comedunt, multi amicas habent: ut inter istos nomen invenias, opus est
non tantum luxuriosam rem sed notabilem facere; in tam occupata
15. civitate fabulas vulgaris nequitia non invenit. Pedonem Albinovanum
narrantem audieramus (erat autem fabulator elegantissimus) habitasse se
supra domum Sex. Papini. Is erat ex hac turba lucifugarum.
'Audio' inquit 'circa horam tertiam noctis flagellorum sonum. Quaero
quid faciat: dicitur rationes accipere. Audio circa horam sextam noctis
clamorem concitatum. Quaero quid sit: dicitur vocem exercere.
Quaero circa horam octavam noctis quid sibi ille sonus rotarum velit:
16. gestari dicitur. Circa lucem discurritur, pueri vocantur, cellarii, coqui
tumultuantur. Quaero quid sit: dicitur mulsum et halicam poposcisse,
a balneo exisse. "Excedebat" inquit "huius diem cena." Minime,
valde enim frugaliter vivebat; nihil consumebat nisi noctem.' Itaque
Pedo dicentibus illum quibusdam avarum et sordidum 'vos' inquit
'illum et lychnobium dicetis'.
17.   Non debes admirari si tantas invenis vitiorum proprietates: varia
sunt, innumerabiles habent facies, conprendi eorum genera non
possunt. Simplex recti cura est, multiplex pravi, et quantumvis novas
declinationes capit. Idem moribus evenit: naturam sequentium faciles

good dinners which he earned by his scathing tongue, called out 'And

13. Buta begins to sleep.' Shortly afterwards when Montanus had recited:
'The herdsmen now have put their beasts in stalls,
Now sluggish night begins the sleepy world
To quieten,'
Varus also remarked: 'What's that? It's night now? I'll go and pay my morning call on Buta.'

Everyone was familiar with Buta's inverted life—style, which, as

14. I've said, many of his contemporaries also adopted. The reason why certain people live like this is not that they think that night in itself has superior attractions, but that nothing conventional appeals to them, and daylight is oppressive to a bad conscience, and to someone whose grounds for desiring or despising anything is whether it costs a lot or a little, the idea of having free light is repugnant. What's more, self—indulgent people like their way of living to be a topic of conversation during their lifetimes: if they're not talked about they consider they are wasting their time. That's why every now and then they do something to make themselves notorious. Lots of people squander their property, and lots of people keep mistresses. To acquire a reputation among that crowd you have to do something not just dissipated but really conspicuous: in such a pre—occupied society as ours ordinary vice isn't talked about.

15. We once heard Albinovanus Pedo, a most urbane raconteur, telling the story of how he had lived above Sextus Papinius, the latter being one of this tribe of daylight—exiles. 'About nine o'clock at night I hear the sound of whipping. I ask what he's up to and I'm told he's going through his accounts. About midnight I hear loud shouting. I ask what's happening and I'm told he's exercising his voice. About two o'clock I ask what the sound of wheels means:

16. I'm told he's going for a drive. About daybreak there's a flurry of activity, a summoning of slaves, an uproar among stewards and cooks. I ask what's happening and I'm told he's finished his bath and has demanded his honey—wine and porridge. "So his dinner," it could be said, "extended beyond the limits of his day." Not at all; for he lived very frugally, and consumed nothing but the night.' Hence Pedo's quip, when some people were saying that Papinius was avaricious and mean, 'You'll be calling him a liver by lamplight as well.'

17. You shouldn't be surprised to find so many singularities among vices: they are manifold, they have innumerable aspects, and they cannot be classed. Concern for the right is simple; concern for the wrong is varied and admits of any number of fresh forms. The same is true of character: those who follow nature have straightforward and uncomplicated characters, showing only minor differences; warped

sunt, soluti sunt, exiguas differentias habent; [his] distorti plurimum et
18. omnibus et inter se dissident.   Causa tamen praecipua mihi videtur
huius morbi vitae communis fastidium.   Quomodo cultu se a ceteris
distinguunt, quomodo elegantia cenarum, munditiis vehiculorum, sic
volunt separari etiam temporum dispositione.   Nolunt solita peccare
19. quibus peccandi praemium infamia est.   Hanc petunt omnes isti qui,
ut ita dicam, retro vivunt.   Ideo, Lucili, tenenda nobis via est quam
natura praescripsit, nec ab illa declinandum: illam sequentibus omnia
facilia, expedita sunt, contra illam nitentibus non alia vita est quam
contra aquam remigantibus.   Vale.

18. characters are mostly at variance both with themselves and with everyone else. But to my mind the main cause of this disease is disdain for a normal life. Just as these people cut themselves off from the rest of us by the way they dress, by the refinement of their dinners, and by the elegance of their carriages, so they aim to isolate themselves even in the disposition of their timetable. Those who aim at notoriety as the prize of their excesses are not interested in ordinary excesses — and notoriety is what all these people want who

19. are, as it were, living in reverse. And so, Lucilius, we ought to stick to the path which nature has laid out for us and not deviate from it. If we follow it, all is easy and straightforward; if we struggle to go backwards, life is just a constant rowing against the stream.

COMMENTARY

LETTER 7

Seneca warns Lucilius of the moral dangers of associating with crowds and illustrates his point with an experience of his own, when he unintentionally attended a revolting gladiatorial exhibition.

This avoidance of mass–contact is not inconsistent with the Stoic ideal of public service (Epictetus gave a similar warning, *Diatr*. 3.16), and it must be distinguished from Epicurean quietism, though there are superficial resemblances. Seneca is here talking about the positive advantages of allowing time for philosophical retirement, *secessus*, which Lucilius should use for contemplation and self–improvement, and the theme is alluded to elsewhere in the Letters and in the treatises *De Otio, De Ira* and *Naturales Quaestiones* (see references below). The scathing attack on the gladiatorial contests shows an attitude which is not, of course, characteristic of the ancient world, though it is rightly compared with a famous letter of Cicero (*Fam*. 7.1.), attacking the butchery of man and beast which occurred at the games celebrating the opening of Pompey's theatre in 55 B.C. S. reveals a similar feeling towards the arena at *Brev. Vit*. 13.6–7, and it seems of a piece with the humanitarianism towards slaves we find expressed in 47. Gibbon approved, and, referring to 7, remarked 'Seneca shews the feelings of a man': *Decline and Fall*, Chap. 30 (Bury ed. Vol III, p. 259).

1. **you ask me:** as often S. suggests an occasion for the letter in a question or comment of Lucilius (see Introd. p. 2). The sequence of letters on the subject of crowds continues with 8, which is S.'s reply to Lucilius' reply to 7.

   I will confess: S. constantly advises Lucilius from the standpoint of one who is himself a more advanced *proficiens*, or Stoic trainee, battling for moral self–improvement. The phraseology here recalls *Tranq*. 17.3 'conversatio dissimilium bene composita disturbat'. Gray remembered this letter in his own letter to Wharton of 11 Dec. 1746: 'Seneca says (and my Pitch of Philosophy does not pretend to be much above Seneca) numquam... ... redit.'

   invalids... ... spiritual illness: S.'s frequent use of medical metaphors and the comparison of moral with physical failings is an inheritance from the diatribe tradition, and from thinkers as diverse as Plato (*Gorgias* 480 b) and Epicurus (fr. 221 Us.) For another characteristic Senecan use see *Ira* 1.15.1 'corrigendus est itaque qui peccat... ... sine ira; quis enim cui medetur irascitur?' See also 104.18, 115.6.

2. **associating with crowds...:** the same thought in *Ira* 2.8.1 '(when you see a large crowd) hoc scito, istic tantundem esse vitiorum quantum hominum', and *NQ* 4a pr. 3 'fac ergo, mi Lucili, quod facere consuesti: a turba te, quantum potes, separa'. S.'s point here,

stressed by the verbs *commendat, imprimit, adlinit, subrepunt*, is our unawareness of the damage done to us when part of a crowd.

3. **inhuman... ... humans:** the paradox is a favourite with S. (115.3 'in homine rarum humanitas bonum', 90.45, 95.33), and it illustrates one kind of verbal play in which Silver Latin delighted.

   midday show: it is not clear what sort of spectacle S. expected to find. The morning show consisted of fighting against wild animals (cf. 70.20), which was a sufficiently brutal spectacle; but as it turned out the midday interval show was far worse, exhibiting condemned criminals forced to fight without defensive armour until they killed each other. Unlike S. the emperor Claudius enjoyed this brutality (Suet. *Claud.* 34), and as we are told here the spectators usually rated it above the regular gladiatorial matches (*ordinariis paribus*) and the special star turns (apparently the meaning of *postulaticiis*).

4. **what's the point of:** *quo* is frequently used elliptically like this with an appropriate verb understood, e.g. *Tranq.* 9.4 'quo innumerabiles libros...?' and Hor. *Ep.* 1.5.12 'quo mihi fortunam...?'.

   fire and steel: this seems to mean that reluctant combatants were prodded back into the arena by swords and brands until they were killed at last in the fights. The idea is developed in the exhortation below to some games official: 'Occide, verbera, ure... Plagis agatur in vulnera.'

5. **'But', you say:** the imaginary objector or interlocutor (whether or not to be identified with Lucilius) appears constantly in the Letters. This is a device inherited from the tradition of declamation, the ethical diatribe and the Platonic dialogue, and was constantly used by Horace, for example, in his *Satires* and *Epistles*, where, as in S.'s Letters, it varies and enlivens the stylistic tone and helps the argument along with greater vividness.

   evil examples recoil: a recurring moral adage in S.: 81.19 'sicut mala exempla recidunt in auctores', *Tro* 870—1 'ad auctorem redit/sceleris coacti culpa', *HF* 735—6, *Thy* 311.

6. **Socrates or Cato or Laelius:** all three are standard *exempla* in the Letters (in this selection see 24, 104, 122). This Cato is probably Cato 'the Censor' (234—149 B.C.), whose strict moral code was proverbial; but his great—grandson Cato of Utica is also referred to several times. Laelius, nicknamed Sapiens, was a close friend of Scipio Aemilianus and consul in 140 B.C.

7. **malice:** for *rubigo* (literally 'rust') in this sense see Statius *S.* 1.3.103 'liventem satiram nigra rubigine turbes', Martial 12 pr. 14.

8. The argument that one should avoid hatred is interesting and perceptive, and S. elaborates it elsewhere. In *Ira* 1.14 he remarks that it is dangerous to hate *errantes*, as we must then end up by hating ourselves; in *Tranq.* 15.2 he argues that all faults should be regarded as laughable rather than hateful.

The sentence *neve similis... ... dissimiles sunt* is a good example of the kind of complex balance and antithetical word—play of which S. is so fond, and which reflects the mannered style of his age: cf. 104.26.

retreat into yourself: given as an Epicurean maxim at 25.6; see also 56.12, *Ot.* 1.1.

9. **readings and lectures:** the readings would be of Lucilius' own writings, the lectures on philosophical topics. In 19.3 S. claims that these talents of Lucilius have already made him well known: 'in medium te protulit ingenii vigor, scriptorum elegantia'. These glimpses of Lucilius' character and interests show the basis of the strong bond between the two men.

you acquired it for your own: the view of some later Stoics was that at least we should not parade our knowledge: see Epictetus *Ench.* 23, Marc. Aur. 10.9. But was S. also having a dig at Nero? According to Suetonius (*Nero* 20) he used to justify his musical recitals by quoting a proverb to the effect that a hidden musical talent went unregarded.

10. **three excellent sayings:** S. regularly rounds off the letters in the first three books with a quotation, often from Epicurus: see Introd. p. 3 and 12.11, 24.22. He refers lightheartedly to these tags as a payment Lucilius expects with each letter (*in debitum* and *antecessum* here, *peculio* 12.10), a financial metaphor of a kind very common in the Letters, e.g. 21.11, 25.3, 28.9, 36.5, 81.17, 118.1, 119.1.

Democritus: the fifth—century atomist philosopher: he reappears in 79.13, 90.32.

The three quotations all make the point that the value of praise or appreciation from others depends on their discernment and not on their numbers. We find this attitude expressed also by Antimachus, who according to Cicero (*Brut.* 191) said 'Plato mihi unus instar est centum milium', and by Heraclitus (fr. 49 D—K: to me one is as good as ten thousand if he is first—rate). It is a short step from this to the conclusion that the opinion of the majority is in fact worthless: 'ut contemnas... ... venientem' here, 99.17 'populo... ... nullius rei bono auctori', *Vit. Beat.* 2.2 'vulgo veritatis pessimo interpreti'.

12. **let your good qualities face inwards:** because they should be satisfying your own standards, not impressing the world: cf. *Prov.* 6.5 'non fulgetis extrinsecus, bona vestra introrsus obversa sunt'.

LETTER 12

A visit by S. to his country estate prompts reflections on the fact that he is growing old. But old age has its own pleasures and consolations, and we should face death with a cheerful fatalism, and treat each day as if it were the end and consummation of our life.

Moralizing on old age and death was of course common coin among philosophers and cut across distinctions of schools. We know, for example, of lost treatises on old age by the Peripatetics Theophrastus and Demetrius of Phalerum (Diog. Laert. 5.43 and 81), and we have Cicero's attractive discourse *De Senectute*. It is a repeated theme in Horace (appearing also in Epicurus) that we should not worry about or try to see beyond to−morrow: see below for detailed references. The important point is that S. is here characteristically adapting to himself and imparting to Lucilius some stock arguments of consolation and commonsense used by a wide variety of writers. He himself was probably in his 60s when he wrote the Letters, and we must remember that in antiquity people on the whole aged sooner and died younger.

1. **my country place:** we know of two of S.'s villas, at Nomentum and at Albanum (each about 14 miles from Rome): 104.1, 110.1, 123.1.

2. **venting my spleen:** in similar terms Cicero mentions to Atticus the bad temper arising from feeling one is growing old: 'amariorem enim me senectus facit. stomachor omnia.' (*Att.* 14.21.3). Resemblances to Cicero's letters to Atticus have an added interest if we bear in mind the possible influence that correspondence may have had on S.'s Letters (Introd. p. 1).

   shrivelled... wretched... rough: S. is a landed proprietor, and he uses words which are technical or semi−technical when applied to plants or land: see 86.18, and *OLD* on *retorridus* a, *tristis* 8, *squalidus* 3.

   my guardian spirit: each man's Genius (and each woman's Iuno) was an inborn attendant spirit who looked after the individual's desires and presided over his fortunes, much like our 'guardian angel': in Horace's words, 'Genius, natale comes qui temperat astrum,/naturae deus humanae... (*Ep.* 2.2.187−8). It was conventional when making a strong appeal, especially to a master or social superior, to call upon his Genius as the most divine element within him: Hor. *Ep.* 1.7.94−5 (an appeal to a *patronus*) 'te per Genium dextramque deosque Penatis/obsecro', [Tib.] 3.11.8, and commonly in Petronius and the Comedians.

3. **that old fossil:** S. sees an ancient figure in the doorway of the villa (perhaps acting as *ianitor*) and makes an elaborate joke, comparing him to a corpse laid out for burial in the conventional position with the feet facing the exit (*foras spectat*, for which the standard parallels are Homer *Il.* 19.212, Persius 3.105). *alienum mortuum tollere* has a proverbial ring, and similar phrases are quoted from

Petronius 54 'alienum mortuum plorare', *Clem.* 2.64 'alienis funeribus gemitus'.

toy figures: these *sigillaria* were little figures in pottery, conventionally given as presents during the festival of the Saturnalia (Martial 14.182, Suet. *Claud.* 5). By reminding the mortified S. of them and by using the diminutive *deliciolum* Felicio stresses that he was at least not older than S. The word (and *delicium* below) may suggest that they were sexual playmates too.

losing his teeth: S. indulges in a similar joke at 83.4.

4. **fruit are sweetest:** for this thought Summers quotes Shakespeare, *Richard II* 2.1.12 'The setting sun, and music at the close,/As the last taste of sweets is sweetest last.'

5. **on the brink:** the metaphor seems to continue the picture suggested by *devexa* and *praeceps*: here old age has slipped to the edge of a tiled roof (*tegula*), but not yet fallen to oblivion.

    their place is taken...: a very Senecan paradox: see 18.10 'summa voluptas est posse capere etiam ex his (bread and water) voluptatem', 90.34, *Prov.* 6.5 'non egere felicitate felicitas vestra est'; but Cicero used it too: *Sen.* 47 'non caret is qui non desiderat: ergo hoc non desiderare dico esse iucundius'.

6. **the register:** the *census* was the censors' register of citizens, who were classified as *seniores* and *iuniores*. The idea that death is no respecter of youth is stressed elsewhere by S.: 26.7, 63.14, *Rem.fort.* 4.1 (where the phrase 'non citamur ex censu' also occurs).

    lifetime... ... concentric circles: this patterning of the divisions of a human lifetime seems unique to S., and the sections are an odd blend of the phases of human growth and decay and the calendar divisions of solar and lunar time. The point is that each is a complete cycle in itself. His six stages were not canonical: Solon (fr. 19) suggested ten; Hippocrates *Hebd.* 5 (like Shakespeare) seven.

7. **Heraclitus:** a celebrated philosopher from Ephesus who flourished c. 500 B.C. He regarded fire as the archetypal form of matter, and he viewed the universe as an apparent equilibrium concealing an underlying tension of elements which were in a state of ceaseless change and interaction. The nickname S. refers to was ὁ σκοτεινός ('The Dark One'): he earned it by the notorious obscurity and ambiguity of his aphorisms, of which the one quoted here (fr. 106 D–K) is a typical example. S.'s own use of a similar concept to 'One day equals all' can be seen at 101.9: 'stabilita mens scit nihil interesse inter diem et saeculum'. On Heraclitus see Kirk–Raven–Schofield, *The Presocratic Philosophers*, 181 ff.

    The translation assumes that some word like *alius* (Gemoll) has fallen out between *enim* and *parem*. There is a more serious textual problem at the end of the section, for which different supplements have been proposed. I have translated what seems to be the general sense of the sentence, assuming that *ista* refers to day and night.

8.   **every day... ... our life:**   a conventional thought which is amplified below (9).

   Pacuvius: legate of Aelius Lamia, governor of Syria who was not allowed by Tiberius to take up his duties.   Pacuvius therefore acted as his proxy, and is thus said to have acquired rights over Syria by occupation (*usucapio*).   See 88.12 for *usu*, and for the facts, Tac. *Ann*. 2.79, 6.27.

   celebrated his own death: the verb here alludes to the Parentalia, a festival in honour of the family dead held on February 13−21.   The most famous parallel to this bizarre performance is in Petronius (78), when the drunken Trimalchio invites his dinner guests to observe an impromptu rehearsal of his own funeral.   For people who unwittingly anticipate their deaths see 122.3: 'mortem timent, in quam se vivi condiderunt?... ... iusta sibi faciunt'.   The chant βεβίωται may have been a common Greek 'tag', as we find Cicero using it in his letters to Atticus (12.2.2, 14.21.3).

9.   The quotation is from Virgil *Aen*. 4.653 (Dido just before her suicide), and is used also at *Vit. Beat*. 19.1.   S. might also have quoted Horace, *C*. 3.29.41 ff. 'ille potens sui/laetusque deget, cui licet in diem/dixisse "vixi"...'.   The thought is a favourite of Horace (see also *C*. 1.9.13, 1.11.8 (with Nisbet−Hubbard's note for other parallels), *Ep*. 1.4.13−4, 1.11.22−3), and of S. himself (93.6, *Thy* 619−20), who was no doubt familiar with Epicurus' remark (fr. 490 Us.), that the man who has least need of the morrow approaches it with the most pleasure.

10.   On   S.'s   habit   of   ending   with   quotations   and   on   *peculio* ('money−allowance', 'pocket−money') see 7.10 n.   The quotation is from Epicurus, but the thought and S.'s commentary on it are in tune with Stoic teaching on suicide as under certain conditions a justifiable way of escape from an intolerable life.   See on 24.11 and 24.   Similar sense and phraseology are found in 51.9 'ego illam (fortunam) feram, cum in manu mors sit?', *Phoe* 153 'mille ad hanc (mortem) aditus patent', *Ira* 3.15.4, Lucr. 3.940−3.

11.   **somebody else's property:**   S. frequently and unashamedly admits to borrowing from the founder of the rival school (2.5, 14.17, 22.13), and as frequently defends his practice by stating that Epicurus' aphorisms are not exclusively his, but common property (8.8, 21.9, 33.2: cf. *communia* here).   S. was no partisan Stoic ('non enim me cuiquam emancipavi, nullius nomen fero' 45.4), and he shows a genuine, if qualified, respect for and understanding of Epicurus: 28.9, 33.2, *Vit. Beat*. 12.4.   Epicurus had the gift for stating universal truths memorably and was worth quoting.

   swear allegiance: the full phrase can be seen in Hor. *Ep*. 1.1.14 'nullius addictus iurare in verba magistri'.

LETTER 24

Lucilius is worried about a troublesome lawsuit and S. writes to offer advice on how to face this trouble and anxieties generally. But his suggestions are not on the lines he has taken before, that Lucilius should hope for the best and not anticipate troubles: rather he must picture to himself the worst that could happen and be ready for that. A series of examples (Rutilius, Metellus, Socrates, Mucius, Cato) show what extremes of endurance are possible — even death is not to be feared. S. makes no excuse for using many traditional and well—worn themes and *exempla* here: the important thing is for Lucilius to take it all in and act accordingly, so giving the lie to the charge that philosophers deal only in words (15).

There are several points of resemblance between this letter and 110.

1. **lawsuit:** we cannot tell if this was real or an invented pretext for the letter, and it does not really matter. If the latter S. is again keeping up the semblance of a genuine correspondence.

    view the future...: this was the advice given in 13.4−5 (cf. 74.33), but this time S. proposes to tackle the problem from the opposite angle. Lucilius must imagine the worst eventuality and gird himself to face it. As this requires a tougher mental approach, the implication is that Lucilius has made some advance in his philosophical schooling and can now take this treatment.

2. **either not great or not long lasting:** in this respect the object of fear is like pain: see 14 below.

3. **philosophical maturity:** S. frequently uses *profectus* (for the Greek προκοπή) in the almost technical sense (not noted by *OLD*) of the philosophical or moral progress made by the *proficiens*: see 11.1, 20.1, 33.7, 72.9, 95.36, 100.11, 115.18, *Const. Sap.* 17.3.

4−6 The listing of *exempla*, well—known historical or legendary individuals who offer patterns of behaviour or salutary warnings, was a well established technique in the traditions of rhetoric, the *consolatio*, and the diatribe. S.'s moral treatises and letters and the Latin satirists (notably Juvenal) made much use of the device, and there were favourite illustrations who crop up repeatedly in different contexts. The *exempla* in our letter are conventional: Rutilius, Mucius, Socrates and Cato all reappear together at *Prov.* 3.4; Rutilius, Socrates and Cato at *Cons. Marc.* 22.3 and *Tranq.* 16.1.

   P. Rutilius Rufus was a pupil of the Stoic Panaetius, a legate of the Metellus mentioned below, and consul in 105. In 92 at a politically instigated trial he was convicted of extortion when governing the province of Asia and went into exile, living as an honoured citizen at Smyrna. Q. Metellus Numidicus, consul in 109, was forced into exile by his political enemies Marius and Saturninus in 100, but managed to return a year or two later. The story of C. Mucius Scaevola (see Livy 2.12−13, with Ogilvie's notes) was one of the most cherished legends which the Romans preserved from the time of the war with the Etruscan Porsenna about the end of the sixth century. S. gives the salient details of the story: Mucius unflinchingly burnt his right hand because he had failed to kill Porsenna — and to show Porsenna the spirit of the other three hundred Romans who had also sworn to kill him. Socrates' arguments for refusing to escape from prison are recounted at length in Plato's *Crito* 48 c ff. (see also Xen. *Apol.* 23). For Cato see also 7.6 n.: this is the younger Cato ('Uticensis'), who committed one of the most famous suicides in history. He was in charge of the Pompeian troops at Utica on the North African coast, and after Caesar defeated the Pompeians at Thapsus in 46 B.C. he killed himself. His suicide and the uncompromising high principles by which he lived his life qualified him in the eyes of Stoics as one of the very few who had achieved the status of *sapiens*.

6. **'these stories... ... rhetorical schools':** such *exempla* played a large part in the training in declamation, as S.'s father's collections of exercises bear ample witness. At this point in the letter it is indeed S.'s intention to come to death as an escape from evil, and one which we need not fear: the theme is developed in 11 ff. below. Meanwhile he treats the *exemplum* in detail so as to stress the important motive in Cato's noble action — that no one but himself should decide whether he lived or died.

    decantatae suggests wearisome repetition, as at Cic. *de Orat.* 2.75 'Graeco aliquo doctore qui mihi pervulgata praecepta decantet', Hor. *C.* 1.33.2−3 'neu miserabilis decantes elegos'.

    Plato's dialogue: the *Phaedo*, according to Plutarch (*Cat. Mi.* 68), in which Plato recorded Socrates' discourse on the immortality of the soul, and his death.

8. **let forth/cast out:** the same verbal contrast between *emittere* and *eicere* is found at 110.8, where S. compares the deaths of the unhappy and the happy man.

9. **Scipio:** Q. Metellus Scipio commanded the Pompeian forces when they were defeated at Thapsus (see note on 4−6: Cato). He was descended from a famous family, two of whom had served with great distinction in the wars against Carthage: Scipio Africanus Maior (236−184/3), and Scipio Aemilianus Africanus Numantinus (185/4−129), who finally destroyed Carthage in 146.

11. ff. From here on S. concentrates on death, which is not only not to be feared itself but sets us free of all other fears ('adeo mors... .. timendum sit'), since suicide offers the ultimate escape. cf. 12.10, 30.6 'mors adeo extra omne malum est ut sit extra omnem malorum metum', and on 24 ff. below. The only thing fearful is fear itself, and if we can but see through the appearance of things our fears may dissolve (13). We come back to the point of the letter, Lucilius'

lawsuit, in 12 and 16 (*istam sollicitudinem*), but the advice widens to cover life's worries in general.

14. The effect of this powerful section is achieved by the vivid apostrophes to death and pain, and by S.'s linguistic virtuosity in describing the horrors of torture and other forms of physical agony. But pain faces us all, and it is either bearable or short—lived. This was a famous and much quoted maxim of Epicurus: see *Kuriai Doxai* 4, *Ep. Men.* 133, fr. 447 Us.; but another Stoic, Marcus Aurelius, has the same thought (7.33, perhaps also from Epicurus); and see also Aesch. fr. 352N, and other Senecan uses of the adage at 30.14, 78.7, 94.7.

15. **practical proof:** S. anticipates the objection that he is uttering common—places by agreeing that he is saying nothing new: what matters is for Lucilius to act on it and disprove the charge against philosophers that they are all words and no deeds. (On this theme see 20.2, 108.35, *Vit. Beat.* 20.1.) Practical action for Lucilius is not to give way to depression over his worrying lawsuit, and to adopt the right attitude to the pains and distresses that are a condition of our existence. Particular examples of disasters follow in 17, with appropriate responses drawn from the tradition of the consolation. Even death is shown to bring its blessings, as the section closes with the pungent tricolon *desinam... desinam... desinam...*

18. **Epicurean refrain:** one of the great lessons of Epicurus was that men need have no fear of either the gods or death, since the gods are indifferent to us and there is nothing beyond the grave. This teaching was elaborated in Lucretius' *De Rerum Natura*, where at 3.976 ff. the poet, making the same point as S. that punishment after death need not be feared, suggests that the stories about the famous sinners suffering forever are simply symbols of men's evil passions during their lives. S. repeats the message elsewhere (82.16, *Cons. Marc.* 19.4), as does Cicero (*Tusc.* 1.10, *ND* 2.5): both imply that most people did not believe the old stories anyway, but presumably there were vague residual fears of post mortem horrors which could be assuaged philosophically by reference to the familiar legends.
death either destroys us or sets us free: some Stoics at least believed in the survival of the soul, though different souls would survive for different lengths of time: see 57.7 n. But either way we need not worry, as neither good nor evil will affect us. (Similarly 36.9—10, 71.16, 93.9—10.)

19. **your own verse:** another reference to Lucilius' literary activities (7.9 n.): S. slyly hints that Lucilius knows all this anyway.

22—23. Once more the quotable Epicurus summarizes S.'s arguments for him (cf. 7.11, 12.10—11): here he berates the stupidity of planning suicide for the wrong reason, boredom rather than contempt for life (*taedio vitae*: so *fastidium/ odium* in 26).

makes the same point: *nota* is literally a brand or stamp which classifies something: see *OLD* s.v. 5 c for this kind of extension of the meaning.

24. **reason persuades us to end our lives:** for orthodox Stoics there were three types of condition which justified a suicide according to reason (εὔλογος ἐξαγωγή: the technical term): (1) when circumstances prevented a man living his life in accordance with nature (e.g. intolerable pain); (2) when death was required by obligations to one's country or friends; (3) when one would otherwise be compelled to say or do disgraceful things. S.'s own views have been subject to much scholarly debate, but he does seem to have accepted a fairly wide range of circumstances which would justify it. The letters are remarkably full of thoughts on suicide, and it is not hard to imagine that at the time they were written he could foresee a situation in which it would be a real issue for himself. For Stoic views on suicide and S.'s in particular see J.M. Rist, *Stoic Philosophy*, 233−55; M.T. Griffin, *Seneca, a Philosopher in Politics*, 372−88.

25. **a brave and wise man:** the ideal Stoic, who knows how to face life and death — the ideal which Lucilius will himself realize if he follows the advice in this letter.

26. **boredom with it:** the *taedium vitae* of 22. The futile repetition of the daily round is a commonplace (77.6, *Tranq.* 2.15, *Brev. Vit.* 7.9), but the depression it can lead to is real enough, and it is the achievement of the *vir fortis ac sapiens* that he would not suffer from it, and would certainly not end his life even if he did.

<u>LETTER 47</u>

S. praises Lucilius for his humane treatment of his slaves, and defends such kindness on the grounds that slaves are our fellow−humans, that the early Romans treated their slaves decently and gave them privileges, and that at any time we ourselves may become slaves to someone or something.

This letter is rightly regarded as showing a creditable humanitarianism in S., and it is indeed much warmer than most earlier discussions of slavery, which, even when they recommended fair treatment for slaves, usually did not go beyond their basic rights. Aristotle in the *Politics* (1255 a 2−3) argued that slavery is a 'natural' condition; and the pseudo−Aristotelian *Oeconomica* (1344 a 29 ff.), while asserting that slaves should be treated fairly and offered the prize of freedom, speaks of the slave's life as one of work, punishment and food. The Athenian in Plato's *Laws* (777 d) stresses that slaves ought to be treated decently, though he stated earlier (757 a 1) that slaves and masters could never be friends. The agricultural writers Cato (*RR* 5.2 and 142) and Columella

(1.8.17–18) prescribe a fair allowance of their material needs (food, clothes, warmth) – a realistic attitude, of course, in view of the tough work required of country slaves. The early Stoics seem to have been lukewarm. Their physical theories would have entailed the natural equality of men, and that therefore slavery has no basis in nature, but no strong humanitarian principles seem to have emerged from this. According to S. (*Ben*. 3.22) Chrysippus defined a slave as a permanent hireling, 'perpetuus mercennarius', and Cicero (*Off*. 1.41), accepting this, concludes that he should in fairness be treated like one: 'operam exigendam, iusta praebenda'. Later on Epictetus (*Diatr*. 1.13.3–4) takes the Senecan line that our slaves are our brothers; and S.'s own views reappear consistently at 31.11, *Cons. Marc*. 20.2, *Clem*. 1.18, *Ira* 3.35, *Ben*. 3.21. But despite the injunctions of philosophers and theorists there was clearly much ill–treatment of slaves, at least in Rome and Italy. Otherwise there would have been little force in S.'s harangue, and no point to the innumerable references in Roman Comedy to beatings and general ill–treatment of slaves. At the same time Comedy also gives us glimpses of the devotion which slaves could feel towards the family who owned them, so that there must always have been other masters like Lucilius, however small a minority they formed. (For a good discussion of Stoic and Senecan views on slavery see M.T. Griffin, *Seneca, a Philosopher in Politics*, Chap. 8 and Appendix E.)

1.   **your culture:**   it is an important point that Lucilius' *eruditio*, his philosophical learning, suits his attitude to his slaves.

'They are slaves'...:   the rapid–fire repetition of imaginary objection and response gets the letter off to a lively start. The objector is not, of course, strictly Lucilius, who shares S.'s views.

3.   **even to speak:**   at *Ira* 3.35.1 S. points out the inconsistency of a man's complaining of the loss of liberty in the state when he curbs this liberty of speech at home. Several writers stress the freedom of speech enjoyed by slaves at Athens, e.g. Demosthenes *Phil*. 3.3, [Xen.] *Ath*. 1.12, and Plutarch explicitly comments on the advantage the Athenian slave had in this respect compared with the Roman slave (*De Garrulitate* 511 e).

all night: S. is fond of using the ablative (*nocte tota*), instead of the accusative, to express duration of time. It is found occasionally in Republican Latin, and more freely from the Augustan period onwards: see E.C. Woodcock, *A New Latin Syntax*, 37–8; K–S I 360–1.

4.   **face execution:**   S. quotes an actual example of a slave doing this at *Ben*. 3.25, using the same phrase 'stretch out the neck' for execution.

5.   **the common proverb...:**   it is quoted as a proverb also by Festus (p. 314 Lindsay). See also Otto, *Sprichwörter* s.v. 'servus', for related *sententiae* in Greek and Latin.

one slave... another...:   these unpleasant tasks of the table slaves are referred to at *Brev. Vit*. 12.5, where skill in poultry–carving is also mentioned: it was clearly an important feature in entertaining, as we see in Juvenal's account of Virro's ostentatious banquet (5.120—4).

7. These unfortunates whose duties alternate between table and bed are referred to again at 95.24: 'puerorum infelicium greges quos post transacta convivia aliae cubiculi contumeliae expectant'; see also 122.7.

8. **earn them another invitation:** just as the *parasitus*, the professional hanger—on, of Roman Comedy earned his dinners by his entertainment value, and Varus in 122.12 won his invitations 'improbitate linguae'. The modest eater and polite talker is a dull guest.

   masters... from these ranks: the anecdote about Callistus which follows illustrates one of the many ex—slaves who under Claudius and Nero worked their way up to positions of power, and often became a by—word for parvenu arrogance. Callistus was a freedman who achieved great influence as a political schemer under Gaius and then Claudius (Tac. *Ann.* 11.29, 38; 12.1—2). He became very wealthy, and the threshold his former master tried to cross was presumably the entrance to his splendid dining—room which Pliny the Elder refers to (*HN* 36.60).

9. **a job lot:** *reicula* is Muretus' convincing conjecture for the MSS *ridicula*, meaning 'rejected as worthless'. The words 'in primam decuriam... experitur' further stress the wretched quality of the consignment which included Callistus.

   apologavit is an adaptation of the Greek ἀπολέγω, apparently unique but perhaps currently used in commercial speech.

   cost him dear: the full construction would be 'domino quam multa Callistus constitit' (see *OLD* s.v. 'consto' 11).

10. **perhaps you should:** *vis* is regularly used like this, with a wide range of emphasis from polite suggestion to strong exhortation.

    your slave comes from the same seed: this was Epictetus' view too (see introductory note), and it is a statement consistent with the Stoic belief that all men have a share of the cosmic *pneuma*.

    Varus: P. Quinctilius Varus was legate of the Rhine army in A.D. 9, when he was trapped and his three legions totally destroyed by the Cheruscan chieftain Arminius in the Saltus Teutoburgiensis (Dio Cassius 56.18—22, Vell. Pat. 2.117—20). The Romans remembered the disaster with horror for generations afterwards. Since our sources suggest that the Roman slaughter was total, S. may be bending the facts to draw his moral; or he may have read another account that some of them escaped.

    distinguished birth... military service: in the imperial era apart from special nominees of the emperor only sons of senators could become senators, and they began their preliminary training for entry into the senate by serving for a year in the army as *tribuni laticlavii*.

    if you can: this translates *nunc*, which often introduces ironically a suggestion made ridiculous by some previous statement of the speaker: see *OLD* s.v. 10 b.

11. **topic:** a *locus* or *locus communis* (hence 'commonplace') was a rhetorical term for a general treatment of a subject, not restricted to a particular use. S. does not want to enter on a discussion of the wider abstract ramifications of his theme, but to advise Lucilius in plain practical terms about his day—to—day treatment of his slaves.

12. We have here the familiar list of *exempla* to underline an argument. Hecuba was the elderly consort of Priam when she was enslaved after the sack of Troy, and she became like Priam a byword for the tragic fall of the once rich and mighty. Croesus was the last king of Lydia, being defeated and over—thrown in 546 B.C. by Cyrus, ruler of the Persians. The mother of Darius III was Sisygambis: she was captured when Darius was defeated by Alexander at the battle of Issus in 333 B.C. There are several anecdotes relating that Plato was sold into slavery. The main tradition records that it happened in Aegina while he was returning from his first trip to Sicily in 387 B.C.: see Diog. Laert. 3.19, Diod. Sic. 15.7, Plut. *Tranq. An.* 471 e, Jerome *Ep.* 53.1 (whose version states that Plato was captured by pirates). Diogenes the Cynic too was the subject of a similar tradition. He was reported to have been captured and auctioned by pirates, but he remained in command of the situation and himself told his captors the man to whom he should be sold: Diog. Laert. 6.74, Plut. *Tranq. An.* 466 e, *An vitiositas* 499 b.

13. **kissing the hands:** in order to win their support in gaining favours from their influential masters: cf. *Ben.* 3.28 'negas tibi a servo tuo beneficium dari posse, cui osculum alieni servi beneficium est?'.

14. **they called the master...:** S. makes the same point by implication at *Ira* 3.25.2: 'et loquatur (servus) et taceat et rideat. coram domino? inquis: immo coram patre familiae'. In fact *familiares* meaning slaves survived rather more widely than in the mimes S. mentions: see *OLD* s.v. 1 b.

    a holiday: the Saturnalia (beginning on December 17), the most uninhibited festival in the year, when amidst the general jollification slaves were given temporary freedom to do as they liked. So Horace invited his slave Davus to 'enjoy the liberty of December' and speak his mind (*Sat.* 2.7.4—5). See 12.3 n.

15. **slavish qualities... respectable men:** the thought reverses the familiar 'evil communications corrupt good manners' of Euripides (fr. 1024 N), Menander (fr. 218 K), and St Paul (1 *Corinthians* 15.33). Here Lucilius' table will provide an improving influence for those who need it.

16. **purchaser... horse itself:** S. uses the same illustration in 80.9, as does Horace, more flippantly, in *Sat.* 1.2.86 ff. (choose your women as you would choose your horse).

17. **pantomime — dancers:** *pantomimi*, dancers who acted traditional stories in dumb show, first appeared in Rome in 22 B.C. Their performances became highly popular and they themselves attracted a devoted following among their audiences, rather like modern pop stars. The subjects and style of their entertainments were often regarded as demoralizing to the public, and there were rowdy encounters between partisans of rival artists: see Tac. *Ann.* 1.77 for attempts by the senate to deal with the problem in A.D. 15. Referring to the popularity of the *pantomimi* at *NQ* 7.32 S. tells us that they gave private lessons to both men and women, who competed in learning immodest dances. For a brief general account of the subject see *OCD* s.v. 'Pantomimus'.

18. **freedom for slaves:** the *pilleus* was a felt cap worn by slaves on being set free, and *vocare ad pilleum* was a technical phrase for manumission.

    love and fear cannot go together: the same thought is varied at 123.16: 'superstitio error insanus est: amandos timet'; and Cicero says there is no place for friendship in the tyrant's life: 'quis enim aut eum diligat quem metuat... ?' (*Amic.* 53).

19. **words... beatings:** the Latin illustrates a typically Senecan word — play, *verborum/ verberibus* — one of the hallmarks of the declamatory style (see Summers, lxxxii ff.).

    exactly please our fancy: *respondere* on its own can mean 'to turn out as one wished' (*OLD* s.v. 10 a), so here *ex voluntate* adds strong emphasis.

20. **pride of tyrants:** from the days of the early kings of Rome *rex* was regularly a dirty word to the Romans, suggesting tyrannical arrogance; and behind S.'s phrase also lies the unscrupulous tyrant as a stock figure in the exercises of the schools of declamation.

LETTER 54

An acute attack of asthma induces thoughts of death, but S. comforts himself with the reflection that non — existence after death is no different from non — existence before birth.

Apart from his asthma S. seems by his own account to have been a martyr to various forms of ill — health for most of his life. In *Cons. Helv.* 19.2 he mentions with gratitude the loving care of his aunt which saw him through a long bout of illness as a child. In the Letters there are several allusions to his disorders, either incidentally or with the purpose of drawing a moral lesson: 65.1 (an unspecified ailment); 78.1 (chronic catarrh); 77.9 (fainting fits); 104.1 (a fever). Dio Cassius (59.19) records that only the report that S. was dying of consumption (perhaps his asthma) saved him from the fatal malice of the emperor Gaius.

There are many discussions of asthma in medical writers from the ancient world, the earliest apparently being an Egyptian medical papyrus (the Ebers papyrus of c. 1550 B.C.), which has been interpreted as specifying remedies for asthma. It is mentioned in the Hippocratic writings (fifth/fourth centuries B.C.), and Celsus (early first century A.D.) classified it with other forms of breathing difficulty; but it was Aretaeus of Cappadocia (late second century A.D.) who first recognized asthma as a separate condition and gave a detailed clinical description of it. For further details and discussion of all this see R. Ellul—Micallef in *British Journal of Diseases of the Chest* 70 (1976) 112—16.

It was an important Epicurean doctrine that there is nothing after death (and therefore we need not fear it): see Epicurus *Kuriai Doxai* 2, *Ep. Men.* 125. The refinement on this argument which S. advances here, that the conditions after death and before birth are equivalent, is not found explicitly in Epicurus' surviving writings but clearly derives from him, and it appears in works which are based on Epicurean thinking: [Plat.] *Axiochus* 365 d; Lucr. 3.830—42, 972—7; Cic. *Tusc.* 1.90—1. S. uses the argument elsewhere at 77.11 'haec paria sunt: non eris nec fuisti; utrumque tempus alienum est'; *Cons. Polyb.* 9.2; *Tro* 407—8. In our own time a greater mind than S.'s thought similarly: towards the end of his life Einstein wrote in a letter, 'there is no risk of any accidents to one who is dead or not yet born'. (Quoted by Banesh Hoffmann, *Einstein*, Paladin Books, 1975, p. 261.)

1. **respite:** *commeatus* is properly 'official leave', 'furlough'. the transferred sense here may be a colloquialism, as we find it in a letter of Cicero, *Att.* 13.41.2.

   its Greek name: the learned S. deprecates the need to make a display of learning, so he refers to ἄσθμα as *suspirium*. He makes the same point more elaborately at *Tranq.* 2.3: no need to use the Greek term εὐθυμία when he can say *tranquillitas*, for 'res ipsa de qua agitur aliquo signanda nomine est, quod appellationis Graecae vim debet habere, non faciem'.

2. **'rehearsal for death':** S. must be giving a wry and heartfelt twist to a commonly quoted dictum of Socrates, that the wise man regarded life as a practice or rehearsal for death: Plato *Phaedo* 67 d, 81 a; Cic. *Tusc.* 1.74; and elsewhere in S. at 26.10, *Brev. Vit.* 7.3, *Cons. Marc.* 23.2.

3. **gasped for breath:** S. uses a technical medical term: see *OLD* s.v. *suffocatio*.

4. **long ago:** *diu* by itself in this sense (for *iam diu, diu est quod,* and the like) is fairly rare and perhaps colloquial: see *OLD* s.v. 1 e.

6. **so long as... .. emotional ones:** literally 'so long as I am not really, or genuinely, sighing'. S. is punning on two meanings of *suspirare* and *suspirium*, 'breathing heavily' and 'sighing' as a symptom of emotional turmoil, which would be unbecoming the tranquillity of the

sapiens. Thus in Cic. *Tusc.* 4.72 the wise man is allowed to love if it is 'sine sollicitudine, sine desiderio, sine cura, sine suspirio'. (See also 57.3 n.)

7. **never assume a full day:** cf. *Cons. Marc.* 10.4 'nihil de hodierna nocte promittitur', and the similar thought at 12.9.
    the man: S. generalizes, as he is certainly not saying that life is still sweet for himself. But he claims at least some merit for his own attitude to imminent death ('est et hic virtus'). On the other hand at 78.2 he tells us that though worn out by illness he made himself go on living — which was in the circumstances an act of courage.
    he escapes necessity: one of many formulations of the Stoic wise man's tranquillity, which he achieves by understanding and living his life voluntarily in conformity with Nature's decrees: cf. 61.3 'quidquid necesse futurum est repugnanti, id volenti necessitas non est'.

LETTER 56

S. describes the noisy uproar he can hear in his lodgings from the public baths below him. However this does not bother him: turmoil around us is of no concern to the tranquil mind, and conversely there is no true peace and quiet unless we have inner calm and our passions are under control. (See also Letter 55 for this theme.)

The idea of tranquil mental detachment has been common to many philosophical creeds, and S. has used it to compose a lively letter with an amusing twist at the end ('I'm going to move'). The description of the noisy baths and the types who frequent them is vivid and well observed, and offers fascinating details for the social historian of the period. We have here a vignette of Italian life which is comparable to the pictures we see in Petronius, especially the episode of Trimalchio playing ball before his bath (27—8).

1. **I can't for the life of me:** literally 'may I die if'. *peream si* and similar expressions (*dispeream si, inteream si*) are colloquial, being found for example in letters (Cic. *Fam.* 8.15.2, 15.19.4) and Horace's *Satires* (1.9.38, 47; 2.1.6).
    I live...: presumably in lodgings he took while visiting Baiae.
    hearty types... dumb—bells: S. did not disapprove of physical exercise in moderation, as he makes clear in Letter 15, where he actually mentions the use of weights or dumb—bells ('cum aliquo pondere manus motae' 15.4) as the sort of activity which can give you a lot of exercise in a short time — but it is exercise of the mind that is really important.
    game—scorer: the *pilicrepus* appears to have kept the tally of balls which were thrown or caught in the game of 'catch' called *trigon*. This is implied in the description of Trimalchio's game (see

introductory note), at which a eunuch 'numerabat pilas, non quidem eas quae inter manus... vibrabant, sed eas quae in terram decidebant', suggesting a variation of the usual method of scoring. Private baths as well as public ones had an area for ball−games, the *sphaeristerium* (Pliny describes one in his own villa, *Ep.* 2.17.12, 5.6.27), as this was a regular form of exercise before bathing. For details of the *trigon* game see Daremberg−Saglio, *Dictionnaire des Antiquités*, IV 477.

2. **brawler:** *scordalus* is a rare and colloquial word (also at 83.12). It means 'behaving like a game−cock', being derived from Greek σκόρδον, garlic, with which game−cocks were fed before fighting. We meet some of the other pests S. complains of elsewhere in Latin literature. Bath thieves were notorious (Plautus *Rud.* 382−5, Cat. 33.1, Petron. 30) − to such an extent that special penalties were decreed for them in the *Digest* 47.17, while at Athens this crime carried the death penalty ([Arist.] *Problems* 29.14). The man who liked the sound of his voice was either singing or reciting aloud his own or others' compositions, as we hear much about this habit too: Petron. 73, 91; Martial 3.44.12; Hor. *Sat.* 1.4.75−6 (where the reason given is that the echoes in the baths are good). Theophrastus listed singing in the bath as one characteristic of the boorish man (*Char.* 4.13).

the depilator: plucking the arm−pits was regarded as routine hygiene, e.g. it is implied among Ovid's injunctions to young men to make sure they are nice to be near (*Ars* 1.522). This seems to be the only occurrence of *alipilus* apart from an inscription. *biberarius* (if the reading is right), *botularius, serrarius* and *pausarius* below are similarly unique.

3. **Chrysippus:** *nostrum* indicates that this must be the famous Stoic philosopher (c. 280−207 B.C.: the third head of the Stoa) but the story is otherwise unknown.

I don't care... ... waterfall: there is a very similar declaration of his indifference to noise at 83.7, where he regards it 'pro fluctu ... ... aut vento silvam verberante'.

a people... ... Nile cataract: S. repeats this at *NQ* 4.2.5 (part of a dramatic description of the Nile cataracts), and Ammianus similarly reports it (22.15.9). Cicero (*Rep.* 6.19) and Pliny (*HN* 6.181) say that the noise of the cataracts caused deafness in those living nearby.

4. **the man who tunes horns:** 'horns' translates Gruter's conjecture *tubulas* for the obscure *tabulas* of the manuscripts. But Summers' *tubulos* (waterpipes) ... ... *ut tibias* is attractive: the man is testing the ducts of the fountain (to see if they are clear) as if they were reed−pipes − but the resulting racket is not in the least musical. This interpretation gives a neat explanation of the reference to the fountain, which in our text must be taken as just a landmark giving the whereabouts of some dealer in musical instruments. The Meta

Sudans must have been a conical fountain in Baiae of a type we know from the remains of one which survived in Rome until 1936, just south–west of the Colosseum: see Platner–Ashby, *A Topographical Dictionary of Ancient Rome*, II 340–1; and for another view of the passage J.M. May in *CQ* 37 (1987), 240–3.

5. **the boatswain's hoarse cry:** this must have been a notorious nuisance to the sensitive: in praising a friend's villa built up on the Janiculum Martial lists among its advantages that you cannot hear the *nauticum celeuma* from the Tiber (4.64.21).

    what is the good ... ?: a commonplace thought, e.g. 55.8 'non multum ad tranquillitatem locus confert: animus est qui sibi commendet omnia'. The quotation is from the *Argonautae* of the first century B.C. poet Varro Atacinus (fr. 8 Morel), who was here adapting Ap. Rhod. 3.749–50.

6. **a virtuous mind can unwind:** for a similar use of *explicare* see 65.16 '... animum qui gravi sarcina (the body) pressus explicari cupit'.

8. **rest is restless:** *quies inquieta* is an oxymoron of a common type, whether or not the elements of the phrase are cognates as here. The mannerism appealed to the sophistication of Silver Latin style, and for similar examples in S.'s treatises see *Tranq.* 12.3 'inquietam inertiam', *Brev. Vit.* 12.2 'desidiosa occupatio'.

9. **great generals:** S. might be thinking of Alexander the Great: according to Curtius Rufus (7.1.4) Alexander was 'satis prudens otii vitia negotio discuti' — but the similar phrasing of the idea there also suggests that it may have been proverbial. The *otii vitia* here are of course to be distinguished from the praiseworthy kind of *otium* which is devoted to the study of philosophy and is the subject of the treatise *De Otio*. With *discuti* ('dispelled') S. as often uses a medical metaphor (*OLD* s.v. 3 b): for other examples of the word see 55.2 and *Ben.* 6.8.1 (both literal), and 28.1 'non discussisti tristitiam gravitatemque mentis' (metaphorical).

11. **in retirement:** *otiosi* in the laudable philosophical sense (see previous note), the state in which we acquire *cogitationes bonas, solidas... .. certas*.

    and yet: S. rather affects this slightly adversative use of *et* in the sense of *atqui* (*OLD* s.v. *et* 14 a), e.g. 57.1, 63.1, 78.3, *Med* 135.

    if we have sounded the retreat: for the use of this metaphor in a similar context see Cic. *Tusc.* 3.33 'vetat igitur ratio intueri molestias, abstrahit ab acerbis cogitationibus... ... a quibus cum cecinit receptui...'.

    as I said: in section 5 above.

12–14. **detachment:** the advice he gave Lucilius in 7.8 (see note there). The quotation is from Virgil, *Aen.* 2.726–9, where Aeneas is making a perilous journey of escape through the streets of Troy while the triumphant Greeks are burning and plundering it: he is carrying his father on his shoulders and leading his son by the hand. The elaborate parallel S. draws is firstly, between the earlier intrepid Aeneas (referred to in the first two lines) and the *sapiens* who is impervious to startling sounds; and secondly, between the present fearful Aeneas and the *inperitus*, the man who has not yet learnt philosophy's lessons. The *sarcinae* ('burden') are his father and son in Aeneas' case, and the disquieting cares of the *imperitus*: the link is made explicit with *trahentibus/portantibus*. (*sarcinae* is used in a very similar metaphor in 44.7: 'sollicitudinis colligunt causas et per insidiosum iter vitae non tantum ferunt sarcinas sed trahunt'.)

14. **lulled to rest:** the translation assumes that *compositum* here picks up *composta* (in the quotation) and *composuit* in section 6 – but the repetition may be coincidental.

15. **I'm going to move:** S. comically sabotages the whole moral lesson of the letter: this particular *proficiens* could only manage to test himself for a time before taking an easier solution. Ulysses protected his companions from the seductive song of the Sirens by stopping their ears with wax (Homer, *Od.* 12.173−7). S. refers to the story to make a different point at 31.2 ('sapiens eris si cluseris aures, quibus ceram parum est obdere: firmiore spissamento opus est quam in sociis usum Ulixem ferunt'), and see 88.7 for another use of the Ulysses legend.

LETTER 57

In this letter Seneca records an unpleasantly dark and dusty journey through a tunnel. This leads to reflections on the nature of the irrational shocks and aversions which even the bravest people are subject to, and these thoughts lead in turn to a strong affirmation of the immortality of the soul.

1. **return to Naples from Baiae:** on the journey to Baiae Seneca tells us in 53 that he was agonizingly sea−sick: hence his anxiety now to avoid a second voyage. Baiae was the most fashionable holiday resort for well−to−do Romans, but it had a bad reputation for immorality, as Seneca tells us elsewhere (51) – and other writers bear him out (Cic. *Cael.* 35, Suet. *Nero* 27).

   and yet: cf. 56.11 n.

   anointment/sand−dusting: the translation tries to preserve a rather involved play on words in the Latin. Seneca compares his successive experiences of mud and dust with two stages of a wrestler's preparations for a bout: rubbing himself over with oil for suppleness and then sprinkling himself with sand to make gripping possible. For this practice see Ovid *Met.* 9.35 ff., Statius *Theb.* 6.847 ff., Lucian *Anacharsis* 1−2. *ceroma* and *haphe* are Greek loan words naturalized in Latin. They belong to the vocabulary of gymnastics, a typically Greek activity.

the Naples tunnel: part of the alternative land route by which Seneca could avoid the longer sea voyage around the coast. This tunnel, now called the *Grotta Vecchia*, was built under Augustus to facilitate the journey between Naples and Puteoli. It is long since closed but two other famous travellers visited it and recorded their impressions. In 1343 Petrarch saw it and remembered this letter of Seneca (*de rebus familiaribus* 5.4.6: quoted by Summers); and three centuries later John Evelyn travelled through it — and he also commented on the excessive dust there (*Diary* for 8 February 1645). Petronius (fr. 16) reported that people had to duck their heads to go through the tunnel.

2. **longer/prison ... gloomy/torches:** the words are juxtaposed in the original (*carcere longius, facibus obscurius*) to underline the paradoxical expressions, so characteristic of Silver Age Latin: a prison is usually cramped and lights usually dispel darkness — but not here.

3. **mental shock and confusion:** Seneca chooses his words carefully, excluding fear here and *perturbatio* below (6). As a Stoic he would be unwilling to admit to suffering from a deep—rooted mental or emotional disturbance (*pathos*): the experience is more a 'thrill' or mild 'frisson' of horror, *mutatio* perhaps suggesting a feeling of alienation or losing one's bearings. See also 54.6 n.

a perfect one: this refers to the Stoic ideal human being, the *sapiens* or the true *vir bonus*, who by endless striving and philosophical contemplation has achieved a life—style which is entirely in harmony with reason. Thus by definition he has no inclination to go wrong, and so too he is no longer a plaything of Fortune. The Stoics themselves admitted that examples of the *sapiens* in history were extremely hard to find (Cato the Younger for his life and his celebrated suicide at Utica was allowed to be a rare instance): nearly all disciples of the school were *proficientes*, novices attempting with varying success to make progress towards the ideal. This is the stance which throughout the Letters Seneca adopts for himself and for Lucilius. (For similar disclaimers see 87. 4—5, summing up his present condition as 'parum adhuc profeci'; *Cons. Helv.* 5.2; *Ben.* 7.17.1.) In spite of the extremely rare appearance of this philosophical phoenix his character and qualities were much discussed, e.g. by Seneca himself (besides the Letters) in *De Constantia Sapientis* and *De Providentia*: the latter treatise argues that no evil can afflict the good man, which is in line with the statement in our letter that Fortune no longer controls him.

even his mind: the *sapiens* himself experiences reactive physical and mental jolts (though by definition not *timor*), so *a fortiori*, as the next two sections illustrate, even the bravest people suffer from quite irrational shocks and physical reactions. The word translated 'courage', *virtus*, covers a range of moral qualities as well — goodness, integrity, highmindedness. Seneca suggests that those who embody such qualities receive in this way intimations of bodily mortality (though the individual *anima* is not subject to death: sections 7—9).

4—5. Even in the comparatively relaxed style of a letter there is a certain formal artistry in the grouping of the illustrations of instinctive revulsion: three examples — a comment on the nature of the reactions — three more examples (all involving blood).

6. **not ... a serious disturbance:** as before (note on 3) Seneca is implicitly careful to characterize his feeling as consistent with his philosophical stance.

the same end awaits us all: the thought lodged increasingly in Seneca's mind in his last years, as other occurrences in the Letters reveal: 'mors quidem omnium par est. per quae veniunt diversa sunt: in quod desinunt unum est' (66.43); '(ratio) nos docet fati varios esse accessus, finem eundem, nihil autem interesse unde incipiat quod venit' (70.27). Even closer to our letter is the remark in another work from this period of his life, the *Natural Questions*, in a discussion about the particular fear people have of dying in an earthquake: 'tamquam non omne fatum ad eundem terminum veniat ... nihil itaque interest utrum me lapis unus elidat an monte toto premar' (*NQ* 6.1.8—9).

watch—tower: this seems to be the only literary occurrence of *vigilarium* (the other instances are in inscriptions: *OLD* s.v.), so the exact nature of the structure must remain uncertain.

7. **do you imagine ...:** Summers thought there was something wrong with this section because there is not a strict logical connection with the preceding sentence 'erunt ... spectat', and because there is no other evidence that the Stoics held this belief about the soul. However, we should not always expect logical tidiness in the loose texture of a letter: Seneca takes up the new thought of the soul's survival which has an associative link with the last paragraph of a heavy weight crushing out life. Regarding the theory alluded to, the Stoics certainly believed that the soul was released from the body at death. Souls were in origin portions of the *pneuma*, the fiery breath pervading all the cosmos, and therefore they survived death, some of them lasting until the *ekpyrosis*, the universal conflagration which ended and renewed successive cycles of creation. (See Diog. Laert. 7.156—7, Cic. *Tusc.* 1.77, F.H. Sandbach, *The Stoics* 82—3.) So if our text is sound Seneca must refer to a qualified version of the Stoic view (elsewhere unrecorded) which applied to this particular form of death and from which he strongly dissents. Yet he himself is not always consistent. We find other statements in line with our letter,

e.g. 24.18 'mors nos aut consumit aut exuit. emissis meliora restant onere detracto...', several of them occurring in the Consolations, understandably in view of their purpose (*Cons. Marc.* 23.1, 24.5, 25.1, 26.7; *Cons. Polyb.* 9.3). But elsewhere when it suits his argument death is seen as final extinction, without mention of a surviving soul (54.4—5, 77.11, 99.30).

8. **flame ... air:** these analogies are naturally suggested by the Stoic conception of the soul as a portion of the fiery air, *pneuma*, which pervaded the universe. This derivation of the soul accounts for its extremely rarefied texture (*tenuissimo, subtilitatis*).

    it returns through a tiny opening: the thunderbolt was generally believed to depart skywards after striking (Xenophon *Mem.* 4.3.14, Pliny *HN* 2.142), and Seneca adds this same detail at *NQ* 2.40: (one type of bolt) 'per id foramen quod ingressum est redit'.

9. **be sure of this:** the argument is that if the soul is exempt from the death of the body (as it is) it is exempt from any death, since we cannot attach any reservation (*exceptione*) to immortality. The words 'propter quod non perit' should be either transposed to follow the clause 'si ... corpori' (Préchac) or deleted as an intrusive gloss on that clause (Summers).

LETTER 78

S. sympathises with Lucilius during an illness and offers some thoughts on how we can face the pain and the disruption in our lives which are caused by illness.

This letter has features in common with 24, which also offers consolation to Lucilius, and with 54, in which S. also tells us about his own bad health. It is indeed S.'s hypochondria at least as much as his sympathy for Lucilius which prompts the detailed series of arguments which should induce the right attitude to illness. These are the thoughts 'quae mihi tunc fuerint solacia' (3), and he deals with the problems of illness under three heads (6): fear of death, physical pain, and interruption to our pleasures. The three topics are not treated very systematically — fear of death (4—6, 25—27), pain (7—10, 12—19), interrupted pleasures (11, 22—24) — but this broken up sequence of themes suits the unstructured character of a letter. The arguments of consolation which S. offers are traditional (for example, Panaetius wrote a letter *de dolore patiendo* (Cic. *Fin.* 4.23), and Cicero devoted the second book of his *Tusculans* to the same topic); so S. as usual is giving a lively turn to unoriginal thoughts, which he claims at least to have personally tested.

1. **I too suffer:** for S.'s varied ill health see introductory note to 54. The severe catarrh he here complains of suggested one of his many medical similes at 75.12: (repeated indulgence in undesirable mental

impulses leads to permanent vices) 'sicut destillatio una nec adhuc in morem adducta tussim facit, adsidua et vetus pthisin'.

2. **my most loving father:** a similar feeling for family sympathy appears at 104.2, where S. says that he looks after himself out of consideration for his wife. Seneca the Elder died in his nineties around A.D. 40.

an act of courage: similarly in 54.7 S. claims 'est et hic virtus' when he faces death in the right way.

3. **and yet:** see 56.11 n. for this sense of *et*.

4. **handing it on to them:** this was the thought which, according to Tacitus, S. left with his friends when he was actually about to die. He said that the one thing, and the best, which he could bequeath to them was the pattern of his life, 'imaginem vitae suae' (Tac. *Ann.* 15.62).

5. **breathing tubes and receptacle:** the arteries, according to ancient medical theory, as S. himself tells us at *NQ* 3.15.1: (in our bodies) 'et venae sunt et arteriae, illae sanguinis, hae spiritus receptacula'.

stimulate your internal organs: *concutere* is a medical term, as we see from its use in Celsus (e.g. 3.21.12 'concutiendumque multa gestatione corpus est'). S. uses it similarly at 15.6, recommending a drive in one's carriage as a change from poring over books, since 'gestatio et corpus concutit et studio non officit'; and at 55.2 he takes a tiring drive: 'mihi tamen necessarium erat concutere corpus' in order to clear himself of catarrh.

6. S. here gives a rough summary of the themes of the letter, which are not, however, followed through in formal sequence (see introductory note). Death is now for the time being dismissed with a few remarks on the stock consolation theme that it is inevitable.

feeling that death was near...: this piquant thought is found also at *Tro* 489—90 'haec causa multos una ab interitu arcuit, / credi perisse'.

7. The consoling thought that severe pain cannot last long is one to which S. often returns: see 24.14 n.

intermissions: the same word *intervalla* is used of S.'s asthma attack at 54.6.

8. **vital force:** *spiritus* here is the life force or vital energy, the non—corporeal part of the body, which distinguishes the animate from the inanimate. It is also the individual's share of the Stoic *pneuma*, as defined by S. himself at 41.2: 'sacer intra nos spiritus sedet, malorum bonorumque nostrorum observator et custos'.

eliminate themselves: *elidere* is another medical term (like *alienatio*, 'numbness' 9, *refectio*, 'convalescence' 17), used of driving out a disease, as at Hor. *Ep.* 1.15.6, and regularly in Celsus (*OLD* s.v. 4a).

9. **a sharp pain:** *verminatio* is a strong but rare word, used also by S.

at 95.17 of a sharp headache.

10. **the unphilosophical:** as usual in S. *inperiti* has the almost technical sense of people who are not strengthened and comforted by (Stoic) philosophy. They are contrasted with the *vir magnus ac prudens*, another way of defining the advanced *proficiens* who knows the relative values of his mind and his body.

11. This section on pleasures we are forced to forego briefly interrupts the discussion of pain, which resumes at 12, and S. returns to pleasures at 22.

    objects somebody: the use of *inquit* without a stated subject to introduce an objection reflects a similar mannerism with non—specific φησί in Greek diatribes. (See also 20 below and 88.11.) The technique dramatizes and enlivens a homily, and was popular in many sermonizing contexts, e.g. Hor. *Sat.* 1.3.126, 1.4.79. (See Lejay's notes on both these passages, and Summers on 28.8.) We also of course have the frequent use in the Letters of quoted objections without *inquit* or any similar verb, as at 7.5, 47.1, 56.15, where the editorial quotation marks simply clarify what is obviously a countering point.

12. S. returns to pain with the admonitory *adice quod... adice quod...* and the play on words *intermittitur/ remittitur* (cf. 14 below).

13. **thinking about it:** S. is realistic in condemning the habit of increasing our troubles by false beliefs about them (this is implied by *opinio*, the Greek δόξα); and he makes the same point forcefully elsewhere: 13.4 'plura sunt, Lucili, quae nos terrent quam quae premunt, et saepius opinione quam re laboramus'; 42.10 'scies non damnum in iis molestum esse, sed opinionem damni'; *Const. Sap.* 5.2. It is a natural argument too in the repertoire of the consolation: *Cons. Marc.* 7.1, 19.1.

14. **what was bitter...:** a good example in the Latin of the crisp antitheses of meaning and tense which are possible in an inflected language: *acerbum/ iucundum, fuit/ est, ferre/ tulisse.*

15. This celebrated quotation is from Aeneas' speech of encouragement to his shipwrecked followers (Virg. *Aen.* 1.203). It is the most familiar statement of a commonplace thought which goes back to Homer (*Od.* 15.400—1) and Euripides (fr. 133 N): see Austin's note ad loc. S. produced his own version at *HF* 656—7 'quae fuit durum pati/meminisse dulce est'.

16. **athletes:** this is a popular comparison in which the toughness and stamina shown by athletes and prizefighters is adduced to strengthen a moral injunction to make some effort ourselves: see 80.3, *Prov.* 2.3, *Ira* 2.12.5, 2.14.2, Cic. *Tusc.* 2.40—1. This section has been seen by some scholars (e.g. Summers) as a likely source of the spurious correspondence between S. and St. Paul, presumably by comparing it with such passages as *I Corinthians* 9.24—7. But a direct link here

seems tenuous, though any imagery which was seen to be common to S. and the apostle would have helped to strengthen a supposed association between them. (See Introduction p. 5.)

17. **lets us off:** *donat* has here the sense (quite common in Silver Latin) of 'forego', 'waive a claim to', like *condono*: the disease is said to release us for long intervals during which it might have made us suffer.

18. **the nôble rôles:** for *partes* used of the theatre of life see 14.13 'ultimas partes attigi Catonis', *Ben.* 1.2.4 'partes boni viri exsequere'.
    the very thing which angered them: if we read *hoc* (not *ob hoc*: see Apparatus) it is an internal accusative with *irati* ('angered over this precisely'). It is a rare construction with this verb, but cf. Cic. *Att.* 15.17.1 'nihil irascor'. In general when a verb takes an internal accusative it is often, as here, a neuter pronoun or adjective (K−S I 279−80).

19. **or worse...:** in passing from physical ailments to the agony of torture S. is indulging the declaimers' taste for describing this sort of horror. We know from his father's collection of *Controversiae* (e.g. 2.5.3−6) that detailed descriptions of beatings and mutilation by torturers were one of the rhetorical exercises in linguistic virtuosity, and S.'s own considerable talent for this shows here (as in 24.14). The heroic fortitude of the victim was one of the stock features of these descriptions.

20−21. These sections are a slight digression in which S. deals with the complaint that illness interrupts our *officia*. His answer is that our minds can still be active during physical ailments, and that in fact illness provides a challenge to the mind to prove its mettle under suffering.

21. **courage even in the sick−bed:** cf. *Rem. fort.* 6.1 'non in mari tantum aut in proelio vir fortis apparet: exhibetur etiam in lectulo virtus'.

22−24. S. resumes (from 11) the theme of pleasures we are supposed to be deprived of during illness. His arguments are that only physical, not mental, pleasures are affected; that in fact the enjoyment of eating and drinking is increased by enforced abstinence; and that we gain the benefit of learning to eat moderately and to do without a surfeit of luxurious food ('cenabis... aliquando tamquam sanus' 24).

22. **there is more enjoyment...:** similarly in Plato's *Gorgias* 496 c−d Socrates makes a careful distinction between the painful states of hunger and thirst and the pleasures of eating when hungry and drinking when thirsty.

23. **melt snow into his wine:** in the absence of more sophisticated methods of refrigeration this was a common device for cooling wine: *Prov.* 3.13, *Ira* 2.25.4, Athen. 3.124d, 125c. The connoisseur Martial has several references to the practice: 5.64.1−2, 12.17.6, and (very

close to our context) 6.86.1–2 'Setinum dominaeque nives densique trientes,/quando ego vos medico non prohibente bibam?'.

Lucrine oysters: these were widely regarded as having the best flavour (Pliny *HN* 9.168) and they are often mentioned (e.g. Hor. *Epode* 2.49, Mart. 3.60.3, 5.37.3, Juv. 4.141–2). The Lucrine Lake from which they came was close to Baiae, so they would have been a local delicacy for S. himself on his visits to Campania.

cooks... bustling around: the bustle of busy kitchens typifies extravagant living elsewhere in the Letters: 114.26, 122.16.

our leathery palates: S. moralises in very similar vein at *NQ* 4b.13.10 'sed quid sentire possunt emortuae fauces et occallatae cibis ardentibus? quemadmodum nihil illis satis frigidum, sic nihil satis calidum est'.

24. **'What a pity...':** the repetition is ironical, as S. proceeds to point out that the result for the invalid will actually be a much healthier diet.

whole birds are now considered a vulgar sight: cf. 110.12 'luxuriae iam tota animalia fastidientis'.

25–27. S. returns to the fear of death (see 4–6) by way of the invalid and his food.

25. **the boundaries between good and bad things:** similarly at 44.6 the hallmark of a man who is truly *liber* is 'si mala bonaque non populo auctore distinxeris'. (This is the meaning of the phrase here, whereas *fines bonorum et malorum* as a recognised topic of philosophical enquiry, like Cicero's treatise of that name, means the extremes of good and evil in life.)

27. **even if it is premature:** S. frequently endorses the Stoic view that it is the quality of a man's life that matters, not its length. This is the theme of 93, and see also 70.4–5 'sapiens vivet quantum debet, non quantum potest... cogitat semper qualis vita, non quanta sit'; 77.20 'quomodo fabula, sic vita: non quam diu, sed quam bene acta sit, refert'; 92.25; 101.15; so too Cic. *Fin.* 3.46.

pleasures which are empty and therefore cannot be completed: another often repeated text is that the true requirements of nature are limited (as Epicurus also taught): 16.9 'naturalia desideria finita sunt: ex falsa opinione nascentia ubi desinant non habent; nullus enim terminus falso est'; *Cons. Helv.* 10.11 'cupiditati nihil satis est, naturae satis est etiam parum'.

28. **Posidonius:** Posidonius (c. 135 — c. 50 B.C.) was the most celebrated Stoic philosopher of his generation. He and his teacher Panaetius were the main representatives of the Middle Stoa, and they both introduced fundamental modifications to earlier Stoic theories. Posidonius taught and influenced Cicero, and S. many times quotes or refers to him: in the present selection of Letters see 83.10, 88.21, 90 *passim*, 92.10, 104.22. The protreptic remark quoted here is like the

paean to philosophy at Cic. *Tusc.* 5.5: 'est autem unus dies bene et ex praeceptis tuis actus peccanti immortalitati anteponendus'. The fragments of Posidonius have been edited by L. Edelstein and I.G. Kidd, *Posidonius: the Fragments*, Cambridge, 1972.

29.· **hang on to it:** *mordere* ('get your teeth into') is unusual in this metaphorical sense, but *tene... morde...* together mean exactly *mordicus tenere*, which Cicero favours in his philosophical works.

whatever you have expected...: a frequent injunction in the Letters and elsewhere: 76.35 'hic (sapiens) levia facit diu cogitando', 88.17, 107.4 'nemo non fortius ad id cui se diu composuerat accessit', 113.27, *Const. Sap.* 19.3 'omnia leviora accident expectantibus', *Tranq.* 11.6, *Cons. Marc.* 9.2.

LETTER 79

S. writes to Lucilius, who is on a tour of Sicily, asking him for a detailed account of Charybdis. He suggests that Lucilius would also enjoy making a scientific excursion to Mount Etna and including an account of it in a poem, as other poets have done whom Lucilius may want to emulate. With this theme of rivalry the letter shifts direction (8), as S. asserts that (in contrast with literature) wisdom and virtue do not involve rivalry: all who have achieved them are equal. Moreover (13) virtue is a joy in itself, and gains the rewards of fame though this may not come during our lifetime.

Lucilius' interest in natural phenomena is also suggested by the fact that S. dedicated the *Natural Questions* to him, but it is his literary talents which give this letter much of its interest. Firstly, the letter has been used as evidence in the long debate over the authorship of the *Aetna*, a didactic poem about the volcano, wrongly attributed to Virgil and of uncertain date, but probably written in the first century A.D. The reference in the letter to the Augustan poet Cornelius Severus may have led to the ascription to him of the poem in some fifteenth century manuscripts (accepted by Scaliger, 1572); while Lucilius himself has been put forward as a candidate for the authorship (Wernsdorf, 1785). All this is speculation, and both suggestions run into the difficulty that S. seems to be suggesting a virtuoso episodic treatment of Etna as part of a longer poem (*locum* 5: on the lines of Ovid's and Virgil's handling of the theme), whereas the *Aetna* is a full—scale poem of 645 lines. Secondly, sections 5—6 of the letter contain one of the most important statements we have of the Latin writers' attitude to their predecessors, and the principles which should be followed in treating topics which had been dealt with before. This was what literary 'originality' involved — tackling a theme which was not 'exhausted' but 'well prepared', and putting your own stamp on it so as to 'produce a new effect'. Thus S. clearly acknowledges and explains the relationship of the Latin writers with both their Greek models and their own forbears.

1. **your trip:** presumably an official tour of the island in connection with his duties as procurator.

 Charybdis, Scylla: in legend these were respectively a fearsomely dangerous whirlpool and a sea—monster inhabiting a cave, opposite to each other in the Straits of Messina. They are described with gusto by Circe to Odysseus at Hom. *Od.* 12.73—110, whence arose their proverbial application to a choice between two undesirable courses. Ovid, like S. here, rationalized Scylla as a rock, but one that *is* dangerous to sailors (*Met.* 14.73—4).

 one wind: the south wind called Auster was usually thought to activate Charybdis (14.8, *Cons. Marc.* 17.2, Ovid *Met.* 8.121).

 Tauromenium: a Greek city on the eastern coast of Sicily (now Taormina), about 30 miles from the straits. The geographer Strabo (6.2.3) has the same story, telling us that fragments of ships wrecked by Charybdis were washed up at Tauromenium.

2. **it is... .. gradually sinking:** Aelian (*VH* 8.11), arguing that decline and decay are a law of the natural order, instances the shrinking of mountains like Etna, Parnassus and Olympus. Accepting the sailors' reports about Etna S. impartially offers two suggestions to account for the phenomenon.

 the mountain... .. being consumed: the author of the *Aetna* argues emphatically that its fire is nourished by volcanic rock or lava—stone (*lapis molaris* 400 ff.). S. does not suggest what 'other material' the fire might feed on.

3. **Hephaestion:** Pliny the Elder also comments on the fires in this volcanic area of Lycia (*HN* 2.236, 5.100). They would have been caused by inflammable gases issuing from the crevices in the ground, so that feeding on these gases they did not consume the surrounding vegetation. The name Hephaestion derives from the local phenomenon, Hephaestus being the Greek god of fire.

4. **obsession:** *morbus* has here the softened sense of 'weakness' or 'failing' (*OLD* s.v. 3), like νόσος occasionally in Greek. The construction understands *curam* with *daturus*.

5. As a poet himself (see notes on 7.9, 24.19), living in Sicily and also having a strong interest in the world of nature, Lucilius could well have been keen to write about Sicily's most dramatic natural feature, and S. implies that he already has a poem on hand which could incorporate it. (This may be the poem of Lucilius from which S. quotes lines describing the river Alpheus coming to Sicily, *NQ* 3.1.1.) S. encourages the project, and urges Lucilius not to be deterred but encouraged by the fact that previous poets tackled the same theme. Lucilius' treatment of it can be interestingly different, and he can make his own original contribution to the literature on Etna. S.

makes a similar point about philosophical enquiry at 33.11: no need to imagine that other theories have precluded new and fresh speculations: 'qui ante nos ista moverunt non domini nostri sed duces sunt. patet omnibus veritas; nondum est occupata; multum ex illa etiam futuris relictum est'.

Virgil described Etna at *Aen.* 3.571−82, when Aeneas calls at Sicily on his journey westwards; and Ovid at *Met.* 15.340−55, where Pythagoras teaches that Etna like all natural things will change. The Augustan poet Cornelius Severus wrote an epic, *Bellum Siculum*, on the war between Octavian and Sextus Pompeius, 38−6 B.C., which might naturally have included a description of Etna. (See also introductory note.)

subject: *locus* is a topic or theme available for all to handle (cf. 47.11 n.).

6. **well prepared:** like ground properly dug or ploughed, the literal meaning of *subactam:* for the metaphor cf. Cic. *de Orat.* 2.131 'subacto mihi ingenio opus est'.

re−arrange to produce a new effect: cf. Horace's advice to writers on giving freshness to familiar words, *Ars.* 47−8 'dixeris egregie notum si callide verbum/reddiderit iunctura novum'.

(The bracketed words 'iurisconsulti... .. capi' are excluded as an intrusion from 88.12.)

7. This section is pivotal in the letter, as it introduces the idea of literary rivalry, which shifts to philosophical rivalry (8 ff.) and the rewards of virtue with which the rest of the letter is concerned.

making your mouth water: the Latin phrase, like the English, seems to be colloquial: a variation is found in Petronius (48.2).

lofty: *grandis* is a standard term in rhetorical writers for a lofty or exalted style: see 114.11, *OLD* s.v. 6.

your modesty: Lucilius' self−depreciation, real or pretended, appears elsewhere in the Letters: 43.1 'quid ergo? inquis, tantus sum ut possim excitare rumorem?'; 44.1 'iterum tu mihi te pusillum facis'.

8. Men can rival each other in their efforts to achieve wisdom but not once they have acquired it, as there is nowhere further to rise to. This criterion of the perfect state, and the formulation *non est incremento locus*, are found elsewhere: 66.9 'quid accedere perfecto potest?... crescere posse inperfectae rei signum est'; *Const. Sap.* 5.4 (discussing the wise man's *virtus*) 'in summum perducta incrementi non habent locum'.

they have come to a halt: this translates *statur*, which is strictly an impersonal passive singular ('there is a stopping'). This is a common construction, but it might be used here to add a generalizing force to the statement.

9. **natural gifts:** *dos*, literally 'dowry', is quite often used metaphorically of a personal quality or talent (*OLD* s.v. 3). These gifts admit of

comparison between individuals, but wisdom is an absolute at which all who have attained it are level — 'stata magnitudo est' (10).

11–12. There is another extended comparison at 102.28 of the light visible to our mortal eyes and the immeasurably greater light which will be visible to our soul after death. S.'s point here is that this revelation can be achieved even before death if we acquire the supreme *virtus* of wisdom.

restored to the heavens: the divine part of the body returns to its home, as explained fully at 102.22: 'cum venerit dies ille qui mixtum hoc divini humanique secernat, corpus hic ubi inveni relinquam, ipse me diis reddam'; cf. 44.1 'omnes, si ad originem primam revocantur, a dis sunt'.

its bodily prison: *custodia* (like *carcer*) is used of the body as the prison of the soul, e.g. *Cons. Helv.* 11.7, Cic. *Amic.* 14. See also 88.34: the idea derives from the Orphics (Plato, *Crat.* 400 c).

13 ff. The rest of the letter develops the theme which is summarized in section 18: 'nulli non virtus et vivo et mortuo rettulit gratiam': virtue is its own reward and delight, and whether the fame which will inevitably attend it comes before or after death does not matter. The usual string of *exempla* help to make the point, all of whom we have met before: Socrates, Cato of Utica and Rutilius in 24; Socrates and Democritus (for a quotation) in 7. (See notes on these letters). Our surviving sources on the whole attribute cheerfulness and fortitude to Democritus, rather than madness, and later antiquity christened him the Laughing Philosopher; but Hippocrates, *Ep.* 14 (Hercher) records that he was supposed to be mad because he could not stop laughing. The statement that Cato was only appreciated by his country after his death presumably alludes to the fact that he never achieved the consulship, but that he became a legend after his famous suicide and a symbol of republican ideals.

14. **enlightened conduct:** the translation assumes that *profectus* has its special sense of philosophical progress, which best suits the context: see 24.3 n.

15. **'lived unnoticed':** a reference to Epicurus' motto, λάθε βιώσας, the prescription for a quiet life withdrawn from the rat—race of political affairs.

Metrodorus: Metrodorus of Lampsacus was one of the most distinguished and devoted of Epicurus' disciples (Diog. Laert. 10.22). Epicurus' high regard for him was shown by his dedicating two works to Metrodorus, and leaving instructions in his will ensuring the welfare of Metrodorus' children. Many fragments of Metrodorus' own writings survive. S. refers to him several times, and at 52.3 he quotes Epicurus' own opinion that Metrodorus was not an original thinker but a good disciple.

17. At *Brev. Vit.* 15.4 also S. develops the thought that the sage's works

and influence survive him indefinitely, since envy is only for the here and now. (Note *invidia* in section 13, *malignitas* and *livor* here.) We find this idea elsewhere: Velleius Paterculus suggests that as a general rule 'naturaliter audita visis laudamus libentius et praesentia invidia, praeterita veneratione prosequimur' (2.92); and it is a stock complaint of writers that fame will not come to you until you are dead (Hor. *Ep.* 2.1.18 ff., Mart. 5.10, Pliny *Ep.* 1.16).

18. **pretence... truth...:** the same sermonizing lesson to Lucilius is found at 120.19: 'vero tenor permanet, falsa non durant'; and to Nero at *Clem.* 1.1.6: 'nemo enim potest personam diu ferre. ficta cito in naturam suam recidunt. quibus veritas subest, quaeque, ut ita dicam, ex solido enascuntur, tempore ipso in maius meliusque procedunt'.

LETTER 83

S. describes his daily round to Lucilius, the more willingly because it is always a good thing to review one's life. He then turns (8) to reflections on the sophistries of philosophers, like Zeno's argument against drunkenness which S. counters by illustrations and anecdotes from life. His own way to attack drunkenness is to expose the vices, wicked actions and disasters to which it leads, again using examples (17−26). Not even the sage is exempt from these dangers: he too must avoid drunkenness (27).

Here a question from Lucilius gives S. his cue to talk about his everyday routine (a natural topic for a letter), which is treated light−heartedly and in turn sets up the main reflective theme. S. adopts the stance of a pragmatic realist, attacking the abstract syllogisms of the philosophers (even the founder of his own school), and showing that if you look at real life things are different: 'instruenda est enim vita exemplis inlustribus' (13), and 'ostende rebus, non verbis' (27). This is the way to draw the practical moral lessons we can live by.

1. The notion that we should live as if the world were watching us appears also at 43.5: 'bona conscientia turbam advocat... si honesta sunt quae facis, omnes sciant...', though there it is not god but your own self−awareness which you cannot avoid.

   god... is present: a familiar precept: see 41.1−2 'prope est a te deus, tecum est, intus est. ita dico, Lucili: sacer intra nos spiritus sedet'. cf. 79.12 n.

2. **review my day:** at *Ira* 3.36 S. recommends a review each evening before bed−time of the day's activities to pass judgment on the *animus*, and specifically so that angry passions will be moderated during the day if they know they will be called to account at the end of it: 'quicquam ergo pulchrius hac consuetudine excutiendi totum diem?...' (when the lights are out and his wife has stopped talking)

'totum diem meum scrutor factaque ac dicta mea remetior.'

3—4. This passage is a pleasant example of S.'s light—hearted style, where he makes ironic fun of himself, and introduces us to one of his slave boys by way of enlivening the theme of his own declining ability to take exercise. We recall the conversation with the farm steward and Felicio in 12.1—3: there is even the same joke about losing teeth in youth and old age.

3. **tires me out... the limit of exercise:** similarly 15.4: 'sunt exercitationes et faciles et breves, quae corpus... lassent'.

4. **trainers:** S. adopts a pure Greek word, *progymnastes*, which is rare even in Greek (cf. *crisin* and *psychrolutes* below). The name Pharius suggests that the boy was Egyptian, in which case his quip may show a national characteristic: Quintilian (1.2.7) mentions the sauciness allowed by their owners to Alexandrian pet slaves.

I'll be changing him: *mutabitur* might also mean 'he will change', i.e. become less *amabilis*.

stage of life: *crisis* (again a Greek term, applied to the crisis of a disease) is a critical or turning point in life, a climacteric. Pharius is credited by S. with using a learned word.

5. **a dead heat:** *hieran*, transliterates ἱεράν (sc. νίκην), literally 'holy victory', a term applied to a drawn contest at the Greek games because the prize was given to a god (see *L—S—J* s.v. ἱερός 7). S. is again being facetiously learned.

cold bath enthusiast: S. may have invented *psychrolutes* (from ψυχρολουτεῖν, 'bathe in cold water'), and he applies it to himself also at 53.3 along with the phrase 'vetus frigidae cultor'. There was more than one canal called Euripus: this was probably the channel which brought water from the Aqua Virgo to the Thermae Agrippae. The Aqua Virgo was one of Rome's aqueducts: its water was notoriously cold (Ovid, *Ars* 3.385, Mart. 7.32.11), presumably because it was one of the lowest of all the aqueducts. (See Platner—Ashby on 'Euripus Thermarum Agrippae' and 'Aqua Virgo').

the first of January...: the Romans believed in principle that activities and occasions should begin under good omens, and the start of the year was no exception. People offered each other good wishes, as we say 'Happy New Year', to induce favourable omens (Ovid, *Fasti* 1.175—6, Pliny *HN* 28.22), and there was a feeling that starting to do something at the New Year would bring success. Columella (11.2.98) says that farmers begin work of all kinds on the Kalends of January 'auspiciendi causa', and this thought lies behind S.'s list of his New Year's Day activities.

6. **short nap:** S.'s routine can be compared with that of Pliny the Elder, as recorded by his nephew (*Ep.* 3.5.8—15): he too indulged in cat—naps — and he had an even more ferocious obsession than S. for not wasting time.

7. S. is immune to the distractions of sound, as he explains at greater length in 56: see the commentary on that letter and particularly 56.3–5: 'istum fremitum non magis curo quam fluctum aut deiectum aquae... animum enim cogo sibi intentum esse nec avocari ad externa'.

8. The rest of the letter is about drunkenness as an example of a vice against which you should argue not with abstract philosophical sophistries but with common sense and actual examples. Elsewhere S. takes the line that one should drink moderately and not excessively: *Tranq.* 17.8 'non nunquam et usque ad ebrietatem veniendum, non ut mergat nos sed ut deprimat; eluit enim curas et ab imo animum movet et ut morbis quibusdam ita tristitiae medetur'; 59.15 'ebrietas quae unius horae hilarem insaniam longi temporis taedio pensat'. This theme of moderation was a poetic as well as a philosophical commonplace: see Homer, *Od.* 21.293 ff., Theognis 211–12, 479 ff., Hor. *C.* 1.18.7 ff.

9. **Zeno:** not surprisingly S. frequently refers to Zeno (335–263 B.C.), the founder of Stoicism (hence 'nostri' below 10). Zeno was born in Cyprus and came to Athens as a young man, where he taught in the Stoa Poikile which gave his philosophical school its name.
   a similar counter–argument: S. demolishes Zeno's false syllogism by offering an absurd one of his own, which is no more illogical than Zeno's. He then considers and rejects Posidonius' attempt to explain and make sense of Zeno's argument. (For Posidonius see 78.28 n.)

11. **its conventional meaning:** that is, by 'drunk' Zeno meant a man who was actually drunk at the time, whether or not through addiction.
    if Zeno understood it in this sense: that is, in Posidonius' sense of 'qui soleat ebrius fieri' (cf. 'sane hoc senserit...' below); but do we read *noluit* or *voluit*? With *voluit* the sense is that if Zeno wished us to understand this meaning, he was deceptively obscure in expressing himself; with *noluit* the sense is that if he did not wish us to understand it (so that we would need an interpreter like Posidonius), why did he have to cloud the issue like that? *noluit* has better manuscript support, but *voluit* looks more straightforward in sense.

12. **I mean the Caesar:** S. distinguishes the Dictator Julius Caesar from the Emperor Gaius Caesar. Tillius Cimber took a leading part in the assassination, and he is mentioned by S. also at *Ira* 3.30.5 as a man who had previously been one of Caesar's strongest supporters.

13. **life should be furnished with notable examples:** S. himself regularly followed this precept, and (like the Letters) nearly every page of his treatises is furnished with *exempla* to endorse and embellish the current lesson.

14. **Lucius Piso:** Lucius Calpurnius Piso was consul in 15, and died in 32 after being (according to Tac. *Ann.* 6.11) *praefectus urbi* for twenty

years (S.'s 'urbis custos').   Suetonius tells us that he and Tiberius indulged together in long carousals (*Tib.* 42), and Pliny (*HN* 14.145) remarks that it was his staying power as a toper that recommended him in Tiberius' eyes for the appointment.   Velleius Paterculus endorses S.'s judgment of his efficiency ('diligentissimum atque eundem lenissimum securitatis urbanae custodem', 2.98).   He was sent to Thrace to deal with a major revolt, which he quelled after three years' fighting.

15. **Cossus:**   this was probably the Cossus Cornelius Lentulus who was consul in 1 B.C., but it may have been his son, consul in A.D. 25 (see *PIR* II, 333−5).   Both father and son are mentioned with respect by Velleius Paterculus (2.116.2).

16. **those set speeches:**   S. quotes an invented exercise (*declamatio*) which might be delivered by a student in a rhetorical school as a set−piece against drunkenness.   No doubt he is making fun of the turgid style of such exercises, instanced here by the elaborate correlative constructions *quemadmodum... sic..., quemadmodum... ita...*

17. **it is much better...:**   S. now turns from the sophistic and demonstrably false attack on drunkenness to the real case that can be brought against it − the horrors and brutality it leads to.
    moderately good man... ideal sage: the phrasing here is very like S.'s description of himself at 57.3: 'multum ab homine tolerabili, nedum a perfecto absum'.

18. **drunkenness... madness:**   see 59.15, quoted at 8 above.

19. **Alexander... stabbed Clitus:**   the incident is related in detail by Plutarch (*Alex.* 50−1), who also stresses Alexander's agony of remorse; and S. refers to it at *Ira* 3.17.1 (an example of the evil effects of anger), and apparently at 113.29 ('occiso amico').
    drunkenness inflames and exposes all our faults...:   Fielding, who was well grounded in the classics, must surely have had this passage in mind for his own disquisition on drunkenness in *Tom Jones*, Bk. 5, Chap. 9: 'Drink, in reality, doth not reverse nature, or create passions in men which did not exist in them before.   It takes away the guard of reason, and consequently forces us to produce those symptoms, which many, when sober, have art enough to conceal.   It heightens and inflames our passions...'.

20. **weakness:**   *morbus* is here used of sexual perversion (*OLD* s.v. 3b): cf. 79.4 n.

22. **disasters... from drunkenness in a nation:**   the idea is something of a rhetorical commonplace, whether or not historically true: see Tac. *Germ.* 23 (on the Germans) 'si indulseris ebrietati suggerendo quantum concupiscunt, haud minus facile vitiis quam armis vincentur'; Pompeius Trogus (Justin.) 1.8.7 'priusque Scythae ebrietate quam bello vincentur'.

23. **goblet of Hercules:**   a huge tankard such as Hercules might have

drained, which thus symbolically describes a massive imbibing. Plutarch (*Alex.* 75) uses the same phrase in his account of Alexander's death in order to deny that Alexander drained the cup of Hercules, and he censures historians who invent details like that in order to dramatize the death of a famous man. For the Ἡράκλειον, or cup of Hercules, see Apollodorus 2.5.10, who says that the Sun gave Hercules a golden goblet in which he crossed the Ocean. Athenaeus (11.469 d) derives the name from the fact that the hero delighted in large cups, and suggests that its size led to the fanciful story of Hercules using it as a boat. See too the portrayal of the carousing Hercules in Euripides' *Alcestis* (747 ff.).

25. **Marcus Antonius:** S. gives the standard portrait of Antony, who had a bad press because of his entanglement with Cleopatra, and was also notorious for his heavy drinking: see Plut. *Ant.* 9, Pliny *HN* 14.148 (who reports that Antony wrote a book *de sua ebrietate*). Presumably S. here refers to the killings under the proscriptions that followed the establishment of the Triumvirate in 43 B.C. of Octavian, Antony and Lepidus, and in particular to one of the first victims, Cicero.

26. **roughened:** again S. uses a medical term in *exasperare*. *morosos* is Hense's conjecture to mend a defective text: that or something like it must give the required sense.

27. The *sapiens* provides a coda for the letter: like the rest of us he is as prone to the effects of swallowing too much drink as of swallowing any strong drug. And even in his case your arguments must be practical, 'rebus, non verbis'.

his footsteps... his speech...: the language here is similar to Virgil's account of the effect of potent grapes which 'temptatura pedes olim vincturaque linguam' (*G.* 2.94).

LETTER 88

In this important letter S. discusses the 'liberal arts' and their relationship to philosophy. They are, he claims, merely preliminary studies for the acquisition of *sapientia* and are not to be confused with it, for they do not lead the mind to *virtus* but only clear the path for it (20).

The terms *liberalia studia* and *liberales artes* were the Latin equivalents of the Greek educational system usually called ἐγκύκλιος παιδεία, (hence the English 'encyclopaedia') i.e. the ordinary or everday education, the general education which provided a basis for more advanced studies (cf. section 23). The constituent subjects came from different sources of Greek educational theory: arithmetic, astronomy, geometry and music (in medieval times called the Quadrivium and derived from Hippias of Elis and Plato), and grammar, rhetoric and dialectic (the medieval Trivium, derived ultimately from the sophists and Isocrates). These are the subjects which were subsequently named the Seven Liberal Arts by Martianus Capella in the fifth century, and they became the staple educational syllabus of the Middle Ages.

Philosophical attitudes to 'general education' varied. Epicurus disliked it (Usener 117, 163); early Stoics disagreed about it, Zeno disapproving of it as useless, while Chrysippus took the opposite line (Diog. Laert. 7.32 and 129). Posidonius' views are given in detail by S. at 21 ff.; and S.'s own position that liberal studies are only propaideutic to philosophy was that of Isocrates (*Antidosis* 266 ff.) and Cicero (*Hortensius* fr. 92 Grilli). For further discussion of all this see H.I. Marrou, *A History of Education in Antiquity*, Pt. 2, Chap. 8; E. Norden, *Die Antike Kunstprosa*, II 670 ff.; C.S. Lewis, *The Allegory of Love*, 78—82 (on Martianus Capella and the Middle Ages).

S. begins with a statement of his own highly critical view of the so—called *liberalia studia* (1—2). He then considers the question whether they can produce the good man, and rejects in turn the claims of grammar (3—8), music (9), geometry (10—13), astrology (14—17), and — extending the normal range of the curriculum — the arts and athletics (18—19). Conclusion: liberal studies can only prepare the mind to acquire virtue (20). He then reports Posidonius' fourfold division of *artes* (21—3). He rejects the claim that the liberal arts are a part of philosophy (24—31): things can assist us without being parts of us (25); the philosopher understands basic principles which are beyond the grasp of geometry and mathematics (26—8); the highest moral qualities are achieved by knowledge of good and evil, untaught by liberal studies (28—30); you should distinguish liberal studies as a prerequisite but not an assistance to virtue (31). It is even arguable that wisdom is attainable without liberal studies as virtue is not learnt through them, and the range of philosophical speculation is so vast that everything superfluous should be banished from the mind (32—5). We must not waste time over the trivial and useless learning of many grammarians (36—41), or the dreary sophistries of many philosophers (42—6).

We have in this letter a glimpse of what was clearly a vigorous debate about the educational function of liberal studies and their relation to philosophy. Much of the letter is illuminated by Letter 90 in which S. sets out his own view of the philosopher's task: the philosopher is not concerned with practical skills but with ethics and the basic truths of nature and the gods.

1. **liberal studies:** the first words of the letter indicate the theme, suggesting that it is an important one; and, as often, a question by Lucilius is supposed to have prompted it. S. also uses *artes* (e.g. 23) in the same sense as *studia*.

2. **liberal... free man:** the point is partly a linguistic one in the Latin, *liberalis/liber*, but the idea had been long and widely held among educationists, e.g. Aristotle, *Pol.* 1338 a 30—32, said that the young

should be trained in a kind of education (παιδεία) which was not useful or essential but ἐλευθέριον (*liberam*) καὶ καλήν. The same ideal was expressed in the famous Stoic paradox that only the wise man is free.

disgraceful... teachers: S. does not spell out his objections to them, but he also complains about the shortage of good teachers at *Tranq.* 3.3 ('in tanta bonorum praeceptorum inopia'). Here both the subjects and their exponents are dismissed as worthless.

some people: a vague reference to the long—standing philosophical debate: see introductory note.

3. **the study of literature:** at the second stage of their education the *grammaticus* taught Roman children grammar and literature among other subjects, his topics including, as we learn from Cicero, *de Orat.* 1.187, 'poetarum pertractatio, historiarum cognitio, verborum interpretatio, pronuntiandi quidam sonus'. Quintilian divided *grammatice* into two parts, 'recte loquendi scientiam et poetarum enarrationem' (1.4.2), both of which are covered by S.'s list (*curam sermonis/ carmina... versuum*). S. suggest elsewhere, perhaps not very seriously, that some of the linguistic preoccupations of the *grammaticus* were a bit tedious: 58.5 (after a discussion of archaic word forms) 'non id ago nunc hac diligentia ut ostendam quantum tempus apud grammaticum perdiderim'. *historiae* are the stories and legends which formed the subject matter of the works studied and which the *grammaticus* was expected to explain in detail — hence *fabularum memoria* below. *carmina* is elucidated by *versuum lex ac modificatio*.

which of these ...?: we find the same appeal for practical guidance in 109, where S. says that certain abstract questions of moral philosophy are only useful for sharpening our wits: 'totiens enim illo revertor: quid ista me res iuvat? fortiorem fac me, iustiorem, temperantiorem' (109.17). Fear, desire and passion were three of the emotions that Stoic teaching aimed chiefly to curb.

4. The text here is disputed. Some think that the sentences 'ad geometriam ... frustra scit' are an intrusive anticipation of the sections on music and geometry (9, 10), as S. is still concerned with *grammatice* down to 8. But we do not expect a tidy thematic structure in the Letters, where S. often outlines a point to which he later returns more fully. However, some word or words are clearly lacking before *utrum doceant*: the translation assumes the loss of *videndum* or *quaerendum* or something of similar sense. (For a discussion of the problem here see Stückelberger 21.)

formally teaching: *consederint* refers to the teacher expounding formally from his official chair, *cathedra*.

5. **Homer:** to the Greeks Homer was not only the greatest of poets but also the fountain—head of wisdom and ethical teaching. In the fifth

century B.C. we are told that Anaxagoras took the theme of Homer's poetry to be virtue and justice (Diog. Laert. 2.3.11). The Stoic Chrysippus claimed the authority of Homer for his own doctrines (Cic. *ND* 1.41): 'refusing even immortality' here is an allusion to Odysseus' rejection of Calypso's offer of immortality as a lure to stay with her (*Od.* 5.206 ff.). The Epicurean Homer usually derived from Odysseus' speech in praise of the hedonistic life—style of the Phaeacians (*Od.* 9.5 ff.), which was alleged to have inspired Epicurus' ideal (Athen. 12.513 a; schol. on *Od.* 9.28). The words 'condition ... in banqueting and song' refer of course to Odysseus' description of the Phaeacians. The Peripatetic division of goods into three classes, mental, bodily and external (see, for example, Cic. *Ac.* 1.19−22), was thought to be exemplified by Priam's words to Hermes at *Il.* 24.376−7, complimenting him on his bodily beauty, his understanding and his parentage. (See schol. on the passage, and on *Il.* 17.238 ff., another passage claimed as a source for Peripatetic dogma.) 'An Academic, stating that nothing is certain' refers to the sceptical phase of the Academy, which began in the middle of the third century B.C. under the headship of Arcesilaus. As a Homeric prototype statement of scepticism editors usually quote *Il.* 2.486 (mortals, unlike the Muses, know nothing but hearsay), but many such passages admitting human ignorance could have been adduced from Homer.

6.　S. tartly dismisses the sort of hopelessly academic questions which pedantic grammarians debated. See also his scornful account of Didymus' interests at 37 below; and *Brev. Vit.* 13.2−3, where he complains that the Romans are becoming infected with the Greek love of useless enquiry (like the priority in composition of the *Iliad* or the *Odyssey*, and the number of Ulysses' oarsmen). The emperor Tiberius may have been partly responsible: he used to expect the grammarians to know things like who was Hecuba's mother, the name the disguised Achilles adopted, and the song the Sirens sang (Suet. *Tib.* 70). Later on Juvenal complained that teachers are expected to know this kind of detailed and trivial information (7.229 ff.: Mayor's note has many references). Quintilian made S.'s point more pungently: 'mihi inter virtutes grammatici habebitur aliqua nescire' (1.8.21).

　　The relative priority of Homer and Hesiod was much debated in antiquity from the fifth century B.C. onwards (see Gellius 3.11). Hesiod is usually assumed to have been writing around 700 B.C., but scholars still disagree whether Homer (i.e. the *Iliad* and *Odyssey* in something like their present form) should be put before or after that date. (The point is discussed by M.L. West in his edition of Hesiod, *Theogony*, pp. 46−7.) The paradoxical assumption that Hecuba was younger than Helen, or at least about the same age (in Homer she is clearly much older), is explained in Lucian's *Gallus* 17 by the statement that Helen had previously been Theseus' wife a whole generation before the sack of Troy by the Greeks.

7. **would you rather know ...?:** there was much argument among ancient critics about the precise track of Ulysses' wanderings, e.g. were they within or outside the Mediterranean Sea: see Gellius 14.6.3, Apollod. *Epit.* 7.1. S. draws a parallel between Ulysses' storm—tossed trials and our own far more relevant moral failings, a parallel much favoured by earlier philosophers, especially the Cynics, like Diogenes (Diog. Laert. 6.27) and Bion (Stob. 3.4.52). Readers of the *Odyssey* will recognize the references here to Calypso, the Sirens and the Cyclopes, among Ulysses' other ordeals. The Odyssean parallel here was convenient for S., as shipwreck was a standard Stoic metaphor for a moral test or ordeal: see Stückelberger's note here, and *Cons. Marc.* 6.3 'ille vel in naufragio laudandus quem obruit mare clavum tenentem et obnixum'.

8. **Penelope:** her reputation for patient virtue was later assailed by stories of relations with the suitors and with Hermes, both linked with the allegation that she was the mother of Pan: Hdt. 2.145, Apollod. *Epit.* 7.38−9, Cic. *ND* 3.56. Penelope talks to the man who turns out to be her husband at *Od.* 19.100 ff.

    chastity ... is in the body or in the mind: by S.'s time this question was a philosophical commonplace, e.g. the *sententia* from Publilius Syrus (710): 'voluntas impudicum non corpus facit'. But earlier, at least until the fifth century B.C., moral purity was generally regarded as a physical, not a mental, attribute: see Barrett on Eur. *Hipp.* 317 χεῖρες μὲν ἀγναί, φρὴν δ' ἔχει μίασμά τι.

9. The power of music to affect the emotions or to educate the character had long been recognized: see Plato, *Rep.* 3.398 c ff., 7.522 a; *Ira* 3.9.2 'Pythagoras perturbationes animi lyra componebat'. A natural development of this was the concept of the soul itself as a harmony, and S. is here again tapping an old metaphor which we find in Diogenes (passage cited on 7: musicians who have their strings in harmony but not their souls).

    notes: the word understood with *acutae ac graves* could be either *chordae* or *voces* ('strings' and 'voices') make equally good sense). *voces* is added in some later manuscripts.

    learn how to harmonize: *quomodo* in this final sense is rare and perhaps colloquial: cf. Ter. *Phormio* 756 and Hofmann−Szantyr 650. Its use here is suggested by the need to parallel the preceding *quomodo. consonare* is used in a similar musical metaphor at 31.8 'aequalitas ac tenor vitae per omnia consonans sibi'.

10. It suits his purpose here for S. to be dismissive of the materialist uses to which geometry is put, but elsewhere he shows a greater respect for the skill of its practitioners: e.g. *NQ* 1.4.1 (discussing the rainbow as an image of the sun) 'rationes, quae non persuadent sed cogunt, a

geometris afferuntur'.   The argument here is that science does indeed teach us about the workings of the world — but it does not teach us to be wise and good.

put my fingers to the service: the reference is to using the fingers for adding up (so too *Ira* 3.33.3), the method the *infelicissimus* below will be reduced to without the aid of accountants.

11. **measuring rod:**   the *decempeda* or ten—foot surveyor's rule appears elsewhere too in contexts suggesting vast domains: see Nisbet—Hubbard on Hor. *C.* 2.15.14.

12. **someone says:**   see 78.11 n.   The section elaborates the moral point before we return to geometry in 13.

if things go well for you: these words may have a sardonic edge, seeing that so many of S.'s contemporaries were obliged for various reasons of prudence to name the emperor as their chief heir.

lawyers ... prescription: under Roman law *usucapio* was the right of absolute ownership of something which was conferred by continuous possession for a fixed period, one year in the case of *res mobiles*, two years for land and buildings.   The exceptions included *res furtivae, res sacrae* and *provincialia praedia* (Gaius, *Inst.* 2.42 ff.). S. is not therefore strictly accurate in saying that the *ager* in question could not be owned, but his aim here is to stress his oft—repeated theme that we are only custodians of our so—called possessions.   This was a philosophical commonplace shared by many schools of thought: Bion (Stob. 4.41.56: Fortune has not given the rich their possessions, only lent them); Epictetus (*Diatr.* 4.5.15: physical objects, unlike mental qualities, are not a man's own); Lucretius 3.971 'vitaque mancipio nulli datur, omnibus usu'; Cic. *Off.* 1.21 'sunt autem privata nulla natura'; and for other Senecan passages see 72.7, 73.7, 120.18, *Ben.* 6.3.2.

13. **reduce ... to a square:**   S. is probably thinking especially of the most famous of such problems, the squaring of the circle, which has fascinated mathematicians from antiquity up to modern times, and remains insoluble.   For ancient attempts to solve it see T. Heath, *A History of Greek Mathematics* I 220—35.

14. Astrology as a science which could explore the influence of the heavenly bodies on human life enjoyed a wide repute from Hellenistic times onwards, and the Stoics accepted it at least to some extent as a respectable study.   S. himself conceded that the stars do influence men's lives: *NQ* 2.32.7—8.   But the more disreputable Chaldaean type of horoscope—mongering, much practised in Italy, was regarded with disfavour by the Roman authorities, who repeatedly and unsuccessfully tried to expel its practitioners (most recently in A.D. 52: Tac. *Ann.* 12.52.3).   In these sections S. is not disputing the claims to knowledge of the astrologers, but he is saying that their information is not worth knowing: the important things are to realize that the course

of destiny is fixed and to be ready for anything.

The quotations here and in 16 are from Virgil, *G*. 1.336–7 and 424–6. The *Georgics* must have been one of S.'s favourite books, if we can judge from the number of times he quotes from them in the Letters (58.2; 86.15, 16; 87.20; 90.9, 11, 37; 95.68; 108.24, 34; 114.23; 122.2; 124.1). The context of these lines is advice to farmers to take warning of approaching storms from weather signs in the sky.

Saturn and Mars are in opposition: a planet is in opposition when it is exactly opposite to the sun in the sky. Saturn and Mars were regarded as unfavourable planets, and Mercury (a favourable planet) is here thought to be adversely affected by Saturn. (See F. Boll, *Kleine Schriften zur Sternkunde des Altertums*, Leipzig 1950, 194–5.)

15. **fixed sequence of destined events:** this is a fundamental Stoic dogma, often endorsed by S.: see 77.12 '(fata) rata et fixa sunt et magna atque aeterna necessitate ducuntur ... series invicta et nulla mutabilis ope inligavit ac trahit cuncta'; *NQ* 2.35.2.

either cause or signalize: a fundamental distinction: cf. *NQ* 1.1.4 'videbimus an rerum omnium certus ordo ducatur et alia aliis ita implexa sint ut quod antecedit aut causa sit sequentium aut signum'. S. goes on to argue that whichever function the planets perform, knowing future events is pointless. (See too the similar argument in Cic. *Div*. 2.21.)

16. The *Georgics* passage should read *lunas* for *stellas* (Virgil is listing weather signs provided by the sun and moon): S. has either made a slip in quoting from memory or deliberately adapted the line to fit his own context.

17. The 'be prepared for anything' argument here recalls 78.29: see the parallels cited there.

18–19. After dismissing the claims of grammar, music, geometry and astrology S. adds a strong moral coda which takes him outside the strict liberal arts syllabus to what we would call the fine arts, and to athletics. This widening of the argument beyond the traditional curriculum may have been intended to counter contemporary educational views and claims: these activities cannot even be regarded as liberal arts, let alone be allowed the philosophical value which S. denies to liberal arts.

18. **oil–and–mud artists:** anointing oil and muddy arenas typified the wrestler's life: see 57.1 n. Cicero also relegates *unguentarii* to the class of 'artes minime probandae' (*Off*. 1.150).

19. **drinking on an empty stomach:** a sign of the hardened drinker, who thus ensured greater potency of his liquor: 15.3 'potionis in ieiuno iturae'; 122.6 'illa ebrietas iuvat quae in vacuum venit'. Pliny the Elder tells us that the practice began during the reign of Tiberius (*HN* 14.143).

trained to stand up straight ...: *exercere* with the infinitive is

extremely rare (elsewhere only at Claudian, *de tert. cons. Hon.* 43
ff.: *TLL* 5.2.1370.62 ff.) *rectam* contrasts with *iacentibus* below, those
who just recline at the table, over—indulging in food and drink (see
OLD s.v. *iaceo* 2 d). *sudem torquere* refers to the drill of practising
spear—throwing with a wooden pole.

    In this section S. pulls out the rhetorical stops to make a
forceful and climactic point, with the hammering questions, the
powerful superlative *effrenatissimis* and the play on words
freno/ effrenatissimis and *vincere/ vinci*.

20. This section summarizes S.'s view of the subordinate rôle of *liberalia
studia*.

contribute... to life's amenities: for the argument and the phraseology
here cf. 44.7 (on the *beata vita*) 'instrumenta eius pro ipsa habent';
95.8 'omnes istae artes circa instrumenta vitae occupatae sunt, non
circa totam vitam'.

used to be called basic grammar: S. alludes to the use of the Latin
litteratura as the equivalent of the Greek *grammatike* (Quint. 2.1.4).
Under the Roman system of eduction the primary schoolmaster or
litterator (reading, writing and arithmetic), and then the *grammaticus*
(grammar and literature), between them covered the subjects which
were dealt with by the Greek *grammatistes*. (See also n. on 3
above.) S. may be implying that the term *litteratura* is going out of
fashion. A similar comparison of the preparatory functions of liberal
arts and of school subjects had already been made by Isocrates
(*Antidosis* 266−7).

21−23. For Posidonius see n. on 78.28. S. quotes his fourfold division
of *artes* in order to take a wide—ranging view of man's technical and
artistic activities, before focussing again on the so—called *liberales* and
redefining them (23: cf. section 2). (Somewhat similar divisions of
artes or τέχναι can be found in other writers: Philo, *Spec. Leg.*
1.335−6; Galen, *Protrepticus* 5; Philostratus, *Vita Apollonii*
8.7.154−5.)

    There are difficulties in the interpretation of this part of the
letter, e.g. the subject of *inquit* 24, but the following points emerge
from S.'s account of Posidonius' views: (a) Posidonius' third class,
pueriles, roughly corresponds to what are currently called *liberales*.
(b) However Posidonius distinguished his *pueriles* and *liberales*, he
clearly included some scientific and physical enquiry among the latter
class. (c) The term *liberales* (better *liberae*) should in S.'s view be
restricted to activities which promote virtue (23).

    (For a detailed discussion of the whole passage see Stückelberger
40 ff., esp. 53−5.)

21. **the craftsman ... no pretence of dignity or grace:** this may be S.'s
gloss on Posidonius, as it reflects a Roman prejudice against trade we
find in Cicero (*Flacc.* 18 'opifices et tabernarios atque illam omnem

faecem civitatum'; *Off.* 1.150 'opificesque omnes in sordida arte versantur'). More clearly Senecan is the explanation 'Herein you would class ... ' in 22.

22. **engineers who devise platforms** ...: the Romans loved spectacular stage effects, many of which were produced by means of the movable platform called *pegma*. There are many references to the versatility — and dangers — of this device: Juv. 4.122 'et pegma et pueros inde ad velaria raptos'; Mart. *Spect.* 2.2. 'et crescunt media pegmata celsa via'; Phaedrus 5.7.7 'dum pegma rapitur, concidit casu gravi'.

   the naïve, who marvel ...: unlike the *sapiens*, whose rational stability is never shaken by anything apparently novel and unusual, as Chrysippus said (Diog. Laert. 7.123), and Cicero after him (*Tusc.* 5.81 'sapientis est ... nihil cum acciderit admirari, ut inopinatum ac novum accidisse videatur').

23. **the Greeks call 'encyclic'**: the full phrase would be ἐγκυκλίους τέχνας (see introductory note).

24. **someone objects**: on this interpretation *inquit* introduces an imaginary objector, as so often, and 25 represents Posidonius' (and Seneca's) point of view. If the subject of *inquit* is Posidonius, he thought geometry was essential to physics, and 25 is S.'s reply. In any case Letter 90 confirms that S. wished to exclude from the philosopher's task anything that was not ethics or basic first principles of theology or physics.

   physics ... ethics ... dialectic: a traditional division of philosophy: Cic. *Ac.* 1.19 (where it is attributed to Plato though it does not appear in his works), *de Orat.* 1.68; Quint. 12.2.10; Sextus Empiricus, *Adv.Math.* 7.16 (who attributes it to Xenocrates, the disciple of Plato). At 89.9−10 S. discusses the triple divison and goes on to say that the Peripatetics added a fourth, *civilis*.

25. **geometry offers us some service**: for S.'s views on geometry see note on 10.

   the craftsman: the instrument−maker who supplies the geometer with his tools.

26. **the philosopher learns ... the causes**: this was also the view of Posidonius, as S. tells us at 95.65: (to other elements which belong to philosophy) 'Posidonius ... adicit causarum inquisitionem'.

   this is not possible for heavenly bodies: their everlasting movement is also stressed at *NQ* 7.25.6 'non licet stare caelestibus nec averti; prodeunt omnia ... opus hoc aeternum irrevocabiles habet motus'.

27. **the sun is large**: there was much disagreement in antiquity about the size of the sun. Democritus must be given credit for believing that it was large (Cic. *Fin.* 1.20), in contrast with more naïve theories like those of Heraclitus (a foot wide) and Epicurus (about as big as it seems).

   first principles: basic abstract assumptions, like the existence of odd and even numbers, which, as Socrates said (Plato, *Rep.* 6.510 c), mathematicians put forward as obvious to everyone and not needing explanation. S.'s point is that mathematicians cannot derive these prerequisite principles from the practice of their own subject.

28. **a lease—holder ...:** a characteristically Roman metaphor, recalling Lucretius' metaphors with *terminus*, the boundary mark of a property (e.g. 5.90).

expand through considering celestial phenomena: for the same idea see 117.19: 'ista (celestial phenomena) ... levant animum et ad ipsarum quas tractat rerum magnitudinem attollunt'.

knowledge of good and evil: a conventional definition of moral philosophy: 71.7 'Socrates ... totam philosophiam revocavit ad mores et hanc summam dixit esse sapientiam, bona malaque distinguere'; Cic. *Fin.* 5.67 'cernatur ... prudentia in delectu bonorum et malorum'.

29—30. **individual virtues:** lists of virtues vary in the Letters, both in their length and in the stress laid on particular ones: e.g. 95.55 (*prudentia, fortitudo, iustitia*), 115.3 (*iustitia, fortitudo, temperantia, prudentia*, followed by *frugalitas, continentia, tolerantia, liberalitas, comitas, humanitas*), 120.11 (*temperantia, fortitudo, prudentia, iustitia*). Here *fides* seems to replace *iustitia* (and according to Cicero, *Off.* 1.23, 'fundamentum autem est iustitiae fides'). The whole passage is a vigorous account of the best moral qualities and their complete independence of liberal studies.

30. **modesty, self—control, thrift:** however they were distinguished by others, Cicero (*Tusc.* 3.16) suggests that *modestia, moderatio* and *frugalitas* (along with *temperantia*) are all possible translations of the Greek σωφροσύνη. The Latin terms, like the suggested English equivalents, certainly shade into each other.

no human being ...: for the sentiment and phrasing see the words of 95.33: 'homo, sacra res homini', and Pliny, *HN* 2.18 'deus est mortali iuvare mortalem'.

31. S. here distinguishes between assistance (*adiutorium*) and prerequisite (*sine quo non*), which is not quite consistent with 25, where he coupled *adiutorium* and what is *necessarium* and distinguished both from *pars*. Cf. 65.13, where he remarks that to a sculptor his chisel and file are prerequisites but not *partes* or *causae* of his art.

32. **a man who is ignorant of books ...:** cf. the example of Homer in section 5.

wisdom hands down deeds not words: the importance of practical rather than theoretical teaching is a recurrent theme of the Letters: 16.3 'philosophia ... non in verbis sed in rebus est'; 20.2 'facere docet philosophia, non dicere'; 83.27; 108.35; 117.33. This was not, of course, an exclusively Stoic attitude: Aristotle also stressed the need for practice compared with theory in acquiring goodness through philosophy (*EN* 2.1105 b 9—18). But this was one of the elements in Stoicism, as they viewed it, which appealed to the temper of the Romans.

memory is more reliable: cf. Plato, *Phaedrus* 274 d — 275 b: according to Socrates, the Egyptian king Thamus once rejected the newly—invented alphabet because its use would ruin the faculty of memory. S. is on firm ground here, as it is well established that pre—literate societies had powers of memory far superior to ours.

33. **wisdom is extensive:** similar large claims for philosophy are found at 90.28 — 9 (see notes there); 117.19 'amplos habet illa spatiososque secessus ...' (followed by a list of topics of enquiry); and in the earnest protreptic at the start of the *Natural Questions* (1 praef. 1 — 3). S. preached what he practised, the long hard slog to wisdom.

the nature of time: the nature of time, and especially the question whether time could be conceived to exist before the universe, was much debated by ancient philosophers. The Stoic Cleanthes wrote a book *On Time* (Diog Laert. 7.174), in which he presumably gave what seems to have been the standard Stoic definition of time as 'an interval in the movement of the universe' (von Arnim, *Stoic. vet. frag.* 2.509 ff.). This implies that time had no existence prior to the world, which is in line with Aristotle's statement that time does not exist outside of the heavens (*Cael.* 279 a 12). The Epicureans, on the other hand, thought it inconceivable that time ever had a beginning (Cic. *ND* 1.21).

34. **questions about the soul:** there is a similar list at 90.29. For the ethical teacher it was naturally a central theme to discuss the soul, its relation to its dwelling—place, the body, and its fate after the body's death. On the latter point see 57.7 n., and for the reference to the Pythagorean doctrine of metempsychosis see 108.19. The body is often called the *domicilium* of the soul (65.17 and 21; 108.19; Cic. *Tusc.* 1.58) or the prison of the soul (79.12 n.). The Stoics, like the Epicureans, considered the soul to be corporeal: 106.4; 113.2.

35. Because of this enormous range of philosophical enquiry we have no time for superfluous things, *supervacua* — a strong word used again below at 36, 37 and 45; also 48.12 'quae dementia est supervacua discere in tanta temporis egestate'. There is a similar attack on the passion for useless knowledge at *Brev. Vit.* 13 ('inane studium supervacua discendi').

36. **the furniture of learning:** *supellex* is often used in a transferred sense: see 58.18 'propria Platonis supellex est' (the doctrine of Ideas); 87.13 'tu ad supellectilem artis, non ad artem venis'; *OLD* s.v. c.

a kind of extravagance: the train of ideas ending in the words 'intemperantiae genus est' is much like 106.12 'paucis satis est ad mentem bonam uti litteris, sed nos ut cetera in supervacuum diffundimus, ita philosophiam ipsam. quemadmodum omnium rerum, sic litterarum quoque intemperantia laboramus'.

37. **learning what is useless:** like the subjects of futile enquiry given in sections 6−7.

   Didymus: a grammarian at Alexandria of the first century B.C. who became a legend for his learning, and was nicknamed Chalkenteros ('Brazen−bowelled') because of his unremitting industry. Much of his work on Homer survives in the existing scholia. The question of Homer's birthplace was much debated (Gellius 3.11.6): seven different cities were alleged to have claimed the honour, though the names vary. We do not hear of any discussion about Aeneas' mother (always stated to be Venus), but perhaps there was minor scholarly controversy deriving from Venus' instructions to Anchises in the Homeric *Hymn to Aphrodite*, 281−5, that he should tell the world that the mother of his child was a mountain−nymph. The dominant themes of Anacreon's (sixth century B.C.) poetry were love and wine: hence Didymus' alleged discussion of his personal proclivities. The background to speculation on Sappho's character is obscure. It may have arisen from lurid accounts of society in Lesbos in her time; or there may be confusion with a courtesan of the same name (Aelian, *VH* 12.19).

   tell me life isn't long enough: a ridiculous idea if you look at what Didymus achieved in his life − futile though his labours were.

38. **our own writers:** Romans, in contrast with Greeks like Didymus.

   a great deal of time: cf. the similar thought at 45.12 'ostendas omnibus magno temporis inpendio quaeri supervacua'.

   a learned man ... a good man: for the same contrast see *NQ* 4b.13.1 'quid istas, inquis, ineptias, quibus litteratior est quisque, non melior, tam operose persequeris?'. S. does not of course mean that we cannot be both, but obsessional concentration on dry−as−dust learning blinds us to the superior claims of a morally good life. Montaigne imitated this passage in his *Essais* 1, 25: 'Criez d'un passant à nostre peuple: O le sçavant homme! et d'un autre: O le bon homme! Il ne faudra pas de tourner les yeux et son respect vers le premier' (quoted by Stückelberger).

39. **the earliest poet:** we get a hint of this debate from Herodotus (2.53), who himself considered Homer and Hesiod the earliest poets (cf. n. on 6). Other candidates would have been the legendary singers Orpheus, Musaeus and Linus.

   Aristarchus' critical symbols: Aristarchus (died 145 B.C.) was one of the most distinguished of the scholars who worked at Alexandria. He founded a school there, and together with Aristophanes of Byzantium he was largely responsible for laying the foundations in establishing the text of Homer as well as many other authors. For his critical work he used various marginal symbols (*notas* here) to indicate different types of error in the texts. His fame was such that he became the type of the rigorous critic: see Horace, *Ars* 450 'fiet

Aristarchus' (with Brink's note). S.'s contemptuous *conpunxit* dismisses the minutiae of literary scholarship as no part of the search for *sapientia*.

40. **Apion:** another Alexandrian scholar and a pupil of Didymus. Pliny the Elder mentions hearing him lecture on Homer in his youth (*HN* 30.18). *circulatus est* suggests the activity of a wandering showman or quack (*circulator*) rather than a serious scholar: cf. 40.3 'vim dicendi rapidam atque abundantem aptiorem esse circulanti quam agenti rem magnam ac seriam docentique', and a similar comparison at 52.8.

   in which he took in ...: the antecedent to *quo* is *principium*, not *operi*: it is the *principium* which contains the two letters and which therefore takes in the whole war.

   two letters: the letters μη from μῆνιν (the first word of the *Iliad*) stand for 48, the number of books in both epics together. With this climax of futile sciolism S. turns from useless grammarians to useless philosophers.

41. **how much time you lose ...:** the thought is recurrent in S., and the formulation here is like *Brev. Vit.* 3.2 (on drawing up a balance sheet of one's life) 'duc quantum ex isto tempore creditor, quantum amica, quantum rex, quantum cliens abstulerit...'; see also 117.32.

42. **use of syllables ...:** S. expresses his scorn of logic—chopping use of language also at 48.4 'tu mihi verba distorques et syllabas digeris'; 71.6 'relinque istum ludum litterarium philosophorum qui rem magnificentissimam ad syllabas vocant'; and he sums up his point at 108.23 'itaque quae philosophia fuit, facta philologia est'.

43—44. S. makes the point by selecting some notoriously paradoxical philosophical statements of the sort which, in his view, no one of ordinary common—sense could take seriously. His aim is not, of course, to dismiss professional philosophy as an intellectual activity, but to attack futile and unhelpful sophistry.

   Protagoras of Abdera (fifth century B.C.) was one of the most important of the Sophists, or professional teachers of philosophy and ortory. Nausiphanes of Teos (born c. 360 B.C.) was an Atomist philosopher who taught Epicurus. Parmenides of Elea (flourished in the early fifth century B.C.) was a thinker of formidable intellect and originality, whose speculations on the nature of being were a landmark in the course of Presocratic philosophy. Zeno of Elea (fifth century B.C.) was a pupil of Parmenides: S.'s summary of his views here is probably an exaggerated over—simplification of Zeno's work, which further developed the ideas of Parmenides and became notorious because of his fascination with paradoxes involving motion. Pyrrhon of Elis (c. 360 — c. 270 B.C.) was the founder of Scepticism. The Megarian school was founded by Eucleides of Megara (c. 450 — 380 B.C.), and their thinking followed ·the lines of Parmenides and his disciples. The Eretrian school began with Menedemus of Eretria (c. 340 — c. 265 B.C.). By Academics S. means the later sceptical phase of Plato's Academy under Arcesilaus (see note on 5). Cicero (*de Orat.* 3.62) groups the Eretrians, Megarians and Pyrrhonians together as schools which have all been superseded by more recent thinkers.

44. **nothing exists except the whole:** the translation assumes the supplement *uno excepto* of Kalbfleisch.

removed the debatables from the debate: to translate the pun more literally, 'put the whole business (of such philosophical enquiry) out of business', — much the same sense as Petr. *Sat.* 56.7 'philosophos de negotio deiciebat'. Perhaps the phrase *de negotio deicere* is colloquial.

45. **useless heap:** the scornful *gregem* is like *turba* in 24 (see *OLD* s.v. 2c).

46. **the whole world is a shadow:** the conclusion we are driven to if we take these theories seriously. *umbra* is used of insubstantial or evanescent existence, like σκιά in Greek, e.g. Pindar, *P.* 8.95—6; Soph. *Ajax* 125—6 (see Stanford's note). The serious polemical tone is maintained to the very end of the letter.

LETTER 90

S explores the part played by philosophers in the earliest days of human society. They were not responsible, as Posidonius thought, for teaching men to acquire practical skills and improved arts and crafts: their instruction has always been of a higher, ethical order — about good and evil, nature, truth and the gods. The end of the letter contains one of S.'s strongest and most characteristic messages: the philosophy that brings *virtus* is only achieved by the struggle of long training and practice. The sequence of ideas is:

1—3 Philosophy leads us to the good life.

4—6 Among primitive men the leaders were *sapientes*.

7—13 Philosophers were not responsible (as Posidonius said) for technological advances.

14—19 The simple life of the wise contrasted with luxury's demand for superfluities.

20—25 Philosophers were not responsible for practical discoveries.

26—29 Philosophy's real task is ethical: as the *artifex vitae* she shows the way to happiness by teaching us to recognize genuine evils, and real greatness, and about nature and the gods and the soul and truth.

30—33 Philosophers were not responsible for practical discoveries.

34—35 Philosophy's real task: to discover the truth about nature and to teach men to follow the universal law.

35-46 This kind of philosophy did not exist in the Golden Age when men acted wisely by instinct. Innocence due to ignorance must be distinguished from the virtue acquired by the trained mind.

As often in other letters this one does not have a strictly logical structure, and important themes are repeated in different places — there are three separate passages refuting Posidonius' claims, and two listing the philosopher's true tasks.

The letter belongs in the tradition of Exhortations to Philosophy (*Protreptikoi*) which was best represented by Aristotle's *Protrepticus* and Cicero's *Hortensius*, both now lost but to some extent recoverable from later writings. It is also an important document for ancient ideas on anthropology, as it is one of our main surviving discussions of the condition of early man and his gradual acquisition of the skills of civilization. S. of course has his own philosophical axe to grind, as did Lucretius in his important account of primitive man in *DRN* 5 (see my notes on 5. 925-87); and S.'s message is emphatically that the early philosophers were not technologists. The letter gives us one of the conventional views of the first human societies: that men once lived in the happy times of a Golden Age, enjoying the earth's bounty without having to toil for it, until moral corruption set in and mankind lost its innocence forever. There are several references in Cicero's works to the part played by either philosophy or oratory in the development of primitive human societies (*Inv.* 1.2; *Tusc.* 1.62, 5.5; *de Or.* 1.33; *Sest.* 91). For an account of Posidonius' views see K. Reinhardt in *RE* s.v. 805-8; and for a good general discussion see A.O. Lovejoy and G. · Boas, *Primitivism and Related Ideas in Antiquity*, Baltimore, 1935.

This letter has also an incidental interest by having provoked a vigorous onslaught from Macaulay in his essay on Lord Bacon. Macaulay derisively attacks S.'s criticism of Posidonius, and goes on: 'For our own part, if we are forced to make our choice between the first shoemaker, and the author of the three books On Anger, we pronounce for the shoemaker. It may be worse to be angry than to be wet. But shoes have kept millions from being wet; and we doubt whether Seneca ever kept anybody from being angry.' (Collected *Essays*, London 1895, 393).

1. **life ... the good life:** *vivere/ bene vivere* is a standard moralizing contrast, reflecting the Greek τὸ ζῆν/τὸ καλῶς ζῆν: see 70.4 'non enim vivere bonum est, sed bene vivere'; *Ben.* 3.31.4; Lucr. 5.17-18.
   philosophy ... bestowed on us by the gods: as Plato said in the *Timaeus* (47 b), which Cicero quotes at *Tusc.* 1.64.
   knowledge ... faculty ...: similarly when discussing our acquisition of 'boni honestique notitia' S. states 'natura ... semina nobis scientiae dedit, scientiam non dedit' (120.4). We have to work to achieve knowledge and wisdom. On not being 'born wise' see *Ira* 2.10.6 '(sapiens) scit neminem nasci sapientem sed fieri'.

3. **virtues ... association:** S. has the same picture of a retinue of virtues at 67.10 'individuus ille comitatus virtutum'.

    tore society apart: *distrahere* (opposed to *contrahere*) is technical for breaking up a partnership or alliance (*OLD* s.v. 7).

    men cease to possess everything ...: conventional moralizing, which recurs in section 38 below, *Cons. Helv.* 11.4 'qui naturalem modum excedit, eum in summis quoque opibus paupertas sequetur'.

4—6. The mention of the consortium of primitive men leads on to a discussion of the rôle of *sapientes* in the earliest societies. They were the leaders among men, chosen for their superior moral qualities, just as among wild animals the leaders are the biggest and strongest. But the presence of *sapientes* seems to introduce a logical fallacy into the argument here: we are told (5) that they checked violence and protected the weak from the strong; but by definition Golden Age society did not need this sort of protection and restraint, as men lived in peace and harmony with each other (see the picture of their life painted in 40—1). Whether this slip in the reasoning is S.'s or Posidonius', it must have arisen from the wish to allot the *sapientes* their task of moral leadership as far back as the beginning of human society, though the need for their services strictly only arose with the start of the moral decline ('societatem avaritia distraxit' 3, 'subrepentibus vitiis' 6).

4. **the worse give way to the better:** this law of nature is applied to the body and the soul at 65.24 'serviant ergo deteriora melioribus'.

    bull ... elephant: familiar illustrations of large and powerful creatures, which also appear together at 60.2; *Ira* 2.31.6; *Ben.* 2.29.1.

6. **laws became necessary:** in Lucretius (5.1136 ff.) the overthrow of kings leads to a period of anarchy, followed by the establishment of the rule of law. Tacitus, like S., envisaged a time of primitive innocence, then a period of despotisms, after which some communities welcomed codes of law (*Ann.* 3.26). Philosophers are also claimed as the first lawgivers by Cicero (*Tusc.* 5.5) and Horace (*Ars* 396—9). Solon was chief archon at Athens in 594—3 B.C., and the most celebrated lawgiver in the Greek world. (Lists of the Seven Sages vary, but they all include him.) Lycurgus (c. 390 — c. 325 B.C.) was another Athenian statesman, who played a major part in fourth—century politics. Zaleucus (probably mid—seventh century B.C.) composed what was thought to be the earliest Greek law code for Locri in southern Italy. Charondas (probably sixth century B.C.) wrote laws for Catana in Sicily. S., like Diodorus (12.20), is anachronistic in making Zaleucus, at least, a pupil of Pythagoras (late sixth century B.C.). No doubt the geographical proximity of Croton, where Pythagoras worked, suggested the link.

7. **taught men ... scattered communities:** the same sort of claim is made for philosophy at Cic. *Tusc.* 1.62, 5.5.

complex multi—storey buildings: even in the time of the late Republic, as Vitruvius tells us (2.17), lack of space in Rome led to increasingly high buildings; and Juvenal paints a vivid picture of the capital's tall and crowded buildings (3.199, 269 ff.). The reasoning is that the difference between building a hut and building a mansion is only one of degree, and the philosopher cannot be associated however indirectly with the trappings of luxury.

fish—tanks: they were a popular feature of villas, and the advantage the fish—fancying owner enjoyed that storms need not endanger his menu is also mentioned by S. in his account of Vatia's villa in 55.6 'cum tempestas piscatoribus dedit ferias, manus ad parata porrigitur', and by Martial, 10.30.19—20.

8.   **keys and bolts:** the implication is that in the innocent days of the Golden Age houses did not have to be locked, as in Tibullus' account of it: 'non domus ulla fores habuit' (1.3.43).

9.   **'For early men ...':** Virgil, *G.* 1.144 — the first of three quotations from that book in the letter (also in 11 and 37): see 88.14 n. Virgil is here talking about skills that men had to learn at the end of the Golden Age.

   a public banqueting—hall: i.e. a private dining—room big enough to be one. 115.8 lists among impressive luxuries 'capacem populi cenationem'.

   in order to support: *ex* is probably instrumental (the trees are to provide columns to prop up the ceilings), rather than indicating source of material (the trees are used to make the ceilings themselves). In moralizing contexts gilded ceilings symbolize pretentious luxury: 114.9; *Cons. Helv.* 10.7; Hor. *C.* 2.18.1—2 'non ebur neque aureum / mea renidet in domo lacunar' (see Nisbet—Hubbard's note); [Lucian] *Cynic* 9.

10.   **in such dwellings ... free from care:** the same important thought is stressed in section 41, and the *culmus* / *auro* contrast is also made at 8.5 'scitote tam bene hominem culmo quam auro tegi'.

11.   **'Then learnt they game ...:** Virgil, *G.* 1.139—40 (for the context see above on 9).

12.   **after forest fires ...:** the same theory is considered by Lucretius (5.1241 ff.). S. does not dispute that primitive metallurgy may have started like this, only that it was the *sapientes* who first saw how to use the metal ores revealed by the fires.

13.   **a bent back ...:** looking up to the heavens is the sign of one who is meditating on noble subjects, gazing at the ground shows the materialists and the money—grubbers, who are thus behaving like animals. Variations on this idea are very widespread: Plato *Rep.* 9.586 a; Cic. *ND* 2.140 (man's upright stature is designed to enable him to know God); Ovid *Met.* 1 84—6; Persius 2.61; Juv. 15.142—7; and elsewhere in S. at 92.30; 94.56; *NQ* 5.15.3.

14. Diogenes (fourth century B.C.) was the founder of the Cynic school: one of his principles was that we should have the fewest possible needs in our lives. Daedalus was a legendary craftsman, credited with numerous inventions. Pliny (*HN* 7.198) also states that he invented the saw, but Ovid (*Met.* 8.244—6) and Apollodorus (3.15.8) attribute it to a nephew of Daedalus. The anecdote about Diogenes is found also in Diog. Laert. 6.37.

15. **jets of saffron:** in Roman theatres and amphitheatres saffron was sprayed on to the stage and the audience, presumably in many cases to conceal less pleasant odours: see Lucr. 2.416; Ovid *Ars* 1.104; Prop. 4.1.16; Pliny *HN* 21.33. At *NQ* 2.9.2 S. refers to the mechanism of the jets: 'sparsio illa quae ex fundamentis mediae harenae crescens in summam usque amphitheatri altitudinem pervenit'.

    channels: a *euripus* (named after the narrow channel between Euboea and mainland Greece) was an artificial canal that often formed an attractive feature of a villa (55.6; Pliny *Ep.* 1.3.1). S. refers here to ingenious devices for simulating a tidal effect in the channels. (See also 83.5 n.).

    revolving panelled ceilings ...: as in Nero's *domus aurea*, which had 'cenationes laqueatae tabulis eburneis versatilibus', causing flowers and perfumes to be showered on the guests (Suet. *Nero* 31). Trimalchio's dining—room ceiling produced a similar spectacular effect (Petr. 60, with M.S. Smith's note).

    imported silks: the wearing of silk was attacked by moralists on the grounds of both its expensiveness and its indecent transparency. *Ben.* 7.9.5 is typical: 'video sericas vestes ... in quibus nihil est quo defendi aut corpus aut denique pudor possit ... ingenti summa ab ignotis etiam ad commercium gentibus accersuntur'.

    on its surface: i.e. without digging for precious metals. S. rings the changes several times on this theme: 94.56; 110.9; *Ben.* 7.1.6.

16. **at any rate very like them:** the qualification is necessary because the perfect *sapiens* was so rare: 57.3 n.

    life's essentials ... luxuries ...: a constant injunction in S., e.g. 4.10—11 'parabile est quod natura desiderat et adpositum. ad supervacua sudatur'. With *sequere naturam* we also have what could be called the motto of the Stoics — a basic rule which they used to support a wide range of ethical teaching.

    ad quaecumque is a compendious expression for *ad omnia ad quae.*

    even to—day: the—*que* in *hodieque* sometimes has this intensifying force: see *OLD* s.v. —*que* 11 c.

    mice: Blankert suggests that *mures* here are martens, and quotes Ammianus 31.2.5 on the Huns, who also dressed in the skins of *silvestres mures*.

17. **the Syrtic tribes:** peoples dwelling near the North African coast,

roughly between Carthage and Cyrene, so called after the Syrtes, two areas of shallow waters on that stretch of coast.

19. **abandoned nature:** *desciscere* is often used in philosophical contexts of abandoning a principle or standard: 122.9; *Ot.* 2.1 'non desciscere me a praeceptis Stoicorum'; Cic *Fin.* 4.43 'Stoici ... desciscunt a natura'; *OLD* s.v. 2.

superfluities ... injurious: a strong pair of words, found also at 89.13 'non tantum supervacuas esse dixit naturalem et rationalem (partes philosophiae) sed etiam contrarias'.

assigned the mind as a slave: *addicere* is technical in this sense, and S. is very fond of the metaphor of the mind as slave to the body or to pleasure: 71.14; 110.10; *Cons. Helv.* 11.6.

paraded around: this is the only occurrence of *circitare* outside of glossaries, though the noun *circitor* is found several times.

sensual dances: perhaps Ionian dances, which were considered lascivious: cf. Hor. *C.* 3.6.21−2 'motus doceri gaudet Ionicos / matura virgo' (a picture of decadent society).

effeminate songs: for *infractos* see 114.1 and n.

20−25. Posidonius got carried away by his own eloquence, *dulcedo orationis*, so that he wrongly claimed all sorts of practical inventions for philosophers. This oratorical self−indulgence seems to have been a notorious feature of Posidonius' style, as Strabo (3.2.9) also comments on it.

20. **firstly ... then ...:** *primum ... ducantur* refers to spinning, *deinde ... iungi* refers to weaving.

threads of the warp: the warp (vertical) threads are fastened to the top of the loom and kept hanging straight by weights attached to them. The weft (horizontal) threads when worked into the warp loosen the tension (*duritiam ... remolliat*) of the warp threads, and are themselves beaten down together by the batten. *tela, stamen* and *trama* all mean warp, and *subtemen* is weft. By way of *variatio* S. adds Ovid's description (*Met.* 6.55−8) of the same technique of weaving − though his memory has garbled and conflated two of Ovid's lines.

clothes which conceal nothing: like those made of silk: see note on 15 above.

21. **initial ploughing ... second ploughing:** both *proscindere* and *iterare* are technical farming terms, e.g. Varro *RR* 1.32.1 'si proscideris (terram), offringi oportet, id est iterare, ut frangantur glaebae'. For S.'s knowledge of agricultural terms cf. 12.2 n.

22. **relegates ... to the bakery:** Summers must be right in suggesting that there is an allusion here to the common practice of punishing slaves by making them work in the pounding mill or bakery.

by imitating nature: whether or not Posidonius rightly credited the *sapiens* with bread−making, the view that nature was the pattern for the arts was long and widely held: Arist. *Meteor.* 4. 381 b μιμεῖται γὰρ ἡ τέχνη τὴν φύσιν; (it was also a theme in Aristotle's *Protrepticus*: see O.C.T. *Fragmenta Selecta* (Iamblichus), p. 44); Cic. *Leg.* 1.26 'artes vero innumerabiles repertae sunt docente natura'; elsewhere in S. at 65.3 'omnis ars naturae imitatio est'; 66.39 'quid est ergo ratio? naturae imitatio'. (See Blankert's note for other references.) The belief was clearly of fundamental importance to the Stoics with their overall ideal of living *secundum naturam.*

23. **regulate the heat:** lit. 'the heat is subservient to control'. For a similar phrase to *serviret arbitrio* see Plaut. *Bac.* 994 'tuos tibi servos tuo arbitratu serviat'.
    even shoemaking: the *reductio ad absurdum* in S.'s view — but see Macaulay's acid comment quoted in introductory note.

24. **reason ... reason in its perfect form:** this is the crucial point: the *ratio* of ordinary men (by which they are separated from beasts) is quite adequate to make inventions; the *recta ratio* of philosophers (by which they are separated from ordinary men) is reserved for other things. *recta ratio* corresponds to ὀρθὸς λόγος, used by Stoics of the reason lying behind the world—process (see *L–S–J* s.v. λόγος III 7).
    fish provided the model: an example of art imitating nature: see above 22 n.

25. **windows ... transparent glass:** S. refers to the comparatively recent development of clear glass, contrasted with the earlier opaque polychrome glass used, for example, in *millefiori* ware. There is evidence of window glass at Pompeii, and in S.'s time windows that let in the light were worth commenting on: see 86.11 '(Scipio) non in caldarium suum latis specularibus diem admiserat'; Mart. 8.14.3–4 (describing a greenhouse) 'specularia puros/admittunt soles et sine faece diem'. *testa* must refer to the *lapis specularis*, some form of mica or gypsum (*OLD*), used in making these windows. (On the whole subject see *OCD* s.v. 'Glass'; D.B. Harden, *G & R* 9 (1934) 140—9.)
    raised bathrooms: these were the *pensilia balnea*, built over a hypocaust or heated vault, which were devised by one Sergius Orata about 100 B.C. (Pliny *HN* 9.168). For details see *OCD* s.v. 'Hypocaust'; and for other references to central heating among the comfort—loving Romans see *Prov.* 4.9 'cenationes subditus et parietibus circumfusus calor temperavit', and Pliny the Younger's complacent description of his villa, *Ep.* 2.17.9 and 23.
    our system of shorthand: the Romans had a system of shorthand, perhaps derived from a Greek one, which Plutarch (*Cato Mi.* 23) says was introduced by Cicero. He apparently worked closely with his freedman Tiro in developing it, and there are surviving lists of signs known as *notae Tironianae*. See E. Maunde Thompson, *An Introduction to Greek and Latin Palaeography*, 71—4.

common slaves: if *ista* refers to the activities in the three preceding questions, S. means that slaves are the builders with marble and stone blocks, and an ex—slave (Tiro) devised shorthand.

26 ff. S. now gives the first of two accounts (26—29, 34—35) of the philosopher's real task (see introductory note).

26. **philosophy occupies a higher seat:** the seat of a teacher of higher things (cf. 88.4 n.): cf. 95.10 'erras enim si tibi illam (philosophiam) putas tantum terrestres operas promittere: altius spirat'.

   the range of musical notes ...: cf. the similar description of horn—playing at 108.10 'spiritus noster clariorem sonum reddit cum illum tuba per longi canalis angustias tractum patentiore novissime exitu effudit'.

27. **art of living:** a favourite description of philosophy: 95.7; 117.12; Cic. *Fin.* 3.4. The phrase *artifex vitae*, 'craftsman of life', is used at *Vit. Beat.* 8.3 of the man who is 'incorruptus externis et insuperabilis'; and at 86.41 the *sapiens* is called 'artifex domandi mala'. The claims made here for philosophy recall 88.28 and 33.

28. **souls brought through to a secondary form of divinity:** the reading *perpetitae* is uncertain, but the general sense seems to be that souls may join a class of gods not belonging to the top rank of divinity. The meaning may be clarified by 110.1 (let us put aside the theory) 'unicuique nostrum paedagogum dari deum, non quidem ordinarium, sed hunc inferioris notae ex eorum numero quos Ovidius ait "de plebe deos" ... singulis enim et Genium et Iunonem dederunt'. (The Ovid quotation is from *Met.* 1.595; and for Genius and Iuno see 12.2 n.) Souls, then, might have a spell of existence as spirits of the rank of *genii*.

29. **the everlasting reason ... the force within all seeds:** *ratio* is the abstract *logos* or controlling principle of the world—process; *vis* is the essential life force which determines the visible structure and activities of things in nature (as in Lucr. 5.76—7 'praeterea solis cursus lunaeque meatus/expediam qua vi flectat natura gubernans').

   the soul: see 88.34 and n.

   the ambiguities in our life: at *NQ* 1 pr. 2 philosophy 'lumen admovet quo discernantur ambigua vitae'.

31. **Anacharsis:** a Scythian prince of the sixth century B.C., who became a by—word for wisdom and virtue and was counted among the Seven Sages. The date of the invention of the potter's wheel is unknown, but it was certainly in use at least by the early third millennium B.C. The reference to the wheel in Homer is at *Iliad* 18.600—1 — a simile in the description of the shield of Achilles. Diogenes Laertius (1.105) also reports a tradition that Anacharsis invented it.

   glass—blower ... after the philosophers disappeared: glass—blowing was invented in the first century B.C.; the philosophers here are the *sapientes* who were leaders among primitive men.

32. **Democritus:** see 7.10, 79.14.
33. **haven't you and your friends forgotten ...:** S. is of course ironic: what else can we think of to credit Democritus with? On softening ivory Summers quotes Plut. *An vitiositas* 499 e (ivory is softened and made workable by soaking it in beer). The term *zmaragdus* or *smaragdus* was applied to the emerald and other green gems. Pliny (*HN* 37.197) refers to the practice of dyeing rock—crystal to imitate *smaragdi*, and the use of counterfeit *smaragdi* was quite common in antiquity: see *Theophrastus On Stones*, ed. Caley and Richards, (Columbus Ohio, 1956), 98, and the note in Diels—Kranz on Democritus, 68 B 300, 14.
34. **eyes ... slow to grasp divine things:** just as at 28 'ad spectacula tam magna hebes visus est'.
    a rule of life: the doctrine that we must accept what happens to us as ordered by the gods is quintessential Senecan Stoicism: see 76.23 'unum illi (viro bono) bonum erit quod honestum ... patienter excipere fatum et facere imperata'; 94.7 'omnia fortiter excipienda quae nobis mundi necessitas imperat'; 120.12 'vir ille perfectus adeptusque virtutem ... , civem esse se universi et militem credens labores velut imperatos subit'.
    weighed all things ... valuation: this is one of the tasks of *philosophia moralis*, as we are told in 89.14 ('aestimans quanto quidque dignum sit').
    pleasures which bring repentance: S. warns against these also at 27.2 'dimitte istas voluptates turbidas, magno luendas'; but the warning was not confined to Stoics, for Epicurus too avoided pleasures that involved greater pains (Diog. Laert. 10.129). The *summum bonum* also 'nec satietatem habet nec paenitentiam' (*Vit. Beat.* 7.4).
    the most fortunate man ...: for the paradox see 98.1 'numquam credideris felicem quemquam ex felicitate suspensum', and 12.5 n.
35. **that philosophy ...:** S. summarizes the three main tenets of Epicureanism, political non—involvement for the individual, relegation of the gods to dwellings between the worlds (*intermundia*), and pleasure as the ideal condition of life. The contrasting Stoicism is similarly characterized, especially in the words *nullum bonum... nisi quod honestum est*, which is a frequent and standard Stoic formula (71.5; 74.1; 76.6; 85.17; 120.3; Cic. *Tusc.* 2.61).
    I do not believe ...: the rest of the letter is devoted to showing that philosophy as just defined did not exist in the earliest societies.
36. **nor in those happy times:** the opening words of the sentence are corrupt, but the translation gives the general sense.
    what philosophers are supposed to do: that is, live according to nature, as the Stoics taught.
37 ff. S. paints a standard picture of the Golden Age (see introductory note) and quotes another one from Virgil (*G.* 1.125—8), to give an

added literary resonance.

38. **then greed burst into this ideal world ...:** the same thought as in 3 above.

39. **the dimensions of provinces:** a characteristically Roman measure of vast properties: cf. 89.20 'ne provinciarum quidem spatio contenti circumscribere praediorum modum', and similar expressions at 87.7; *Ira* 1.21.2.

40. **the stronger had not yet laid a hand ...:** this clearly contradicts 5, 'infirmiorem a validioribus tuebantur'. S. has changed his viewpoint, unless he is reproducing an inconsistency in Posidonius' reasoning (see note on 4—6).

41. **what soft sleep the hard ground gave them:** the commonplace 'uneasy lies the head that wears a crown' has had a long history: *Phae* 520—1 'certior somnus premit / secura duro membra versantem toro'; Epicurus fr. 207 Us.; [Lucian] *Cynic* 9; and a variation in Lucr. 2.34—6. For a similar idea see also 10 above.

42. This is a fine piece of imaginative description, as S. pictures the beauties of the heavens by night and by day, open to the wondering gaze of primitive men. Passages like this show him a master not just of the clipped style of pungent epigram.
    all that mighty creation: for *opus* used of the cosmic structure see *Prov.* 1.2 'non sine aliquo custode tantum opus stare'; *NQ* 7.25.6; Ovid *F.* 5.12.

43. **you tremble:** 'you' (*vos*) the present generation, compared with the innocents of old: Lucilius has faded from view.
    without fearing the house ...: primitive men did not have houses which could, for example, catch fire or fall down.

44. **men ... fresh from the gods:** early men were closer to the gods, whether by their origin or in their innocence: Plato *Philebus* 16 c; Cic. *Tusc.* 1.26, *Leg.* 2.27.
    the earth ... before it was worn out: S. is stating a view which was widely held, that the earth, the original mother, as she aged and became exhausted ceased to bear creatures, or produced creatures which were inferior to those she bore in her youth: cf. especially Lucr. 2.1150—74, 5.826—36. (See Blankert here and my notes on Lucr. 5.826—36.)
    nature does not give virtue: the point the letter started with (1): 'philosophiam ... cuius scientiam nulli dederunt'.

45. **killing their fellow—men ... to provide a spectacle:** as described in Letter 7: see 7.3 n.

46. **innocence ... ignorance:** so at 95.5 people whose minds have not absorbed good precepts 'etiam si recte faciunt, nesciunt facere se recte'.
    justice, practical wisdom, self—control and courage: these are the four virtues into which Cicero subdivides *honestum* (*Off.* 1.15 ff.: see

also *Fin.* 5.67).

virtue only reaches a mind which has been trained: a basic assumption in other contexts: 88.32 'quamvis enim virtus discenda sit ...'; 123.16 'nemo est casu bonus: discenda virtus est'.

LETTER 92

S. meditates on a stock theme: is virtue sufficient for happiness? For the Stoics the *telos*, the goal of life, is virtue and virtuous action, defined as living in harmony with nature. Everything else is indifferent (ἀδιάφορον), but among indifferent things there are some which are preferable (προηγμένα) and which include natural advantages like health and wealth. The sage may choose these provided they do not divert him from the main aim of acquiring virtue. There was much discussion in the Early Stoa on how the choice of natural advantages affected the achievement of the ultimate goal of virtue, and leading Stoics like Chrysippus, Diogenes of Babylon and Antipater of Tarsus offered various formulations to allow such a choice within their definitions of the *telos*. (See A.A. Long, *Hellenistic Philosophy*, 194 ff.)

The sequence of arguments can be analysed as follows (and it may be noted that except at the beginning, there are almost no indications of a letter to Lucilius, but several appearances of the argumentative objector − *inquit* at 11, 14, 17, 21, 24, 27):

1−3   Happiness depends on the possession of *ratio* in its highest form and therefore is a characteristic of the *sapiens*.

4−10   Some people think that irrational or external elements contribute to the happy life, e.g. tranquillity and pleasure: S. allows tranquillity but excludes pleasure.

11−13   We may choose certain external advantages because they are in accord with nature and because of our mental attitude in choosing them.

14−18   To admit that the *sapiens* can be at all happy even if afflicted by physical suffering is to admit that he can be completely happy. The power of *virtus* to overcome external calamities is not limited.

19−26   Physical qualities or afflictions are wrong criteria of happiness. Virtue and therefore happiness do not admit of degrees of intensity, and are not affected even by physical suffering.

27−35   Men have the gift of reason in common with the gods, and the soul, once it is freed of vices and can despise wealth and possessions, aspires to return to its origins in the heavens and has no interest in the death of the body.

1.   **the body is looked after for the sake of the soul:** tnis is the philosopher's view; but for the sensualist the mind becomes the slave

to the body: 90.19 n.

the soul has subordinate parts ... the ruling element: the Stoics considered the soul to have eight parts – the five senses, the parts controlling reproduction and speech, and the governing–principle (τὸ ἡγεμονικόν, *principale* here). The governing–principle is the central and dominant element; it is the seat of consciousness, and it is situated in the heart. The presence of the rational element in this governing–principle is what distinguishes men from the other animals. Chrysippus had said that the whole of the governing–principle is rational; Posidonius, probably influenced by Plato, rejected this and said that allowance must be made for an irrational element. S. here follows Posidonius: see also 8 below. (For further details of Stoic psychology see A.A. Long, op. cit. 171–5.) S. refers to the *principale* also at 113.23; 121.10; *Ira* 1.3.7.

2. **reason in its perfect form:** as acquired by the *sapiens*, who thereby knows how to live according to nature: see also 90.24 n. – *recta ratio* there is equivalent to *ratio perfecta* here.

   guarding us ...: the uncertainty in the text here does not affect the general meaning: see the Apparatus for conjectures.

3. **freedom from care and unbroken tranquillity:** in contrast with *aliena* these depend on ourselves, and are acquired by our own efforts, as S. goes on to say. The cardinal quality in the following catalogue is *voluntas ... intenta rationi nec umquam ab illa recedens.*

5. **some claim that the highest good can be increased:** implying that virtue is not in itself a sufficient condition for the *summum bonum* without natural advantages. These thinkers would include Epicurus (see 85.18 for his view that virtue alone is not enough for the happy life) and the 'Middle' Stoics Panaetius and Posidonius (Diog. Laert. 7.128: we need health, material resources and strength as well as virtue). Antipater of Tarsus (see introductory note) was head of the Stoa for twenty years from about 150 B.C.

6. **tranquillity...:** the Greek term may have been technical philosophical (especially Epicurean) jargon, as surviving examples of its use seem to be confined to such contexts (see *L–S–J* s.v.).

   the trivial to the great: some word or words must have fallen out after *magno*, probably giving a contrasting sense to it.

7. **men of worth:** *viri* are contrasted with *homines* in somewhat the sense of the English 'real men': cf. 31.7 'non est viri timere sudorem'; 104.25; *OLD* s.v. 3.

8. **the irrational part of the soul:** see note on 1 above. The sub–division of the irrational part here ultimately derives from Platonic psychology (in *Republic* 4 the soul is described as having three parts, rational, spirited and appetitive), which seems to have influenced Posidonius, and in turn S.

9. **Scylla:** the quotation is from Virgil, *Aen.* 3.426–8 (Helenus warns

Aeneas of dangers on his journey). For Scylla see also 79.1 n. S. chooses a notoriously horrifying hybrid of mythology to make his point in this rather laboured comparison, though it was Scylla's destructive powers rather than her physical form which became proverbial.

10. **that other condition, tranquillity:** after the extended attack on *voluptas* S. reminds us that *quies* (see 6 above) could be allowed as a contributory aid to the supreme good.

11. **of course I shall:** this is a clear statement of the Stoic attitude to that class of natural advantages which are 'preferable' and which the sage may choose: the key phrases here are *secundum naturam, bono iudicio,* and *rationi convenientem modum*.

13. **nature has enveloped the soul with the body ...:** another variation of the familiar image of the body as the soul's container: see 79.12 n; 88.34 n.

14—18 The argument is that there are no degrees of happiness for the *sapiens*: if it is admitted that he can triumph over pain and distress it must also be allowed that his triumph is complete. S. uses a form of the sorites argument: at what point on the ascending scale of happiness can you say that the sage is this much happy and no more? Such a decision would be quite arbitrary, and it is more logical to say that if he can achieve happiness against obstacles, he can *ipso facto* achieve complete happiness. The *summum bonum* is, after all, by definition supreme; so the sage having achieved that should enjoy correspondingly supreme beatitude.

14. **natural means ... natural goods:** the objector tries to turn the Stoic's own phraseology against him with *naturalia* and *naturalibus*.

17. **a while ago I was saying ...:** in section 5.
   the sun remains unaffected by obstacles: Lucretius carefully explains (5.281 ff.) that fire in the visible form of light is made up of a stream of successive particles, so that the sun, even when blocked by a cloud, continues to pour forth its light particles. S. works out the parallel carefully, making an acute distinction between *obstare* and *impedire* in the physical world and between *opponere* and *detrahere* in the sphere of virtue. The comparison here gains force from the fact that S. likes to refer to virtue or the good life in language reminiscent of the sun: 93.5 (the man who has achieved the *summum bonum*) 'vidit enim veram lucem'; *Ben.* 4.17.4 'virtus in omnium animos lumen suum permittit'.

19—26 The fundamental Stoic belief that underlies the arguments here is that physical suffering and disability are irrelevant to the happiness that virtue brings. Illness and pain are certainly among those 'indifferent' things which the wise man would choose not to have (ἀποπροηγμένα) if he could do so and remain virtuous, but they must not be thought of as even qualifying the intensity of his happiness.

19. **accidentals:** for *fortuita* in the sense of *externa* see 5 above, *fortuitis repugnantibus*.

21. **as you say:** that is, you admit implicitly that this man (the wise man of section 20) remains in a state between happiness and wretchedness — and this makes nonsense of your analogy with hot, cold and tepid.

23. **virtue alone suffices to produce it:** the answer to the central question of the letter.

24. **virtue does not have degrees of intensity:** for the same thought and wording see 71.16 'non est ergo M. Catonis maius bonum honesta vita quam mors honesta, quoniam non intenditur virtus'.
    pleasure is not an end ...: so we must not be tempted by the Epicureans (cf. the arguments of sections 6—10).

25. **it does not need the future ...:** the length of a virtuous life is irrelevant compared with its quality: see 78.27 n.
    apply its name to our vices: and therefore we cannot comprehend genuine virtue when we see it.
    studio: *officina* has here the sense of a training—school, and is used of Epicurus' Garden also at 14.17. The same story is told about Epicurus at 66.47, and Diogenes Laertius (10.22) records that Epicurus, on the point of a painful death from these ailments, wrote to his friend Idomeneus, saying that on that last happy day of his life the physical agony he suffered was matched by his joy in recalling their past conversations together.

26. **these degenerate and petty—minded people:** the Epicureans (in spite of Epicurus' personal heroism under suffering): see also note on 5 above.
    once virtue has taken its stand: *virtus*, the quality of the good soldier or gladiator, is here itself the soldier (gladiator).

27—35 The last part of the letter takes an elevated tone, emphasising man's link with the gods through his possession of *ratio* and the natural urge of the soul to match the wishes of the gods and, unencumbered by vices, to return to its original home.

29. **wickedness of a more violent and deep—rooted kind:** the text is corrupt but the sense apparently is a serious tendency to wickedness contrasted with the lesser *malitiae vis quaedam:* cf. 75.10 'nemo sit extra periculum malitiae nisi qui totam eam excussit; nemo autem illam excussit nisi qui pro illa sapientiam adsumpsit'.

30. The quotation is from Virgil, *Aen.* 5.363 (with *corpore* for *pectore*) — an exhortation to boxers in the Sicilian games. In the following sentences there is the usual Stoic assumption that each human *animus* derives from the cosmic *pneuma*, to which it instinctively longs to return (57.7 n.).
    as our bodies go upright ..: see 90.13 n.

31. **to stock our souls:** for *animum impleri debere* we might have had *se impleri debere*, as *animus* has been the subject of all the main verbs

from *redit* (30).

32. **we can give the soul supreme power** ...: cf. *Ben*. 7.8.1 'cum animum sapientis intuemur potentem omnium et per universa dimissum'.

33. **a necessary burden** ... **a servant of the body** ... **other masters we acquire** ...: all this is common coin of many schools of moralizing, and the language reflects passages in other letters, e.g. 14.1 'multis enim serviet qui corpori servit'; 65.16 'corpus hoc animi pondus ac poena est'.

34. **'Thrown to the dog—fish** ...: S. is presumably misquoting Virgil, *Aen*. 9.485 'canibus data praeda Latinis' (Euryalus' mother laments her dead son).

35. **a corpse displayed** ...: the usual practice with executed criminals at Rome.

     nature has taken care ...: for this sentiment and the quotation from Maecenas see Lucan 7.818—19 (on the unburied dead at Pharsalia) 'capit omnia tellus / quae genuit: caelo tegitur qui non habet urnam'. Maecenas' writings in relation to his life—style are discussed extensively at 114.4 ff. With him the letter ends rather abruptly, but in this last section the soul has spoken S.'s peroration.

LETTER 104

S. takes a trip to the country to recover from an illness. He is duly cured, but the main theme of the letter is that a change of scene is no good for an ailing soul, which takes its faults with it. The only cure is to study and cultivate the wise.

It is a familiar *topos* that you cannot escape from yourself simply by changing your surroundings, and we find many variations on the theme in other writers and elsewhere in S.'s works. (See note on section 7.)

The main sequence of ideas is as follows:

1—6	A trip to Nomentum successfully cures a fever that is afflicting S. He is taking particular care of himself for the sake of his wife.
7—20	Travel will not cure our moral failings and our false values, since we take them with us wherever we go (though travel will show us interesting and unfamiliar sights, 15).
21—22	We should avoid vicious company and choose the examples of the wise and the good.
23—26	Nature endowed us with noble souls: we should therefore be fearless in the face of difficulties.
27—33	Here are two examples for you: Socrates and Cato of Utica.
34	We can emulate them provided we reject pleasures and wealth.

1. **my place at Nomentum:** see 12.1n. Nomentum is the modern

Mentana. On S.'s recurrent ill—health see introduction to 54.

Paulina: S. mentions his wife Pompeia Paulina only in this letter. We hear that he had a son who died young in 41 (*Cons. Helv.* 2.5), and there has been speculation whether Paulina was a second wife. (For a discussion of this see M.T. Griffin, *Seneca, a Philosopher in Politics*, 57—9.) Their strong affection for each other is confirmed by Tacitus' words 'sibi unice dilectam' (*Ann.* 15.63) in his account of S.'s death: Paulina wanted to share her husband's suicide but was prevented by Nero's orders.

Gallio: S.'s elder brother, who was proconsul of Achaea in c. 52 and is best known for his refusal to hear the case brought by the Jews against St. Paul (*Acts* 18.12—17).

2. **her existence depends on mine...:** for the sentiment here see S.'s attitude to his father's feelings in 78.2.

 inside this old man ... a young man: the sense is somewhat obscure, but perhaps S. means that old age has not made him philosophically tough through and through, and that earlier, more vulnerable feelings survive within him which he has to respect, including his reactions to his wife's appeals. For the idea cf. Plato, *Phaedo* 77 e ἔνι τις καὶ ἐν ἡμῖν παῖς, though the reference there is to childish fears that linger within us.

3. **for the sake of our dear ones:** cf. 78.4, where the sympathy and support of his friends helps S.'s recovery from illness.

6. **my vineyards:** the vineyards in the Nomentum area, and S.'s in particular, were famous for their excellence. Columella (3.3.3) praises the region for its vineyards, especially that part owned by S.; and Pliny (*HN* 14.51) reports how S. enthusiastically paid a high price for his vineyards there. S. describes his technique of vine propagation at 112.2.

7 ff. The letter now shifts direction to show the limits to the benefits travel brings — it is helpful to an ailing body, as we have just heard, but useless to cure the ills of a faulty soul. The link is the opening remark that even physical benefits of a change of place depend also on mental self—mastery, *nisi se sibi praestat animus*. This leads on to the moralizing *topos* that the soul cannot escape from itself and leave its faults behind simply by a change of scene. We find the idea expressed pithily by Aeschines, *Ctes.* 78 (the vicious man) οὐ γὰρ τὸν τρόπον ἀλλὰ τὸν τόπον μετήλλαξεν; the theme is a favourite with Horace: *C.* 2.16.18—20 'quid terras alio calentes / sole mutamus? patriae quis exul / se quoque fugit?', *Sat.* 2.7.111—15, *Ep.* 1.11.27, 1.14.13; and see also Lucr. 3.1068—70. There are variations on the idea elsewhere in S. at 2.1; 28.1 ('animum debes mutare, non caelum'); 69.1; *Tranq.* 2.14.

 there is a story ...: the same quip of Socrates is quoted at 28.2.

9. **however much you have ...:** discontent with one's lot was a favourite

theme among Hellenistic sermonizers, e.g. the Cynics, and we have a vigorous treatment of the topic in Hor. *Sat.* 1.1: cf. especially S.'s 'imaginary poverty' with Horace's 'neque se maiori pauperiorum / turbae comparet' (1.1.111—12). The theme of political jealousy and ambition in this section appears also in *Ira* 1.21.3 'ambitio ... non est contenta honoribus annuis; si fieri potest, uno nomine occupare fastus vult, per omnem orbem titulos disponere'; *Brev. Vit.* 20.1.

10. The quotation is from Virgil, *Aen.* 3.282—3. Aeneas and his fellow—exiles on their journey westward have got round to the western coast of Greece, shortly before the final crossing to Italy, and have thus won their way through the hostile territory in their path. S.'s point is that the habit of needless fear will persist even when real dangers are over.

11. **the worst of afflictions ... loved ones:** in S.'s view the death of a friend was the hardest of afflictions, even worse than the loss of a son (99.2—3).

    be reasonable in your view ...: the text is faulty, and probably some further reference to trees and leaves is lost: see the Apparatus for suggestions. This is the typical language of the *consolatio*, and the parallel between falling leaves and perishing mankind goes back to a famous passage in the *Iliad* 6.146 ff. οἵη περ φύλλων γενεή, τοίη δὲ καὶ ἀνδρῶν ...

    they are replaced: the same thought is expressed crisply at 63.11: 'satius est amicum reparare quam flere'.

12. **every day ... alters you:** cf. 58.22 'nemo nostrum idem est in senectute qui fuit iuvenis; nemo nostrum est idem mane qui fuit pridie'.

    don't hope ...: the mannered phrasing of this injunction recalls the slightly different *sententia* at *Med* 163 'qui nil potest sperare, desperet nihil'.

14. **the effect of movement:** though this can be physically beneficial: see 78.5 'viscera molli iactatione concutias', and note there.

15. Travel would naturally appeal to S.'s own thirst for scientific and topographical information (his *Natural Questions* alone are evidence of a voraciously enquiring mind); and for Lucilius' similar interests see the introduction to 79. There is another enthusiastic passage on this theme in *Ot.* 5.1—3 'hoc non erit probatum ... quantam cupidinem habeat ignota noscendi...? navigant quidam et labores peregrinationis longissimae una mercede perpetiuntur cognoscendi aliquid abditum remotumque ...'.

    Nile, Tigris: the Nile is discussed in detail at *NQ* 4a.2, and the Tigris at *NQ* 3.26.4 and 6.8.2.

    Maeander ... on which every poet has enjoyed practising his craft: e.g. Propertius (2.34.35—6), Ovid (*Met.* 8.162—6), and S. himself at *HF* 683—5. The twistings of the Maeander's course were so famous that its name was applied to any maze–like shape — and so came into English usage.

17. **your troubles are following you:** a commonplace thought, e.g. 82.4 'quid deinde prodest secessisse? tamquam non trans maria nos sollicitudinum causae persequantur'.

18. Here we again have the common analogy between bodily and spiritual sickness and the medical imagery so often used by S., and by the Cynics and Stoics before him: see 7.1 n.

20. **your companion:** your own mind and wicked ways.
The idea that you acquire vices by association with the vicious is the theme of Letter 7: note especially 7.2 'nemo non aliquod nobis vitium aut commendat aut imprimit aut nescientibus adlinit'; 7.7 'unum exemplum luxuriae aut avaritiae multum mali facit ...'.

21–22. The advice to turn to the wise and good is underlined by naming the *exempla*, whereas the vicious were characterised as types. We meet the Catos (especially Uticensis) very frequently in the Letters; Laelius at 7.6. Tubero (second century B.C.) was a Stoic, a member of the Scipionic Circle, and a friend of Panaetius. His simple and frugal life–style was noteworthy (95.72–3; 98.13; 120.19; Cic. *Brut.* 117). Socrates, Chrysippus and Posidonius are also very familiar; and for Zeno see 83.9 n.

22. **practical activity ... clever talking:** this is the usual contrast: see 20.2 'facere docet philosophia, non dicere', and 24.15 n.
harbour in the stormy tossing sea of life: for the image cf. Cic. *Tusc.* 5.16. This metaphor was much favoured by the Epicureans, e.g. Epicurus, *Ep. Men.* 128, and Usener 544; Lucr. 5.11–12.

23. **a spirit most like the cosmos:** a reference to the Stoic theory of the connection between the individual soul and the cosmic *pneuma* to which it aspires to return.

24. The quotation is from Virgil, *Aen.* 6.277 — part of a description of the ghastly forms which confront Aeneas and the Sibyl at the Gates of Hell. See 24.12–13 for the idea that things are only fearful until you see through their appearances to the reality.

25. **real man ... any man:** for this distinction between *vir* and *homo* see 92.7 n.

26. **it is not because ...:** the symmetry in thought and phrasing is a favourite with S.: see 7.8 n.

27 ff. S. concludes the letter with two very famous *exempla*, one Greek and one Roman.

27. **Socrates ... who endured so much:** Socrates was famous for his toughness in the face of physical hardship: Plato, *Symp.* 219 e ff. As S. says, his lifetime (469–399 B.C.) spanned a period of great military and political turmoil — the Peloponnesian War (431–404) and the rule of the Thirty Tyrants at Athens after the war. The restoration of democracy in 403 proved to be *libertas saevior* for

Socrates because in 399 he was brought to trial on the charge of introducing strange gods and corrupting the youth. S. stresses this ironic fact elsewhere: *Tranq.* 5.3 'hunc (Socratem) tamen Athenae ipsae in carcere occiderunt, et qui tuto insultaverat agmini tyrannorum, eius libertatem libertas non tulit'; *Ben.* 5.6.7. Many sources testify to Socrates' sufferings from his nagging wife Xanthippe: S. records an episode when she poured dirty water over him (*Const. Sap.* 18.5).

perpessicius is a very rare word, also found at 53.6.

See the Apparatus for conjectures for the corrupt *sivere*, which probably conceals a verb taking *uxorem* and *liberos* as objects. The general meaning of the sentence is reasonably clear.

28. **prison and the poison:** Plato's *Phaedo* gives us an account of Socrates' last hours, spent in lively conversation with his friends.

29. **Marcus Cato:** for Cato of Utica see note on 24.4−6. S. alludes to Cato's involvement in the complex political and military events leading up to and including the Civil War of 49−6 B.C., and it suits his argument to stress Cato's sturdy independence throughout, though Cato in fact took the Pompeian side in the war.

   blocked him ... even in his death: because he was initially prevented in his attempt to commit suicide: see 24.8.

   For *intacta* Gronovius' *in pace* is as good as any suggestion; and the translation assumes something like Haase's conjecture *servituti se eduxisse* for *inseruisse dixisse*.

   Pompey and Caesar and Crassus: the 'First Triumvirate' in 60 B.C.

30. **political defeat:** at the consular elections for 51. He had been praetor in 54.

   making an accusation: notably against Murena and against the Catilinarian conspirators (both in 63).

   his province: at the time of his death Cato was governor of Utica, the capital of the Roman province of Africa.

   with Caesar lined up on one side ...: cf. the very similar picture of Cato's position at 14.12: 'videtur tibi M. Cato modeste philosophari ... qui furentium principum armis medius intervenit? qui aliis Pompeium offendentibus, aliis Caesarem, simul lacessit duos?'.

31. Another Virgilian quotation, *Aen.* 1.458 (with *Atriden* for *Atridas*), part of the description of the pictures on Dido's temple to Juno, depicting scenes from the Trojan War. Achilles is of course Cato, but which of the others represents Caesar and which Pompey is not obvious — and hardly matters.

33. This section summarizes Cato's tremendous physical and moral toughness, and the repeated *vides* gives a rhetorical flourish to the climax.

34. The moral: we too can act like this if we get our values right.

LETTER 110

This letter is an eloquent plea for a sane outlook on life, and, with the aid of philosophy, for the strength of mind to reject groundless fears and reduce our needs to a minimum.

1–2   You should cultivate a healthy state of mind and be on good terms with yourself.

3–4   It is essential to measure and evaluate our affairs correctly: frequently we mistake how things will turn out and indulge too much in hopes and fears.

5–7   In any case our fears are illusory.

8–10   Enlightenment comes through the study of philosophy, but we have turned away from it and become slaves to avarice and pleasure.

11–13   The cure is to learn to distinguish the essential from the superfluous and to despise even essentials.

14–20   Attalus once described how the sight of a brilliant procession suddenly convinced him of the vanity of riches: real wealth is to be content with little, and if you reduce your wants to nothing you are equal to the gods.

Many of these thoughts are familiar, and in particular this letter can be compared with 24, for example in the insistence that we should not be deceived by appearances and tormented by false fears. The heart of the lesson in 110 is that we can dispel our mental darkness only by the light of wide and intense philosophical study (8–9).

1.   **my place at Nomentum:** see notes on 12.1 and 104.1.

wish you health of mind: a variation on the usual wish for physical health. (S. talks about conventional greetings in letters at 15.1; and cf. Plato, *Ep.* 3.315 b.) Here *mens bona* is defined as having the gods well disposed to you: elsewhere S. often uses it in the sense of wisdom and virtue, e.g. 16.1; *Brev. Vit.* 3.5.

S. dismisses as irrelevant for the time being two questions, whether we are endowed with guardian spirits and whether the gods look after humans in their daily lives. More important than these speculations is the aim to achieve the right state of mind ourselves.

a god appointed to him as a guardian: see 12.2 n. for Genius and Iuno, and Pliny *HN* 2.16 'singuli quoque ex semetipsis totidem deos faciant Iunones Geniosque adoptando sibi'. These guardian spirits correspond to what the Greeks called *daimones*, or semi–divine beings not given the full rank of gods. In the Ovid passage (*Met.* 1.595) Jupiter is asserting his own powers in contrast with lesser divinities. See also 90.28 n.

our ancestors ... were essentially Stoics: because like the Stoics they believed that a divine element of some sort was incorporated in

2. **we shall see presently ...:** in fact S. does not return to the question in this letter, and he is probably just postponing the point indefinitely.

3–4. It was commonly observed that apparent prosperity could simply intensify a subsequent disaster, and conversely that troubles were often blessings in disguise. Variations on the idea can be found from Homer (*Od.* 16.211–12) to Claudian (*In Rufinum* 1.21–3). Horace is typical: *C.* 1.34.12–14 'valet ima summis / mutare et insignem attenuat deus, / obscura promens' (see Nisbet—Hubbard for many parallels); and the Claudian passage is much like ours: 'iam non ad culmina rerum / iniustos crevisse queror: tolluntur in altum / ut lapsu graviore ruant'.

3. **turn out well ... badly:** S. is contrasting *contingere* and *accidere*, used here respectively of fortunate and unfortunate occurrences, though the distinction is not generally a firm one in the use of these verbs.

4. **thrown out ... let out:** another linguistic point: the verbs *eicere* and *emittere* are contrasted as in the account of Cato's death at 24.8 (he too, like the *felix* here, 'spiritum non emisit sed eiecit'). The lesson is that we should remember our mortality and not expect to prolong our state of being, whether it is happy or unhappy.

5–7. These sections further develop the point about our fears (*istuc malum*): they are in any case groundless, and might actually on close inspection reveal something of value (*bonum*) or an element of reassurance (*tuta*).

6. S. quotes Lucretius (2.55–6), who was also concerned to dispel illusory fears, though his method was by the Epicurean not the Stoic *ratio*. S. characteristically goes one better and suggests that our darkness, as well as our fears, is self—induced.

8. **daylight can come ...:** S. continues the metaphor with philosophy providing light (*lucescere*) in the darkness of our moral confusion. But mere superficial dabbling in the subject is not enough: we must thoroughly immerse ourselves in all aspects of philosophy, physics and cosmology as well as ethics.

9. **from this divine spectacle we have withdrawn our minds:** this is a familiar Senecan contrast between upward—gazing contemplation of celestial things and money—grubbing preoccupation with riches hidden in the earth: see 94.56 '(natura) nihil quo avaritiam nostram inritaret posuit in aperto: pedibus aurum argentumque subiecit ... illa vultus nostros erexit ad caelum et quidquid magnificum mirumque fecerat videri a suspicientibus voluit'; and for *non contentus oblatis* cf. 90.15 'si contenti fuerimus iis quae terra posuit in summo'. With these words the argument shifts to another familiar topic, the attack on luxury and greed.

10. **we have enslaved our souls to pleasure:** see 90.19 n.

11. **distinguish ... the essential and the superfluous:** another characteristic point is S.'s impatience with *supervacua*, which waste our time and

distract our minds from what is important: cf. the strong condemnation of superfluous learning at 88.35 ff. However, the argument is taken further here: the really admirable attitude is to despise even essentials (12) (a more extreme position even than that of the Cynics), and the mention of basic food leads to yet another familiar Senecan target of attack, the luxury of eating (13): cf. 78.23−4; 95.15; 119.13−14; *NQ* 3.17−18, 4b.13.

12. **flamingoes' tongues:** these were famous as a gourmet's dish: Pliny *HN* 10.133; Mart. 13.71.

    disgusted with whole animals: cf. 78.24 'totas (aves) enim videre fastidium est'.

13. **seasoned:** *condīta*, from *condio*.

    one uniform horrid mess ... look at what happens to it: the sort of blunt realism which might be found in a Cynic diatribe drives home S.'s climactic argument against greed. A similar thought occurs in Aristotle, *Protrept.* fr. 59 R: would a beautiful body still appear so to us if we could see the ugliness inside it?

14. **Attalus:** a Stoic philosopher who taught S. (108.3), and was considered by the elder Seneca a man of great eloquence and by far the most acute philosopher of his time (*Suas.* 2.12). S. quotes him admiringly several times in the Letters. This quotation ends our letter with Attalus' meditation on a passing parade as an image of the passing of riches; and his final advice to us to reduce our needs to nothing is a restatement of S.'s point that real virtue lies in despising even essentials (12). For another use of the procession as an image of instability and change see Lucian, *Nec.* 16 (human life is like a passing pageant).

18. **we have water, we have barley: we may vie with Jupiter:** cf. 25.4 'panem et aquam natura desiderat. nemo ad haec pauper est, intra quae quisquis desiderium suum clusit cum ipso Iove de felicitate contendat' (quoting Epicurus: see Usener 602); 119.7 '"at parum habet qui tantum non alget, non esurit, non sitit." plus Iuppiter non habet'; 18.10.

19. **hunger ends hunger:** we die of hunger and so cease to be hungry.

20. **the one over whom fortune has no hold:** the *sapiens* of, for example, 57.3 'in quem fortuna ius perdidit' (see note there). So simply by wanting nothing the philosopher achieves the ultimate goal of equality with the gods, and this equality is a recurrent theme in the Letters: 9.16; 73.13 'deus non vincit sapientem felicitate, etiam si vincit aetate; non est virtus maior quae longior'. Moreover, since the *sapiens* has achieved felicity by his own efforts, in a way he even surpasses the gods: 53.11−12 'est aliquid quo sapiens antecedat deum: ille naturae beneficio non timet, suo sapiens. ecce res magna, habere inbecillitatem hominis, securitatem dei'.

LETTER 114

S. argues for the theory that there is a demonstrable connection between a man's character and his style of speech. This is illustrated by the example of Maecenas — foppish in his behaviour as in his literary style — and the letter continues to show that there are no fixed rules for style, and we find the idiosyncrasies of an influential author imitated to excess by lesser writers.

1—12   S. explores the theme *talis hominibus fuit oratio qualis vita*, using Maecenas as an example.

13—14   There are no fixed rules for style.

15—16   Faults in word—order and rhythm.

17—19   Minor writers sometimes imitate to excess the mannerisms of great ones, e.g. Arruntius and Sallust.

20—23   Faults due to imitation must be distinguished from inborn ones: the latter arise when the mind is unsound.

24—27   So too when the mind has lost self—control we become a prey to greed.

This letter is one of the most important texts in the study of attitudes to prose style in the first century A.D. We have plenty of evidence of concern among writers themselves at what many of them saw as a decline in literary — and more precisely oratorical — standards, and several theories were canvassed to account for this. The *Dialogus* of Tacitus purports to record a debate on this topic, and one of the reasons suggested there, a moral decline in the community, is based on very similar assumptions to those we find in S.'s letter. The same theory too was voiced by the Elder Seneca (*Contr.* 1 praef. 7—8), though he gave as an alternative explanation the cyclic theory that after anything has grown to perfection the only subsequent development must be a decline: this theory was also favoured by the historian Velleius Paterculus (1.17). Again, the treatise 'Longinus' *On Sublimity* (44) discusses what it sees as a decline in literature, and links this closely with a moral decline. Thus our letter must be viewed in the context of a wide—ranging debate which lasted throughout most of the first century A.D. on a subject of crucial interest to its own practitioners.

In other letters S. discusses the right style for philosophical writing and lecturing (40, 100, 115), saying firmly that it is the matter not the manner of such discourses which is important. Letter 114 has a wider application, but its style/character correlation is picked up in 115 with the statement there of the link between *oratio* and *animus* (115.2).

1.   **effeminate sing—song effects:** the Latin words indicate that S. means unpleasantly exaggerated rhythmical effects. We must remember that rhythm and metrical cadences were widely used by skilled writers in prose as well as poetry to achieve a great variety of subtle effects. Seneca's own Letters are highly rhythmical in character: see

226 - COMMENTARY: LETTER 114

Introduction, p. 4. But the techniques could obviously be misused: see on 15—16 below.

allusive: *suspiciosus* (*OLD* s.v. 2 b) and *suspicio* (*OLD* s.v. 1 e) seem to be almost technical terms of the declaimers in reference to the deliberate use of innuendo and veiled allusions.

Greek proverb ...: Quintilian (11.1.30) agrees in attributing the idea to the Greeks, and Cicero (*Tusc.* 5.47) suggests that it was first formulated by Socrates. He was followed by Plato in his discussion in the *Republic* of the rôle of poetry in society, though Plato linked the poet's character with his choice of subject—matter rather than with his style (*Rep.* 3. 396 c, 400 d). The theory that a writer's style somehow mirrors his character has had a distinguished history: it lies behind 'Longinus'' famous dictum 'grandeur in writing is the echo of a noble mind' (*On Sublimity* 9.2), Buffon's 'le style est l'homme même' (*Discours sur le style*, 1753), and Gibbon's 'style is the image of character' (Introduction to his *Memoirs*); and generally speaking it was a popular belief among English critics from the sixteenth to the eighteenth century. See further M.H. Abrams, *The Mirror and the Lamp* (New York, 1953) 229 ff.

3. **mind / moral character:** S. now begins to establish the link between them.

   mad or — what is much the same thing — angry: the visible symptons being often similar: cf. 18.15 'ingentis irae exitus furor est'; *Ira* 1.1.2 'quidam ... iram dixerunt brevem insaniam'; Hor. *Ep.* 1.2.62 'ira furor brevis est'.

4. **Maecenas:** friend and adviser to Augustus, and literary patron notably to Virgil, Horace and Propertius. For the picture of his effeminate character painted here cf. 120.19 'Maecenatem delicis provocant'; and for other criticisms of his literary style see Tac. *Dial.* 26 (Messalla jeers at the 'curling tongs' of Maecenas' style), and Quint. 9.4.28 (Maecenas' contorted transpositions of words). S. quotes from his verses elsewhere at 92.35 and 101.11, but not with the same purpose of illustrating his grotesque style.

   his own appearance was careless: *discinctus* means not having the tunic neatly belted and so slipshod to look at (see 6 below).

   his wife: Terentia, sister of Varro Murena. The marriage seems not to have been happy: S. speaks of Maecenas as 'amoribus anxio et morosae uxoris cotidiana repudia deflenti' (*Prov.* 3.10), and Terentia had an affair with Augustus (Dio Cassius 54.19). The statement below (6) that Maecenas married her a thousand times suggests that there were repeated reconciliations between them.

5. The examples of Maecenas' style quoted here are very obscure and the translations given are tentative. The point to grasp is that S. is condemning his unrestrained use of grotesquely extravagant metaphor, which in S.'s view is a clear counterpart to his foppish character and

behaviour. (See the Apparatus for references to further discussions of the fragments.)

6. **when he was acting for Augustus:** though he never officially held public office, Maecenas acted for Octavian when the latter was abroad, for example in 36–33 B.C.

like a rich man's runaway slaves in a mime: these were stock characters in mimes: Cic. *Phil.* 2.65; Petr. 80; Juv. 13.110–11.

married her a thousand times: see on 4 above.

7. **so carelessly flung down:** for *abicere* used in this way see 75.2 'sensus meos ... quos nec exornassem nec abiecissem'; Cic. *Brut.* 227 'verbis non ille quidem ornatis utebatur sed tamen non abiectis'.

8. Maecenas is condemned on three counts: order of words, choice of words, thoughts ruined in the utterance. The harmful effect of *felicitas* on him is almost a Senecan *topos*: 19.9 'magnum exemplum Romanae eloquentiae daturus nisi illum enervasset felicitas, immo castrasset'; 92.35; *Prov.* 3.10. Sallust generalizes similarly: 'secundae res sapientium animos fatigant' (*Cat.* 11), reflecting a widely held historical theory that military and political success led to moral degeneracy in Roman society.

9–12. The mention of prosperity and the consequent taste for *luxuria* widens the theme from Maecenas to other fashionable excesses of style — writers who indulge in archaism, or extravagantly coin new words, or create harsh effects by curtailing or spinning out their sentences. All this is part of the widespread disdain for the conventional which is felt by a luxury–loving society.

9. **gilded ceilings ...:** a feature of expensive mansions and symbolic of luxurious living: see 90.9 n.

unusual order in presenting dishes ...: cf. Martial's complaint (13.14) 'cludere quae cenas lactuca solebat avorum, / dic mihi, cur nostras inchoat illa dapes?'.

10. **varying the forms:** the translation gives the general sense of an uncertian text. For *deflectere* used of modifying words see *OLD* s.v. 5 b.

11. **guess its import:** see note on 1 for *suspicionem*.

aiming high: for the technical *grande* see 79.7 n.

if it is widespread: this is important, and it was stressed also in section 2: we must not generalize from isolated cases.

degeneracy: *procidere* is here used of a moral collapse, a rare metaphorical sense of the verb (*OLD* s.v. 1 c).

12. **man in the street:** *corona* is a circle of spectators or listeners, especially at a court trial. The word is often used contemptuously, as at *Brev. Vit.* 20.2 'imperitae coronae adsensiones captantem', and here it means ordinary unsophisticated people.

admire ... the faults themselves: cf. Quint. 2.5.10, on the same sort of false taste: 'propter hoc ipsum, quod sunt prava, laudantur'.

There is a certain irony in Quintilian's comment on S. himself, that it was his faults themelves that appealed to his imitators (10.1.127).

their vices and virtues ... stand or fall together: cf. the comments of 'Longinus' (33.4) about the many faults seen even in the genius Homer – yet he is far preferable to the flawless Apollonius.

13. **style has no fixed rules:** S. is stressing historical changes in literary fashion as an inevitable process. In Tacitus' *Dialogus* the speaker Aper makes a similar claim for oratorical style: 'mutari cum temporibus formas quoque et genera dicendi' (18.2; cf. 19.2). So too Horace in his *Ars* (48–72) argues strongly that language must change and new words must be coined as part of the natural process of expressing new ideas. S. goes on to list examples of fashions in corrupt writing habits: excessive archaizing, commonplace triviality, highflown poetic vocabulary.

vocabulary from a different age: S. was not alone in condemning the fashion for archaizing: see too Persius 1.76–8; Quint. 2.5.21; Tac. *Dial.* 23 (Aper again). The habit was not new – in the late Republic Sallust had been a notable archaist – and in the second century A.D. it was a major literary force in writers like Fronto and Apuleius.

The Twelve Tables were the oldest Roman code of laws, dating from 451–50 B.C. Parts of the surviving text are in archaic language, and it is thus a valuable document for the history of the Latin language. Gracchus would be one or both of the famous brothers and reformers, Tiberius and Gaius, who were tribunes respectively in 133 and 123 B.C. Lucius Licinius Crassus (140–91 B.C.) was one of the greatest orators of his generation, who inspired the young Cicero to follow in his steps. Gaius Scribonius Curio was another celebrated orator, and consul in 76 B.C. Appius Claudius Caecus and Tiberius Coruncanius represent the earliest models the archaizers could choose from the dawn of recorded Roman history: Appius was a distinguished and innovating statesman who held the consulship in 307 and 296 B.C.; Coruncanius was a notable early jurist and consul in 280 B.C. (For surviving fragments of the early orators see H. Malcovati, *Oratorum Romanorum Fragmenta*[2], Turin, 1955.)

14. **one shaves ... not even his armpits:** see 56.2 n., and Ovid *Ars* 1.506 'nec tua mordaci pumice crura teras' (i.e. don't be too dandified).

15–16. Variation of word–order to give rhythmical effects can be far more extensive in an inflected language like Latin and Greek than, say, in English: see note on section 1. A highly stylized writer like S. would naturally be interested in techniques of rhythm, and critical of unpleasant effects, and he discusses similar faults of *compositio* at 100.6–7.

15. **jolting sequence of words:** *iunctura* is a rhetorical term for the juxtaposition of words (Hor. *Ars* 48; Quint. 9.4.32 ff.), involving consideration of the sound of succeeding letters and syllables and the use of hiatus.

    singing not rhythm: like the 'sing—song effect' (*cantici*) criticized in section 1.

16. **that lingering cadence, like Cicero's:** the same comment is made about Cicero's clausulae at 100.7. He was criticized specifically for indulging too much in the cadence —uuu—x, e.g. his particular fondness for ending a period with the words *esse videatur* (Tac. *Dial.* 23; Quint. 9.4.73, 10.2.18). *detinens* here is used like *detineant* in 11.

    there is also a fault ...: something seems to be wrong with the text here, and the *OCT* assumes a lacuna after *tantum*, the presumed meaning being 'we find faults not only in rhythm but also in epigrams', i.e. both in the form of sentences and in their content. The use — and over—use — of the *sententia*, the crisp and pungent aphorism, was one of the more obvious features of 'Silver' Latin, S. himself and Tacitus being the most notable exponents of the technique. Part of the force of the *sententia* in Latin lies in the tricks one can play with an inflected language, but comparable effects in English epigrams can be seen almost anywhere in the poetry of Pope and the plays of Oscar Wilde.

    no effect beyond the sound of the words: so too in 40.5 (a certain type of discourse) 'plus sonat quam valet'.

17. **in Sallust's heyday there was a fashion ...:** S. does not imply that Sallust created the style for which he became famous, but he is usually regarded as the major innovator of his time, reacting against contemporary literary norms. At any rate S.'s description of his style accurately highlights its main features, and besides minor plagiarists like Arruntius Sallust exercised a wide influence on later writers, notably Tacitus. Quintilian makes much the same point about slavish imitation: 'acciditque ... ut deteriora imitentur (id enim est facilius) ac se abunde similes putent si vitia magnorum consequantur' (10.1.25).

    Lucius Arruntius: a public figure (consul in 22 B.C.) as well as historian. S.'s description of him as *vir rarae frugalitatis*, which is endorsed by Velleius Paterculus (2.86.2), is important and anticipates the point made in 20 below: faults which arise from imitation and are not inborn are not a sign of the writer's character, so a man of moral austerity can yet exhibit adventitious extravagance in his literary style. The illustrations of Arruntius' use of *facere* are not in fact unidiomatic Latin (examples can be found in good authors): he just overworked the word.

20. For the careful distinction between the imitative and the inborn see on 17 above.

21. The moralizing tone continues as S. returns to the link between effeminate behaviour and Maecenas' style.

    this is the aim ...: *quod* rather loosely anticipates *inritant illos ...* , which explains it, and is picked up correlatively by *talis est oratio Maecenatis.*

    refuse to do anything which might pass unnoticed: like the *luxuriosi* in 122.14. In the following sentence *volunt* is understood with *dum conspici.*

22. **a drunken style:** cf. the description of Maecenas' style in 4 above: 'eloquentiam ebrii hominis'.

23. S. quotes Virgil, *G.* 4.212−13: unity and harmony among bees depends on the welfare of their king (that is, the queen bee). He quotes the same lines at *Clem.* 1.4.2 to illustrate the unifying power of human kings.

24−27. With the mention of the controlling power of the mind the moralizing becomes more general, and the letter ends with an attack on one of S.'s favourite targets, greed.

25. **not being able to force ... down his own gullet:** the same frustration of over−indulgence is pointed out at 89.22: 'infelices, ecquid intellegitis maiorem vos famem habere quam ventrem?'.

26. **our kitchens and our cooks milling around:** see 78.23 n.

27. **he cannot hold much ...:** S. likes to point out that the glutton is simply stupid as well: cf. 47.2 'est ille plus quam capit'.

    turn your thoughts to death: again the theme of life as a *meditatio mortis*: see 54.2 n.

LETTER 122

S. makes fun of people who live topsy−turvy lives by reversing the activities of day and night: this is a clear case of acting *contra naturam* (and therefore defying the paramount Stoic rule of life).

1−4   Some people turn night into day and day into night.

5−9   The reason is that all vice and luxury perversely tries to act against nature.

10−16   Anecdotes about two of these characters who lived by night.

17−19   Vice has many manifestations, and the main concern of these people is to achieve notoriety. Let us stick to nature's course instead.

Most of the letter is lighthearted in tone, especially in the joking anecdotes about Buta and Papinius; but it concludes on a more serious note (17−19), as S. diagnoses the eccentricities under review and draws the moral for Lucilius.

1. **lying half−asleep when the sun is high:** like the sluggards in Persius: 'stertimus ... quinta dum linea tangitur umbra' (3.3−4).

2. **Virgil:** yet another quotation from the *Georgics* (1.250−1, with *illis* for *illic*), a passage describing how light and darkness occur in the northern and southern zones of the earth.

3. **antipodeans:** *antipodes* ('having the feet opposite'), like its Greek original, is used of people living on the opposite side of the earth, whose night is our day and vice versa.
   have never seen the sun either rising or setting: this was a stock description of a profligate life−style: Athen. 6.273 c (the Sybarite Smindyrides claimed he had not seen the sun rise or set for twenty years); Cic. *Fin.* 2.23.
   death ... is what they have plunged themselves into: for this idea see 77.18 'mori times: quid porro? ista vita non mors est?'.
   ill−omened as nocturnal birds: the owl with its mournful cry was commonly regarded as portending evil: cf. *Med.* 733 'maestique ... bubonis' (with my note there); Virg. *Aen.* 4.462 'ferali carmine bubo'.
   many courses ... their own obsequies: another familiar attack on the widespread Roman habit of over−eating and the consequent danger to health: so too 95.18 'multos morbos multa fericula fecerunt'. For *parentatur* see 12.8 n.

4. **birds which are reared for the table ...:** this description of fattened poultry recalls 110.13 'diu pasta et coacta pinguescere fluunt ac vix saginam continent suam'. The practice was widespread: see the references collected by Mayor on Juv. 5.114−15.
   dark surroundings: the translation assumes that some form of *umbra* should be read in this crux; but it might conceal *membra* (see Apparatus).
   for the sake of the dark: that is, in order to live in the dark. S. labours the point somewhat with *caecis* and *oculos*.

5−9. This behaviour is typical of all vice in acting *contra naturam*. The point is driven home powerfully by the repetition six times in 6 − 8 of *vivere* or *vivunt contra naturam*, and it is of course the strongest indictment a Stoic could bring.

6. **drink on an empty stomach:** see 88.19 n. *venae* were regarded not only as blood−vessels (cf. 78.5 n.) but as conveying food and drink in the body (*OLD* s.v. 2 a): hence *inanibus venis* here.
   rustic householders: the type of unsophisticated people scorned by these profligates with their refined pleasures.
   float on food: this use of *innatare* is much like its application to food itself that lies undigested on the stomach: 84.6 'alimenta ... solida innatant stomacho'; Hor. *Sat.* 2.4.59−60.

7. **exchange clothes with women:** perhaps not referring literally to transvestism, but to the wearing of immodest transparent clothes like women (90.15 n.; 114.21).
   a boy never to become a man ...: for the sexual duties of boy slaves see 47.7 and n.

8. **plant orchards on the tops of towers:** roof–gardens were another symbol of wealth: *Thy* 464–5 'nulla culminibus meis / imposita nutat silva'; *Ira* 1.21.1; Pliny *HN* 15.47 'in tecta iam silvae scandunt'. Cicero even tells us of oyster–beds on roofs (*Hort.* fr. 78). For further details see Daremberg–Saglio, *Dictionnaire des Antiquités* III.1 p. 284.

   lay foundations for hot baths in the sea: the sites for these were presumably chosen to trap hot currents for the bathers to enjoy. Suetonius reports that Nero organized the building of a *piscina* into which were diverted the warm waters at Baiae (*Nero* 31). For a similar indulgence see 89.21 'ubicumque scatebunt aquarum calentium venae, ibi nova deversoria luxuriae excitabuntur'.

9. **rejecting her:** cf. 90.19 'a natura luxuria descivit' and n.

10. **untimely ... torches and candles:** they are said to anticipate an untimely end in this way because funerals for children were held at night by torchlight: see *Tranq.* 11.7 'immaturas exequias fax cereusque praecessit'; *Brev. Vit.* 20.5.

    Acilius Buta: otherwise unknown. S. now indulges in one of his favourite techniques of punctuating a moral discourse with anecdotes – often serious, but here lively and lighthearted.

11. **Montanus Julius:** this is virtually all we know of Montanus, but the elder Seneca mentions him admiringly (*Contr.* 7.1.27), and Ovid refers to him briefly (*Pont.* 4.16.11).

    fond of ... sunrises and sunsets: such descriptions were very popular with great and lesser poets alike, and S. satirizes them wittily at *Apoc.* 2.

    Natta Pinarius: a client of Sejanus, mentioned also by Tacitus (*Ann.* 4.34).

12. **plaintive swallow:** if *tristis* is a significant description the bird must be Procne, who in some accounts of the legend was turned into a swallow when pursued by Tereus.

    Varus: usually thought to be Quinctilius Varus, son of the Varus who was defeated by Arminius in A.D. 9. Seneca the Elder heard him declaiming (*Contr.* 1.3.10).

    Marcus Vinicius: son–in–law of Germanicus and twice consul, in A.D. 30 and 45. In the following year he was killed by Messalina's orders. Velleius Paterculus dedicated his history to Vinicius.

    dinners which he earned by his scathing tongue: cf. 47.8 'quos adulatio et intemperantia aut gulae aut linguae revocet in crastinum'.

14. **to be a topic of conversation ...:** for this passion for notoriety see 114.21.

    talked about: *fabula* often has the special sense of gossip or scandal: see *OLD* s.v. 1 b and c.

15. **Albinovanus Pedo:** a poet. and friend of Ovid (*Pont.* 4.10.3–4). S.'s father quotes a passage of his hexameters at *Suas.* 1.15; and Martial

lists him among his models for writing epigrams (1 *praef*.).

Sextus Papinius: he cannot be identified with any of that name.

daylight—exiles: *lucifuga* is a very rare word, used humorously by S. and seriously by Apuleius (*Met*. 5.19). The adjective *lucifugus* was probably coined by Lucilius as an appropriate description of a *nebulo*, a 'shady' character (468 M).

whipping ... accounts: for a similar scene see *Ira* 3.33.3: 'ne propter fiscum quidem sed pugnum aeris aut inputatum a servo denarium senex ... stomacho dirrumpitur'.

16. **uproar among stewards and cooks:** cf. 78.23 n.

honey—wine and porridge: these seem to have been taken together as hors d'oeuvre: Pliny *Ep*. 1.15.2; Mart. 13.6. They formed the frugal Papinius' dinner, which though starting *circa lucem* did not extend beyond his day (that is, other people's night), as the enquirer supposes.

a liver by lamplight: *lychnobius* is a humorous Greek/Latin coinage by S., but if there is a further joke it is obscure. The Budé editors suggest that the stingy Papinius used lamp—oil on his food, in which case we might translate 'a liver on lamp—oil'.

concern for the right is simple ...: this lesson is stressed elsewhere: 16.9 'naturalia desideria finita sunt ... nullus enim terminus falso est. via eunti aliquid extremum est: error immensus est'; 39.5 'necesse est enim in immensum exeat cupiditas quae naturalem modum transilit. ille enim habet suum finem, inania et ex libidine orta sine termino sunt'.

18. **notoriety as the prize of their excesses:** again S. stresses this motive as he did in section 14.

19. **rowing against the stream:** a proverbial expression, as in English: cf. Virg. *G*. 1.201—3 and Otto, *Sprichwörter* s.v. *flumen* (7). The lesson is that nature's course is downstream.

SELECT INDEX TO THE COMMENTARY